TIGERS vs. JAYHAWKS

From the Civil War to the Battle for No. 1

By Mark Godich

Foreword by Joe Posnanski

"Finally, Kansas and Missouri have provided a game to match one of the oldest, bitterest rivalries in college football."

— Chuck Carlton, *The Dallas Morning News*

"Most great college sports rivalries emerge from memorable moments on the field, coaching feuds or recruiting battles, but the annual football game between the Kansas Jayhawks and the Missouri Tigers, to be played tomorrow night in Kansas City, Mo., with unusually high import, taps into a mutual animosity born of a flashpoint in American history."

— Kevin Butterfield, for *The New York Times*

"They have been enemies since the 1850s, when pro-slavery Missouri clashed with abolitionist Kansas in a precursor to the Civil War. Their football meetings have been considerably less momentous. More often than not, the Tigers have underachieved, and Jayhawks football generally has been a messy warm-up act for one of the nation's most prestigious basketball programs. But things will be very different Saturday night at Arrowhead Stadium in Kansas City, Mo., when No. 2 Kansas and No. 3 Missouri square off. The victor will move one win away from the national championship game."

— Herb Gould, *The Chicago Sun-Times*

"As the universities of Kansas and Missouri prepare to play the most important football game in their 117-year-old rivalry, trash talking is rampant here in a metropolis that straddles both states. Yet this isn't just the usual back-and-forth about which quarterback or defense is superior. ... Rather, this trash talking is focused on which state's residents behaved more abominably amid the Civil War."

— Adam Thompson, *The Wall Street Journal*

"This is big. And blindsiding. When the teams agreed to move their '07 and '08 meetings off campus to Arrowhead, it barely registered a blip beyond Lawrence and Columbia. Now it smacks of genius."

— John Helsley, *The Oklahoman*

"Kansas against Missouri is the nation's second-oldest football rivalry. Minnesota and Wisconsin have played 117 times. Tonight will mark the 116th time the Jayhawks and Tigers have played—but never with so much national impact. It is the first time since 1973 both teams are nationally ranked, and the first time ever both are in the top 10 of The Associated Press poll."

— Diane Pucin, *Los Angeles Times*

"It truly does boggle the mind. Neither team was ranked in the preseason Top 25. Kansas didn't get a single vote. You may not see such a dramatic one-season rise in football fortunes in two downtrodden programs for another generation."

— Lee Barfknecht, *Omaha World-Herald*

"The best rivalry in college sports—at least in terms of historical perspective —will be highlighted for the rest of the country Saturday. You can have Texas-Oklahoma, Auburn-Alabama, Michigan-Ohio State or USC-UCLA. But for my money, no rivalry has the basic historical hostility of Missouri vs. Kansas."

— Tim Griffin, *San Antonio Express–News*

"You might have to go back to the Civil War to find the last time Missouri-Kansas meant anything on a national level. Saturday night, it's all in. National title. Heisman Trophy. Prime-time national audience. Kansas City's Arrowhead Stadium. To folks in those precincts, of course, it's always been the equivalent of Ohio State-Michigan or Auburn-Alabama. This time, they get to share it with the rest of the college football world."

— Mike Kern, *The Philadelphia Daily News*

"The rivalry has always been fierce. This time around, it's also important. Really important."

—Doug Tucker, The Associated Press

Stumping on the campaign trail in the spring of 2008, Bill and Hillary Clinton visited Columbia. Dave and Susie Christensen were invited to the on-campus reception and, figuring they might never get another opportunity to rub elbows with a U.S. President, they decided to attend. In the receiving line, Christensen told Clinton what he did for a living, and the ever-personable 42nd President became especially engaged. Clinton mentioned the showdown at Arrowhead. "He said, 'I watched every minute of that game,'" Christensen recalls. "He said it was the best football game he had ever seen."

TIGERS vs. JAYHAWKS

From the Civil War to the Battle for No. 1

By **Mark Godich**

Foreword by **Joe Posnanski**

Requests for permission should be addressed Ascend Books, LLC, Attn: Rights and Permissions Department, 12710 Pflumm Road, Suite 200, Olathe, Ks. 66062.
10 9 8 7 6 5 4 3 2 1

Printed in Korea
ISBN- 978-0-9889964-8-9
ISBN e-book- 978-0-9889964-9-6
Library of Congress Cataloging-in-Publications Data Available Upon Request

Publisher: Bob Snodgrass
Editor: Jeffrey Flanagan
Dust Jacket and Book Design: Cheryl L. Johnson Design
Publication Coordinator: Beth Brown
Sales and Marketing: Lenny Cohen, Dylan Tucker

Every reasonable attempt has been made to determine the ownership of copyright. Please notify the publisher of any erroneous credits or omissions, and corrections will be made to subsequent editions/future printings. The goal of the entire staff of Ascend Books is to publish quality works. With that in mind, we are proud to offer this book to our readers. Please note, however, that the story, the experiences and the words are those of the author alone.

www.ascendbooks.com

To Leigh, the love of my life

CHAPTERS

Foreword

The Rivalry

By Joe Posnanski

Sports always seem at their most magical when the unexpected happens. And the unexpected so rarely happened in Kansas City. I think that's why the 2007 football game between Missouri and Kansas still glows so brightly in our collective memory. Everything about that season still glows. We just didn't see it coming.

You have to understand that in Kansas City in the 2000s, we tended to see everything coming. I had been a columnist at *The Kansas City Star* for more than a decade, but that just meant the same stories annually. The Royals were terrible. Check! The Chiefs lost their playoff game. Check! Kansas lost in the NCAA basketball tournament. Check! Missouri's season, whatever the sport, ended in heartbreak. Check!

When you live in the Midwest for a long time, you get used to the flatness of the land … and you learn to appreciate you can usually see the storms coming from miles and miles away. That's how it was for sports too.

But that 2007 season? No, we were totally blindsided.

Kansas football was an afterthought to all but a few stubborn old Jayhawks fans. I would run into those folks every now and again when speaking at an alumni function; they would regale me with stories of Gale Sayers and John Riggins, and they would talk about the glory years of Kansas football — or, more correctly, the glory year, since they were almost always talking about 1968 and Kansas' stirring 15–14 loss to Penn State in the Orange Bowl. The Jayhawks had tied for the Big Eight championship that year. They would not challenge for another conference title for more than a quarter century. Not that most Kansas fans noticed. They were watching basketball.

And Missouri football, if anything, was an even more troubling mix because Missouri fans actually *did* care about football, care intently, and the Tigers always let them down. It wasn't just the losing, though there was plenty of it. It was the *way* Missouri lost. The Tigers famously lost a game against Colorado in 1990 when officials gave the Buffaloes a fifth down. They famously lost a game against Nebraska in 1997 when a receiver kicked the ball to a teammate. But these are just the ones that cut through the national consciousness. A real Missouri fan can spend hours listing the cruel games fate has played with Tigers football.

And 2007 wasn't expected to play out any differently than any other year. Neither team was ranked when the season began. Kansas was coming off a 6–6 season, one of its best years historically, and Missouri was only a slightly better 8–5. (The Tigers had lost their bowl game to Oregon State, 39–38, in typically horrific Missouri style.) We went into the 2007 season anticipating nothing out of the ordinary.

It's a _different_ rivalry because Kansans and Missourians are still divided by a street named "State Line" and they still look across that line at one another with doubt and distrust.

And, then, illogically at first, more absurdly as time went on, the teams started to win. They were both wildly exciting, with undersized quarterbacks and wide-open offenses. It couldn't last. Everybody understood that. Only Kansas kept winning, Missouri kept winning. And, well, as you will read here in Mark Godich's marvelous book, miraculous things started happening.

I tell people all the time that the Kansas–Missouri rivalry is unlike any other in sports — or it _was_ unlike any other rivalry in sports until greed and conference stupidity broke them apart. I'm not saying it's the best or the most passionate rivalry — there are great and passionate rivalries all over the country, including many that get no press at all.

But Kansas-Missouri is a _different_ rivalry because no other traces back to such an ugly history, to Bleeding Kansas and John Brown and Osceola and Quantrill's Raiders. It's a _different_ rivalry because the states themselves are so different — with Missouri a mix of rural and urban and long viewed as a purple swing state, while Kansas is flat, sparse, right in the middle and one of the reddest of red states in the Union. It's a _different_ rivalry because Kansans and Missourians are still divided by a street named "State Line" and they still look across that line at one another with doubt and distrust.

So it's a rivalry with feeling … and every year, no matter how bad the teams were (and they were often bad), there was something emotional and fervid when the Tigers and the Jayhawks played. Year after year, those of us around Missouri and Kansas often wondered what would happen if their game ever actually meant anything. In 2007, we found out.

Perhaps the strangest part of that week, and the thing I remember most, was how — and I realize this sounds illogical — the game actually brought Kansas and Missouri fans together. Oh sure, Kansas fans desperately wanted to beat Missouri, and Missouri fans wanted to beat Kansas even more, but everybody understood how unlikely it all was, how unique it all was. There they were playing for No. 1 in America. Ridiculous! Impossible! It was all anyone could talk about. I so vividly remember the scene outside Arrowhead Stadium, the madness, the Missouri fans shouting "M-I-Z" across the parking lot and hearing the "Z-O-U" echo, the Kansas fans in their Jayhawks blue barbecuing up a storm. Everybody knew that this game, this moment, would never happen again.

Reliving it all through Mark's words makes me sad to realize that's probably true — it probably never will happen again.

Chapter 1
Four Upsetting College Years

I get paid to watch football. It has been that way since 1979, when I cut my teeth as a reporter and editor at the *Abilene Reporter-News*, and my fall weekends might have included covering a high school game featuring teams from the district of *Friday Night Lights* fame, a Southwest Conference contest and a Dallas Cowboys affair. In the mid-1980s, I was the executive sports editor at the award-winning *Dallas Times Herald* during a time when recruiting allegations shared top billing with football scores and the SMU Mustangs were slapped with the death penalty. As a writer at The Associated Press, I was at Valley Ranch on the Saturday night in February 1989 when Jerry Jones giddily announced he had purchased America's Team. I was drawn to the corner of the packed room where Tex Schramm stood in stunned silence. I wrote about Schramm's anguish and heartbreak as the franchise he had built from scratch was abruptly being ripped away. Since 1995, I have been a senior editor at *Sports Illustrated*. For 10 years, I was in charge of the magazine's NFL coverage, and in 2005 I became the caretaker for college football. I am one of the 900-odd folks who have a Heisman vote. I contend that for a sports fan, there's nothing better than being in a college town on a fall Saturday.

In 2007, it was a good year to be the college football editor at SI. In a season filled with unfathomable twists and turns, the madness began when little ol' Appalachian State knocked off mighty Michigan in the Big House. Many fans on the East Coast did a double-take when they awoke on the first Sunday of October to the news that Stanford, a 41-point underdog, had knocked off No. 1 USC in the Coliseum. The chaos climaxed on the day after Thanksgiving when Arkansas shocked top-ranked LSU in triple overtime in Death Valley. Those, however, were just three of the games that made the 2007 college football season crazier than any other in recent memory. How else can one explain how Missouri and Kansas, basically blips on the college football radar, could both go from unranked at the start of the season to becoming the focal point of the sport — and to playing for No. 1 in the land on the last Saturday of November? And what better setting for a game between bitter rivals than a neutral site on the Missouri-Kansas border, just down the road from where ancestors clashed in the last major Civil War battle west of the Mississippi?

"I was in Berkeley on the first Saturday of the '07 season," recalls *Sports Illustrated* senior writer Austin Murphy, who was on the college football beat that year. "Cal was opening against Tennessee. I'd just finished talking to some Vols fans while standing under a sprawling redwood whose upper branches had become home for tree-sitters protesting the Bears' planned $124 million athletic training center. The Tennessee folks were having trouble wrapping their minds around why anyone would be *against* a multi-million dollar upgrade to the football facilities. A couple of hours before kickoff, I got a 'stop-the-presses!' call from Godich. Appalachian State had just upset Michigan. I needed to hustle home and start working the phones.

In its 121-year history, Missouri football owns exactly 19 victories over top 10 teams. Six of those came under my watch. Not that I was there to see them. Remarkably, they all came on the road.

"One of the many charms of the college game is that it's wilder and woolier and less predictable than the NFL. That said, '07 was simply out of control. I don't even want to think about how many times we had to scrap a planned story on Saturday night in order to chronicle the chaos. It was the most remarkable, entertaining season of football I have ever covered."

He'll get no argument from the editor who was calling the college football shots for SI every week from his 31st floor office in midtown Manhattan. I missed almost all of a dinner party my wife, Leigh, and I were hosting, plotting instead with Murphy on a plan that would make sense of one Saturday of madness. On the second Saturday in November, I had to sneak away from Leigh's 50th birthday celebration for another brainstorming session. I'll admit it. I had a vested interest in the proceedings. I am a graduate of the Missouri School of Journalism. And proud of it.

A native Texan who was weaned on high school football, I headed to Columbia in August 1975 because I wanted to be a journalist. It was the only school to which I applied. I had heard fabulous things about the j-school, but I didn't know much else about the university. I had no idea the mascot had a Civil War connection, that forces from Missouri and Kansas were engaged in guerilla warfare almost a decade before the first shots of the Civil War were fired at Fort Sumter. And though I considered myself an expert on all things football, I was unaware that Kansas had cost Missouri the national championship in 1960, only to be ordered to forfeit the game for using an ineligible player. I didn't know what a Jayhawk was and, quite frankly, I didn't care. So what if Missouri and Kansas had been playing football since 1891, making it the oldest rivalry west of the Mississippi? It couldn't have been anywhere near as intense as Texas–Texas A&M. And Texas–Oklahoma? Puh-leeze!

Nevertheless, I was excited about the opportunity to experience the Big Eight style of play. Football weekends were a big deal. Tailgating hadn't caught on yet, so my fraternity brothers and I would arrive at Faurot Field at least 90 minutes early to wedge ourselves into the Delta Sigma Phi block, which typically accommodated two if not three bodies for every seat. The opponent was usually a brand name. Following through on the precedent set by Don Faurot almost a half-century earlier, the Tigers faced a murderers' row of non-conference foes. *Cupcake* wasn't in the vocabulary.

Playing a physical style of football and knocking off highly ranked opponents were trademarks of the Al Onofrio era at Mizzou. Onofrio was promoted from defensive coordinator after Dan Devine left to coach the Green Bay Packers at the end of the 1970 season. Missouri finished 1–10 in Onofrio's first year, but after losing at sixth-ranked Nebraska, 62–0, in the fifth game of the '72 season, the Tigers, a five-touchdown underdog, won the following week at No. 8 Notre Dame, 30–26. So certain were broadcasters that the score the wire services were reporting had to be a mistake, they reasoned the Irish had to have won, 62–30. In fact, Missouri not only prevailed in South Bend but also beat seventh-ranked Colorado the following Saturday and received the first of two straight bowl bids, this one to the Fiesta.

That was nothing. I would argue that my four years of watching the Tigers as a student were as unpredictable as the 2007 season was chaotic. In its 121-year history, Missouri football owns exactly 19 victories over top 10 teams. Six of those came under my watch. Not that I was there to see them. Remarkably, they all came on the road. Inexplicably, those upsets too often were followed by a stunning defeat to an unranked opponent— often at home.

As luck would have it, for the first game of my college career, the Tigers were in Birmingham for a prime-time, nationally televised meeting with Alabama. It was Labor Day. Mizzou was unranked and a three-touchdown underdog to the second-ranked Crimson Tide, which had won 22 consecutive regular-season games. Legend has it that an ABC executive sidled up to Missouri sports information director Bill Callahan before the game and said he hoped the Tigers could keep the halftime deficit under double digits, concerned that viewers in the Eastern time zone would otherwise call it a night. Sure enough, by halftime, the rout was on. Mizzou led 20–0, and when Callahan bumped into the exec at halftime, he quipped, "There goes the East Coast audience." Tony Galbreath was the star in the 20–7 victory, running for 120 yards and a touchdown. Alabama coach Bear Bryant called the game "a good ol' sound country beating."

Back in Columbia, the post-game celebration spilled into the streets of Greek Town, and my fellow Delta Sigs and I were right in the middle of the party. Sometime after midnight I came up with the brilliant idea to call home. Collect, of course. Mom and Dad knew the Tigers were playing; Dad and I had watched—and analyzed—too many football games to count, and I was eager to get his take on the game. The phone rang several times before he picked up. Yes, he had seen it, and, yes, the Tigers were impressive. Then he had a question for me: Did I have any idea what time it was? I don't remember what else we discussed, only that the conversation was considerably shorter than the one we engaged in the following day.

The Tigers went from unranked to fifth in the country after the upset of Alabama. They won their next two, over Wisconsin and North Carolina, before losing to No. 12 Michigan in Ann Arbor (Crimson Tide, Badgers, Tar Heels, Wolverines…whoa!). But after a 6–1 start, things went downhill fast. Missouri got drilled at home by No. 3 Nebraska—the Cornhuskers broke the game open with their famed fumble-rooski—then lost a heartbreaker to No. 6 Oklahoma, 28–27. As the season finale at Kansas approached, word leaked that a victory over the Jayhawks would earn the Tigers an invitation to the Sun Bowl. Several of my pledge brothers were excited about the prospect of a bowl game in Texas, figuring the Godich household would be a convenient stopover en route to El Paso. I regrettably told them the drive from Columbia to Richardson was shorter than the trek from Richardson to El Paso. That became a moot point after the Jayhawks rolled to a 42–24 victory.

The next season produced more of the same: stirring upsets followed by jaw-dropping defeats. Mizzou opened with a 46–25 victory over No. 8 USC at the Coliseum, came home the next week and lost to unranked Illinois, 31–6, then headed to Columbus for a meeting with second-ranked Ohio State in the Horseshoe. Overtime in college football was still 20 years away, so Onofrio went for the win against the Buckeyes, calling for a two-point conversion attempt with 12 seconds left. After an Ohio State penalty moved the ball inside the two, quarterback Pete Woods dived across the goal line on an option play for a 22–21 victory. Another party in Greek Town. A head-scratching home loss to Iowa State came three weeks later, but the following Saturday the Tigers won at No. 3 Nebraska, 34–24. Woods again made the big play, hooking up in the third quarter with wideout Joe Stewart on what is still the longest play from scrimmage in Missouri history: a 98-yard touchdown pass that those of us huddled around a black-and-white TV in the Delta Sig house heard but did not see. A violent thunderstorm had knocked out the picture on the set. But the crackling description of the play is still vivid, the broadcaster's voice echoing over a stadium gone silent.

The 1976 season, however, would end just as the previous year had—with losses in three of the last four games. Again, the finale was against Kansas, and again a trip to the Sun Bowl was on the line. That loss to the Jayhawks alone was tough to stomach. What made things unbearable was the way the Tigers got pushed around. It was 24–0 at the half and 34–0 after three quarters. KU rushed 83 times for 421 yards. The final was 41–14. In a stadium that

Onofrio didn't lose his job because he failed to take the Tigers bowling in five of seven seasons. He didn't lose his job because of his .481 winning percentage. He lost his job because he couldn't beat Kansas.

wasn't even half full, Mizzou scored with 11 seconds left, and the Kansas players danced around Faurot, celebrating the program's first consecutive winning seasons since 1960–62.

Unless you want to count a 15–0 road victory over No. 20 Arizona State, Onofrio didn't beat any heavyweights in 1977. The problem was that he didn't beat hardly anyone else either, and he was fired at the end of a 4–7 season. I was home for Thanksgiving when I saw the one-column headline in the afternoon *Dallas Times Herald*. It was hardly a surprise; as I left for break, rumors were rampant that Onofrio would be canned. Yes, in his seven seasons he had knocked off Nebraska (three times), Notre Dame, Alabama, USC and Ohio State—all on the road!—while beating nine other teams that were ranked in the top 20 at the time the game was played. He had defeated Bryant, Devine, Bob Devaney, Woody Hayes and John Robinson. He had gone a respectable 37–31 over his last six seasons. Onofrio, however, didn't lose his job because he failed to take the Tigers bowling in five of seven seasons. He didn't lose his job because of his .481 winning percentage. He lost his job because he couldn't beat Kansas. He lost his job because he went 1–6 against the Jayhawks, including losses in the last three meetings, the finale a 24–22 kick-in-the-gut defeat in Lawrence. Even a 20-year-old Texan who was just starting to understand the depth of the hatred between two border rivals knew 1–6 wouldn't cut it.

Bob Dudney could have provided some insight. In 1967, as a senior at Richardson High, just north of Dallas, Dudney took the Eagles on an improbable run to the state semifinals in Texas's largest class. Dad and I took in every snap that season, right down to the 42–6 loss to Jack Mildren and Abilene Cooper High in the Cotton Bowl on the first Saturday in December. I idolized No. 12. An aspiring journalist, Dudney landed a football scholarship from Devine and Missouri, which, in turn, punched his ticket to the j-school. And though the only passes Dudney attempted were for the freshman team in the fall of '68, he lettered as a senior in 1971 and was in uniform for a game against Kansas. Dudney received his journalism degree in 1972 and was working as a reporter at the *Times Herald* when I dropped him a letter. I had just graduated from high school, and I had some questions about Mizzou, the journalism school, fraternity life and the city of Columbia. The reply came in a *Times Herald*-logoed envelope, in a letter dated June 3, 1975. The letter was typed, double-spaced, six pages long, written on the copy paper that was used to craft newspaper stories in the day. Dudney told me what j-school would be like, what he thought of fraternity life. He was candid. His writing was crisp, thoughtful and insightful. One paragraph about the j-school stood out:

Of those 35 hours of straight journalism you are permitted to take, almost all will stress reporting, laying out advertising, reporting, writing magazine articles, reporting, setting type, reporting, editing copy, reporting, reviewing (not criticizing) books, reporting and more reporting. As you know, students staff the city desk (on the Columbia Missourian*) and are under paid, professional editors, and you will be expected to be a professional yourself. What you write in the afternoon will go in the next morning's city newspaper and by noon (when the* Columbia Daily Tribune *hits the newsstand), if you've screwed up, you will have to answer for it. It's that kind of ball game, and it's a good ball game to be in when you're 20 or 21, else you have to learn it when you're 23 or 24, when it's much harder.*

He wrote about the respect the j-school commanded, noting that even in a ridiculously tight job market, "Missouri could still attract recruiters from the best outfits." He suggested I not limit myself to sports writing, pointing out that he headed to Columbia with the same single-track mind, "but I changed and took up other pursuits, including fiction writing." Near the end he wrote: "You'll see that college is not that big a deal, not that hard, not that frightening, not that strange and unusual. Just get on an even keel, go out with the ladies, have a few drinks at the Kai Minh bar or the Velvet Lounge (two of my favorite drinking places), don't be too serious or too outrageous, keep your pants on and don't let anybody sell you a bill of goods." He closed by saying, "I wish you good luck."

No. 12 proved to be dead-on about everything he told me in his correspondence. My first beat at the *Missourian* was the Mizzou wrestling team. Save for the handful of times I curiously tuned in to Channel 11 to watch the Von Erichs "wrestle" at the Sportatorium in Dallas, I'd never seen a wrestling match. Now I was covering a top 20 program. I held my own, or at least I thought I did. I can say I never had to answer for something that appeared in the *Tribune*, not that the afternoon daily had anyone assigned to the beat full time.

As my senior year approached, I believed my work on wrestling had been solid enough to merit a spot on the *Missourian*'s coveted Missouri football beat. Sadly, I was the odd man out in a three-person team, and I was relegated to reporting on the hometown Hickman High Kewpies. I was fortunate to cover running back Gary Anderson, a lightning bolt who would go on to a successful career at Arkansas and in the USFL and the NFL, and I could always count on coach Tom Travis for a colorful quote. (I still pass along how Travis consoled his players after a stunning defeat in the first round of the state playoffs: "I told them that if losing this game is the worst thing that happens to them, they're going to have one heck of a life.") But Missouri high school football was nothing like the game I knew in Texas, and I spent much of the fall of '78 believing I belonged in the press box three miles down Providence Road from Hickman High.

It would have been some year to be on the Missouri beat. The new coach was 37-year-old Warren Powers, one of the hot young names in the coaching ranks, most recently the head man at Washington State. Along the way, he had been an assistant at Nebraska, so he knew what life in the Big Eight was like. Missouri hadn't won a conference championship since 1969—"I still have my Orange Bowl watch," Dudney told me years later— but Powers was confident he could get the program back to the top.

The Powers era began with—what else?—a stunning upset of a top 10 opponent on the road. This time the victim was No. 5 Notre Dame; the Tigers knocked off Devine and the defending national champions in South Bend, 3–0. A defeat at home to top-ranked Alabama followed, and two weeks later Mizzou lost at new No. 1 Oklahoma. But the pollsters rewarded the Tigers for their absurd schedule, and after a 56–14 victory at Kansas State, they were ranked 13th. Powers had his guys playing with a chip on their shoulders. Faurot was rocking. I was finally experiencing, as a student, winning, big-time college football.

Then came the unthinkable, the most crushing defeat I witnessed during my four years as a student. It was homecoming, and Colorado was the unfortunate opponent. An overflow crowd along with an ABC audience watched the Tigers storm to a 27–7, third-quarter lead. Mizzou was loaded on both sides of the ball—tight end Kellen Winslow and running back James Wilder were among the 14 players who would be selected in the next four NFL drafts—and as the Tigers were coasting to their sixth victory of the season, analyst Ara Parseghian told the viewing audience, "I'll tell you. Anybody who doesn't think Missouri is for real …" He stopped in mid-sentence, then praised Wilder, fellow running back Earl Gant and quarterback Phil Bradley. Play-by-play man Keith Jackson, who already had been gushing about the size and physicality of Winslow, Wilder and Gant, added: "I do get the feeling, Ara, that the Missouri people have taken over the line of scrimmage."

Whoa, Nellie. Slowly, the Buffs chipped away, and with a pair of TDs three minutes apart in the fourth quarter, they led 28–27. Suddenly, a botched snap on the extra-point attempt after Mizzou's third touchdown loomed large. With less than five minutes remaining, Bradley found Gant streaking down the left sideline a good 15 yards behind the Colorado defense. Gant, however, dropped the perfectly delivered pass. He pounded his right fist into the turf, then lay face down, motionless, for a good five seconds. "Holy cow," Jackson bellowed. "He drrr-opped it. That will haunt him the rest of his life."

Unfazed, Bradley moved the Tigers into field-goal range, but with about two minutes left, Jeff Brockhaus, who would kick in the USFL and get a cup of coffee in the NFL, missed a 43-yard field-goal attempt that fluttered and fell a couple of yards short of the crossbar. As the clock wound down and the Buffs celebrated their first victory in Columbia since 1966, a camera caught Gant on the sideline. In his distinctive down-home voice, Jackson said, "The man who's going to go to the supper table and to bed tonight haunted by the memories of this ball game will be Earl Gant, who was wide open and home free for a go-ahead touchdown for Missouri. He looked up into the sun, took his eyes off the ball (pause) and he drrr-opped it."

Two days later, Keith Graham, a grad student in the photojournalism sequence, walked over to the *Missourian* sports desk with a shot he had taken a split second before Brockhaus' right foot met the football.

Something looked amiss, and sure enough, frozen in time was the image of holder Jay Jeffrey placing the ball on the grass, *behind* the black kicking platform that was used in the day. The tack-sharp, three-column photo ran in the next day's *Missourian* — fittingly it was Halloween. *Block that kick* took on a whole new meaning. Brockhaus deserved credit just for advancing the ball within a couple of yards of the crossbar.

Mizzou was upset again the next week at Oklahoma State, and just like that, a season that two Saturdays earlier appeared certain to end with an invitation to a marquee bowl was in danger of ending before Thanksgiving for the fifth straight year. Though he took his foot off the gas, Powers got on the alumni's good side with a 48–0 whipping of Kansas at Faurot, and a week later the Tigers headed to Lincoln for a meeting with No. 2 Nebraska. The Cornhuskers were coming off an upset of top-ranked Oklahoma. Only the formality of beating a 6–4 Missouri team stood between the Big Red and a trip to the Orange Bowl to play Penn State for the national championship. Again, the Tigers turned the college football world upside down. They shocked the Cornhuskers, 35–31. The winning touchdown came on one of the most storied runs in the history of the program: a Wilder romp off left tackle that covered all of six yards. Halfway to the end zone, he tossed aside a Nebraska defender as if he were a rag doll. "Did you see that?" analyst Bill Wilkerson shouted on the Tigers' radio network. "Did you see him take that man and throw him down?" Added equally incredulous play-by-play man Dan Kelly, "You will not believe what Wilder did." Nor would anyone have believed the Cornhuskers' fate. Nebraska got its trip to the Orange Bowl, all right — for a rematch with Oklahoma, while the Tigers, suddenly the darlings of bowl reps from coast to coast, accepted an invitation to face LSU in the Liberty Bowl.

All was right with Missouri football. With a new coach and against one of those murderers' row schedules, the Tigers finished the regular season at 7–4, with victories over three ranked opponents. They were headed to their first bowl game since 1973 (and would prevail, 20–15). They had embarrassed the detested Jayhawks, winning for the first time in four years. Things couldn't have been any better. Or could they?

On the night of the victory over Kansas, I was assigned to work the *Missourian* sports desk. Not long after I had settled in for my editing shift, the door on the other side of the newsroom flew open. It was Brian Brooks, the paper's news editor. Brooks was a Delta Sig alum whom I met during my first week on campus. He was (and still is) as big a Mizzou fan as you could find. He was decked out in black and gold, but his face was red, baked, I figured, as a result of being outside on an unseasonably warm November afternoon. Brooks was hot, all right, but it had nothing to do with the temperature. To no one in particular, he said, "I don't care what the score is. Doesn't Warren Powers know that you *never* take a knee against Kansas?"

Chapter 2
The Border War

"You have to start with Osceola," Brooks would say some 32 years later. "Everybody points to what happened in Lawrence, but it all started in Osceola."

In fact, the hostility between Missourians and Kansans dates to the mid-1850s, almost a decade before a band of Jayhawkers rode into the town at the head of the Osage River and burned it to the ground, executing 11 men and plundering $1 million in property. The conflict featured the most gruesome guerilla-warfare tactics of the time, neighbor fighting against neighbor, raids orchestrated by U.S. senators, skirmishes that gave rise to outlaws such as Frank and Jesse James and the Younger brothers, Bushwhackers who fought on the Missouri side even as Buffalo Bill Cody and Wild Bill Hickok rode as Redlegs in support of the Kansas cause. It was the basis for the 1976 movie *The Outlaw Josey Wales*, in which Clint Eastwood was cast in the role of a Missouri farmer who fought for Bloody Bill Anderson after Redlegs murdered Wales' wife and children and torched his house. Eastwood delivers a powerful performance filled with memorable lines, none more endearing to Missouri fans than his response to a comment about the Kansas countryside: "I always heard there were three kinds of suns in Kansas: sunshine, sunflowers and sons-of-bitches."

An innocent family's fate might have been determined by how the head of the household answered a knock on the door, often in the dead of the night. Richard Sunderwirth chronicled the destruction of his hometown in the 2007 book *The Burning of Osceola*. Of the savage fighting that typified the times, Sunderwirth says, "You didn't know who your enemy was. It was all about survival."

Ask for the spark that ignited the border conflict, and historians point to the 1854 passing of the Kansas-Nebraska Act. In *The Causes of the Civil War: The Political, Cultural, Economic and Territorial Disputes Between North and South*, Paul Calore wrote that the act would "fan the flames of turmoil in Kansas, further fracture the Democratic Party, dismember the Whigs, initiate the beginnings of a new national party and launch a Springfield lawyer into political prominence."

Missouri had been admitted to the Union as a slave state in 1821. Kansas-Nebraska, proposed by Illinois Senator Stephen A. Douglas, effectively voided the Missouri Compromise, which, with the exception of Missouri, prohibited slavery in states and territories north of the parallel 36 degrees, 30 minutes. Residents would decide whether their territories would be free or slave, but there was one significant oversight: The legislation did not address how residency, or voting rights, would be established in the territories.

"Spreading slavery west of the Mississippi was problematic," says Stuewe. "If you want to stop something, you stop it before they have it. You don't wait for them to get it."

"This piece of legislation may not have been the most significant in American history, but its impact on America's past is undeniable," Tony R. Mullis wrote in *Peacekeeping on the Plains: Army Operations in Bleeding Kansas.* "Regardless of the act's original objectives, it places the question of slavery extension at the heart of the nation's political being. To many, the future of Kansas represented the future of the nation. Whether one was a free-soiler, a pro-slavery zealot or a disinterested factory worker, Kansas represented a crossroads in the country's destiny."

Missouri was entangled in its own philosophical struggle. A key geographic location because of its proximity to the Mississippi, the state was a study in contrasts. On the eastern side, particularly in and around St. Louis, the makeup was largely German immigrants, liberals who sided with the North. But much of the rest of the state was populated with Southern sympathizers, ardent proponents of state rights. They had migrated from Tennessee, Kentucky, Virginia and Arkansas. Their existence was dependent on farming—and slavery.

"Kansans want to make it about morals," says Joe Beilein, who as a PhD candidate at the University of Missouri wrote his dissertation on guerilla warfare during the Civil War. "Still to this day, they call Missourians slavers. If you're going to have that argument, they're going to win every time. For people of the South, slavery was an engrained part of their world view. Generally today, if we don't like where we're living, we can move. But back then, if you're born in, say, Tennessee, you see economic advancement as someday owning slaves and being part of this larger plantation, agricultural system. People who didn't own slaves were tied to it, too."

Even before the 1854 act was passed, Missourians flocked to Kansas to make land claims, but the new legislation upped the stakes. Missouri was bordered by free states to the north (Iowa) and the east (Illinois), and the prospect of having another such territory or state to the immediate west was troublesome. Likewise, abolitionists feared the admission of Kansas as a slave state would accelerate the westward expansion of slavery. (With its colder climate, Nebraska was deemed unsuitable for an agricultural-based economy.) "Early on, it was not about the abolition of slavery," says historian Paul Stuewe, a Kansas graduate and an authority on the 1863 sacking of Lawrence. "It was about the spread of slavery into the territories. Spreading slavery west of the Mississippi was problematic. If you want to stop something, you stop it before they have it. You don't wait for them to get it."

Southerners knew that the admission of Kansas and Nebraska as free states, coming in the wake of the 1849 acceptance of California, would mean the loss of four more Senate seats. "We are playing for a mighty stake," said Missouri Senator David Atchison. "If we win, we carry slavery to the Pacific Ocean. If we fail, we lose Missouri, Arkansas and Texas and all the territories. The game must be played boldly."

And so the two sides did. In 1854 and '55, the New England Immigrant Aid Society sent 1,400 settlers to Kansas. Lawrence, named after Amos Lawrence, the aid society's treasurer, became the center for free-soiler activity in the territory. (For evidence of the New England influence in Lawrence, look no further than the name of the main downtown drag: Massachusetts Avenue.) The town, Stuewe says, was settled for political reasons and not simply economic factors. "It set up the hostility from the very beginning," he says.

A year later, a second wave of settlers arrived, many of them from Ohio, Indiana, Iowa and other Midwestern states. "They were not abolitionists," says Stuewe. "They were free-staters. Not only did they not want slavery in Kansas, they didn't even want blacks in Kansas. If you had slave systems, they would drive down the price of white labor."

The first general election in Kansas was held in March 1855, and Missourians rushed across the border and stuffed the ballot box. They became known as Border Ruffians. Among their coups: having the county in which Lawrence sits named after Douglas, who not surprisingly, says Stuewe, was unpopular with abolitionists.

"In the North, it's all about building cities," says Beilein. "In the South, it's all about the land. And with land comes slaves. Missourians saw Kansas as the natural extension of Missouri. Before Kansas-Nebraska, Missourians had already set up claims in Kansas. When Douglas gets Kansas-Nebraska passed, the abolitionists and the aid societies start to send those people over, and the Missourians move back. That's when the conflict goes crazy."

New York Tribune columnist Horace Greeley coined the term Bleeding Kansas. The violence escalated after two events in May 1856. First, a band led by Atchison rode into Lawrence and ransacked the Free State Hotel and the offices of the town's two free-soil newspapers. Days later, John Brown, who had moved from Ohio to Kansas because he was disturbed by the success of pro-slavery forces there, led a night-time raid across the border at Pottawotamie Creek. With four of his sons, Brown went from house to house and murdered five pro-slavery residents in cold blood. "These were not killings done in the heat of battle," Donald L. Gilmore wrote in Civil War on the Missouri-Kansas Border. "They were execution-style murders in which the victims were roused, in the middle of the night, forced from their beds unarmed and unsuspecting, to be shot and hacked to death. … Brown's midnight visit broke any remaining trust between the pro-slavery partisans and the Free Staters, prompted increased violence across the territory, and sent emotional tremors across the entire nation, North and South."

Historians agree that the impact of the violence in Lawrence and at Pottawotamie Creek cannot be overstated. In Kansas: A History of the Jayhawk State, William Frank Zornow wrote: "This horrible massacre [at Pottawotamie Creek] was the signal for the beginning of the border war."

Some 26 months later, in an August 1858 election, Kansans voted for territorial status and no slavery over statehood. Raids into western Missouri became more frequent. So intense was the fighting that some have argued the first shot in the Civil War wasn't fired at Fort Sumter; rather it came in one of the countless skirmishes along the Missouri-Kansas border.

"In 1860, when it's clear there are going to be issues between the states, things really picked up again," says Beilein. "That's the birth of what would become the guerilla conflict in Missouri. It started as this neighborhood patrol to protect the property and rights of the slaveholders in Jackson County."

In *Divided in the Middle: A History of the Kansas-Missouri Border, 1854–96*, Jeremy Neely wrote: "As the twin perils of secession and war threatened the future of the American republic, the border between Missouri and Kansas represented the most explosive geographic intersection in the nation."

Kansas was admitted as a free state in January 1861, but only after South Carolina, Florida, Georgia, Alabama, Mississippi and Louisiana seceded from the Union. Three months later, on April 12, the Civil War began. Missourians fought on both sides—100,000 wore the Union blues, compared to the 30,000 who took up arms for the Confederacy. Over the course of the Civil War, Missouri was home to more than 1,200 battles and skirmishes, the third-most in the country, after Virginia and Tennessee.

That's largely because Missouri was home to another kind of struggle. With males of military age off to battle, many households were inhabited by women and their young children. These homes became easy targets for marauding Kansans. Particularly vulnerable were the residents who lived in four border counties along the Missouri River (Bates, Cass, Jackson and Vernon), where slavery was most prevalent. "These people were protecting slavery—or the prospect of someday owning that property," says Beilein.

The neighborhood patrols were effective to a point, but residents were overwhelmed by the scores of enemy forces that flooded across the border. "James Jennison's Raiders and Jim Lane and his guys went into Missouri and put the torch to things," Beilein says. "They started it."

Osceola was one of the most vibrant towns in Missouri; with about 2,500 residents, it was the third-largest city in the state, after St. Louis and Kansas City. About a third of its residents were Union supporters who lived in peace with their Southern sympathizers. In those days, says Sunderwirth, "any town on the river was a town that prospered." Visitors would travel from miles away, waiting for barges that traveled down the Osage stocked with silk, whiskey and other merchandise. Osceola's most famous resident was Waldo P. Johnson. Elected to the U.S. Senate in March 1861, Johnson strongly opposed President Lincoln's policies. In August of that year, Johnson introduced an amendment calling for a convention "to devise measures for the restoration of peace to our country." It failed, 29–9.

James Lane wanted no part of a discussion about peace. He was among the most powerful men in Kansas, the state's first senator, a close adviser to Lincoln. However, long before he was elected, Lane was leading incursions into Missouri, laying waste to towns along the border and claiming others' possessions as his own. Nicknamed the Grim Chieftain, Lane had a particular interest in Osceola, partly because he suspected (incorrectly) it housed a Confederate arsenal but also because it was the town that Johnson called home. Six weeks after Johnson's amendment failed, on Sept. 21, 1861, Lane led 1,200 troops on a midnight raid of Osceola. They stayed for more than two days, burning all but a handful of homes and businesses, and planted the first Union flag in the ashes where Johnson's house had stood. At a mock trial in the town square, a dozen men who had been guarding a bank were found guilty of being disloyal to the Union. All but one died in execution-style shootings. On Sept. 24, the population of Osceola was 183.

"You must march so that the traitors will feel the difference between loyalty and disloyalty," Lane said as he led his troops out of Osceola. They would leave with wagon after wagon of merchandise. Everyone joined in. The Rev. Hugh D. Fisher, one of Lane's chaplains, confiscated the altar ornaments, pews and pulpit from a church, to be hauled back to Lawrence, where his own place of worship was under construction. The plundering continued as the Lane Brigade marched back to Lawrence. There was a one-word term for the thievery: Jayhawking, they proudly called it.

"Having unleashed a uniquely vengeful form of total war—a strategy that prominent generals would adopt after years of fighting—Lane established a ruthless precedent that the border war's antagonists would follow for years to come," Neely wrote. "The Lane invasion marked the beginning of open warfare between Missouri Bushwhackers, Kansas Jayhawkers and the Union troops trying to subdue them. The attacks on Osceola, Butler and other western Missouri towns fueled reprisal raids into Kansas the following year."

One of the more prominent Bushwhackers was a twenty-something Ohioan who initially had supported the free-state cause, had admired Lane, and had even lived in Lawrence for a time. His name was William Quantrill. But in late 1860 he switched allegiances, telling his mother he hated Kansans for their defense of the abolitionist Brown. Early in the

16

Civil War, Quantrill served with Confederate forces, and by 1862 his guerillas, according to Gilmore, were the largest and most powerful partisan force in Missouri. As Jayhawkers continued their attacks in Missouri, Quantrill countered with raids into Kansas.

"He didn't do this for ideological reasons," says Stuewe. "He was an outlaw."

Because it was the center for free-state activity in Kansas, Lawrence topped Quantrill's list. But he couldn't persuade other guerilla leaders to join him. A tragedy in August 1863 changed everything. Jailed for their alleged conspiring with the Bushwhackers, five women died in a prison collapse in Kansas City, Mo. Among the victims were the sisters of Bushwhackers Anderson and John McCorkle.

Seven days later, on Aug. 21, 1863, Quantrill led an army of 450 to Lawrence. "On, paper, this looks like a suicide mission," says Stuewe. "Thirty-five miles inside enemy lines, the Army is patrolling up and down the border. How are you going to get over there, destroy the town and then get back without getting caught? Quantrill convinced them. He had that charisma."

As Quantrill and his band crossed into Kansas in southern Johnson County, they were spotted by Union troops. They knew the only place Quantrill could have been headed with so many men was Lawrence. But rather than send scouts ahead to warn of an impending attack, the Union forces headed north to Kansas City to enlist help. The tactical error gave Quantrill a four-hour head start. He had something else working in his favor.

"He was waiting for the right time," says Stuewe, "and the right time to attack would be one where Lawrence was off guard." Sure enough, the attack came several months after the Battle of Gettysburg and after Grant's victory at Vicksburg. "People had the sense the Civil War was ending," Stuewe adds, "and Lawrence let its guard down."

Quantrill's Raiders arrived in Lawrence before daybreak, split into three units and did an immediate sweep of the town. "The bulk of the plunder from Missouri is there," says Beilein. "There is row upon row of houses filled with property from Missouri. McCorkle even recognizes things like headboards. Not only is Lawrence the ideological center, but it is also the place where the Jayhawkers are taking all of this stuff. There's a reason Quantrill went to Lawrence."

In the weeks before the siege, Lawrence Mayor George Collamore had repeatedly told the townsfolk that Quantrill was coming. But those warnings went unheeded. The city was defenseless; many men were off fighting in the war, and most of the residents' weapons were locked up in an arsenal. "Even in the People's Republic of Lawrence, we're better armed today than they were back then," Stuewe says with a laugh. "Go to the Wal-Mart parking lot and you can find more guns in the backs of cars than they had in 1863."

The raiders carried a list of assassination targets, including Lane and Fisher, and Quantrill, wearing a black hat encircled with a gold cord, later issued the order to "kill every man big enough to carry a gun." Lane and Fisher escaped, but over the next four hours, 182 males ages 14 to 90 were murdered and more than 180 buildings were burned.

Mounting fresh horses they confiscated in town, Quantrill's Raiders fled back across the border ahead of Union troops. From a military standpoint, historian Albert Castel called the sacking a "masterpiece," and a "perfect combination of timing and execution." It was, of course, much more than that. "As a single incident in the whole bloody history of Kansas and the whole bloody course of the Civil War, none exceeds the second sack of Lawrence for unvarnished terror and brutality," Alice Nichols wrote in *Bleeding Kansas*.

To this day, the debate rages. Kansans point to an assault on a defenseless community, the cold-blooded murder of innocent, unarmed residents. Missourians argue the sacking was simply retaliation for the countless, senseless attacks their people had endured for years.

"Here's why it's different, where apologists for Quantrill miss the mark," says Stuewe. "They think somehow they can equate what James Lane did in Osceola with what Quantrill did in Lawrence. [Jayhawkers] would steal your property and burn your house, but they wouldn't shoot you in cold blood. They wouldn't just put a gun to your head and blow you away. The rules of engagement changed."

Beilein, however, contends that it's easy to see where Quantrill got the idea for the attack of Lawrence. "It's a reflection of the Kansas raids into Missouri," he says. "They come over here and kill fathers, burn farms and put mothers and children out." Beilein points to the memoir of William H. Gregg, the reflections of McCorkle and Andrew Walker and *Recollections of Missouri Women in the 1860s* as documented proof that the atrocities families in Lawrence endured weren't any different from the nightmares experienced on the other side of the border. "The men and women living on the Missouri side recount story after story where old men were dragged out and shot, women were assaulted and houses were burned," says Beilein. "Just because Kansans hadn't been exposed to the game, and perhaps didn't fully understand how it was being played in Missouri, does not mean that the rules were changed."

The Union response to Quantrill's raid was swift. Issued by U.S. Army Gen. Thomas Ewing, Order No. 11 called for the immediate eviction of all inhabitants in Bates, Cass, Jackson and Vernon counties and the burning of their homes so they could not harbor Confederate guerillas. Some 20,000 people were evicted, many of them women and children. The strife was depicted in George Caleb Bingham's iconic painting — Ewing sitting on his horse as Union forces, many of them Redlegs, carried out the order. A Missourian living in Kansas City and a staunch Union supporter, Bingham wrote to Ewing: "If you execute this order, I shall make you infamous with pen and brush."

> "Just because Kansans hadn't been exposed to the game, and perhaps didn't fully understand how it was being played in Missouri, does not mean that the rules were changed," Beilein says of the raid on Lawrence.

"Order No. 11 stands alongside the most repressive policies ever implemented by the federal government against its citizens," Neely wrote. "The wartime devastation of the depopulated counties in western Missouri rivaled or exceeded that witnessed anywhere in the South, including the broad swatch of territory destroyed in Sherman's infamous march [to the sea]."

Evictees eventually returned to their property to find acre upon acre of charred terrain, the landscape dotted only by brick chimneys that rose from the ashes. The region became known as the Burnt District.

Among the evicted were the maternal grandmother and the young daughter who would become the mother of Harry S. Truman. So devastating was the order, so humiliating the experience, that when Truman returned from World War I and walked into his grandmother's house proudly dressed in his Union blues, she angrily told him never to set foot in her home in uniform. (Truman delivered his first political speech as a candidate for a judgeship in Jackson County in the early 1920s, at a reunion of Quantrill's Raiders.)

Known as "Gettysburg of the West," the biggest and last Civil War battle west of the Mississippi was fought at Westport in October 1864.

About 20,000 Union forces overwhelmed 9,000 Confederate troops near Kansas City. That is not to say the fighting along the border ended, or even subsided. Missourians refused to acknowledge that the war was over, that Lee had surrendered. "There was no culminating victory, no clear defeat, no catharsis," Michael Fellman wrote in *Inside War: The Guerrilla Conflict in Missouri During the American Civil War*. "The terrible grudges of neighbor against neighbor created in the guerrilla [sic] conflict remained unresolved at the end of the war. No one apologized. No one forgave. Violence remained widespread in 1865 and 1866 as men reopened barely closed wounds."

Those festering wounds gave rise to the James and Younger brothers. All of 16, Jesse James had joined his older brother, Frank, and Confederate guerillas in 1864. The four Younger brothers hailed from Cass County; though he was a Unionist, the Youngers' father had been murdered by Union troops, and Jayhawkers had plundered or destroyed much of the family property and possessions. Missouri became known as the Outlaw State as the James and Younger brothers robbed banks and later trains. The railroad was a symbol of Northern superiority, and many Missourians celebrated those robberies, saying they were justified retaliation for the atrocities inflicted on their people during the war.

The violence essentially ended with the death of Jesse James in April 1882. Less than 10 years later, on Halloween 1891, Missouri and Kansas met on the football field for the first time. But they did not play in Columbia or Lawrence; they squared off in Kansas City, on the Missouri-Kansas border, just down the road from the site of the Battle of Westport. Before a crowd of 3,000, Kansas won, 22–8 — touchdowns in the day were worth four points. According to a report in the Nov. 6 edition of *The Missouri Statesman*, the losing side offered several excuses, including that "the university boys could have won with ease had the game last 30 minutes longer, as they had simply been 'dallying' with their opponents." Lame excuses aside, the result was inconsequential. There was a much deeper significance.

"The timing of the football rivalry is fascinating in that the players are the sons of these guys who had been killing each other," says Beilein. "These people were fighting against and killing each other one generation before this sporting event started."

Joe Beilein knows a thing or two about rivalries. His uncle, John, is the basketball coach at Michigan. "I've become inundated in the

Michigan-Ohio State rivalry," Joe Beilein says. "Sorry, but that's not a rivalry. Those SEC rivalries that are supposed to be so special? Those people didn't fight against each other. This is the one example we have of people who took up arms against each other and were then competing in sporting events against each other."

Or, as *The Statesman* put it, "Thirty years ago the red legs of Kansas and the Pukes of Missouri were waging a warfare along the border that filled hundreds of untimely graves and desolated scores of homes. ... Saturday last at Exposition Park in Kansas City the Kansans and Missourians again came together and a huge grave was again filled to the brim, but this time only with the disappointed hopes of Missourians. No lives were lost but there were bruised shins and sore heads galore."

The Missouri team entered the stadium that day as the Tigers, named after the band of students who protected Columbia during the Civil War. The Kansas mascot was the Jayhawker, a name that later was softened. The Jayhawk is a fictitious bird, a name derived from the hawk and the jaybird, some Kansans suggest. Even the most casual Missouri fan knows better.

Chapter 3

Olive Branch

In 19 of the first 20 years of the series, the teams squared off in Kansas City, the streak interrupted by a 1907 meeting in St. Joseph, Mo. Kansas won 13 times; Missouri, four. There were three ties. Best anyone can tell, the games were fairly civil. Kansas pitched seven shutouts, and in 1899 the Jayhawks won, 34–6, to cap a 10–0 season, the first of two perfect campaigns in program history. The coach was Fielding Yost, who stuck around for a year before moving on and making a name for himself at Michigan. The 1909 matchup was a meeting of unbeatens. The Jayhawkers had allowed 10 points while rolling to eight straight victories, but Missouri prevailed for the first time in eight years, 12–6

Two years later, the unthinkable happened. Missouri officials reached out to their neighbors to the west, inviting their Missouri Valley Intercollegiate Conference foe to play in Columbia. (Iowa and Nebraska rounded out the four-team league.) "Many Missourians who have never seen a football game have read for years of the annual Thanksgiving struggle between Missouri and Kansas on the gridiron, and their sympathies have always been for Missouri," the *Columbia Daily Tribune* reported. "Many of these remember a struggle fifty years ago when the object was not a goal but a life, and many of these 'old boys' will be here — men who now have boys attending the University of Missouri."

There was much more to it than that. The invitation was extended not only to a bitter rival but also to former Missouri students. University officials saw the game as an opportunity to entice alumni to return to campus, where they could reflect on fond memories and reconnect with long-lost acquaintances. And that is how the college football tradition we know as homecoming was born.

"What better name could be found for the gathering of students and alumni at the University [on] Saturday, November 25, than the 'homecoming'?" the *University Missourian* wrote in its Nov. 20, 1911 edition. "While many will come as strangers to watch the game, yet a large number will greet former classmates and look about with familiar eyes."

Determined to make their guests feel as comfortable as possible, university and town officials rolled out the red carpet. The discussion at the Commercial Club and among the faculty was that *Welcome* should replace *Beat* in any Kansas signage displayed around town. During a campus rally, University President A. Ross Hill noted that merchants would decorate their stores in the colors of both schools and, according to the *Tribune*, "requested that students leave the Kansas colors unmolested."

J.C. Jones, dean of the College of Arts and Sciences, told the *Missourian* "it is Missouri's duty to treat the guests in the hospitable manner for which Missourians are noted."

J.C. Jones, dean of the College of Arts and Sciences, told the *Missourian* "it is Missouri's duty to treat the guests in the hospitable manner for which Missourians are noted."

Understanding the significance of the game, the Electric Shoe Repairing Co. announced it would present every player on the Missouri side "a pair of half soles and heels." (The NCAA infractions committee was *not* dutifully notified.) And the Lipscomb-Garth Shoe Co. offered a free pair of footwear to "the lady guessing nearest the score" of the game.

Kansas, fresh off a 29–0 loss to Nebraska that dropped its record to 4–2–1, set up camp in Moberly, 35 miles north of Columbia. First-year coach Ralph Sherman conducted daily three-hour practices on a baseball field, as security guards stationed themselves around the perimeter. At night, the Jayhawkers retired to the Merchants Hotel. A *Tribune* reporter dispatched to the town "found the ancient bird in the best of health and spirits, just preening his feathers into shape and putting the final edge on the sharp bill with which he expects to peck out the eyes and twist the tail of his arch enemy."

Missouri wasn't exactly entering the season finale on a roll. Since opening with a pair of shutout victories, the Tigers had endured four losses and a tie. But the significance of the game wasn't lost on first-year coach Chester Brewer, who during two stints in Columbia spanning 17 years also coached the basketball, baseball and track teams and served as athletic director. So that the Tigers might have a coach for each of the 11 positions, Brewer invited former players to attend practice, and they turned out in force. Fearful of spies who might shuttle secrets back to Moberly, the Tigers trained on Tuesday in a remote area of a golf course.

Then, not unlike teams today that sequester at an area hotel on the night before a game, Missouri coaches and players caravanned after Thursday's practice four miles west of town to the farm of George Evans, quarterback of the 1895 team. That night, players lounged around the house's four large fireplaces. A couple of light practices were held on Friday, and the *Tribune* described what the scene would be like on the eve of the game: "There are baths and rubdowns, and trainers care for the sore spots in muscledom. A hearty supper follows, and the day is finished up by another period of rest before the cheerful fires, where stories of other years in the annals of Missouri football pass current and the older coaches instill in the men the spirit which has always characterized Missouri, especially when battling against Kansas. The players are put to bed at 9 o'clock."

On Saturday morning, the Jayhawkers traveled by train to Columbia for the 2 p.m. kickoff. Midweek rains that turned Rollins Field into what the *Tribune* called "a slip and slide" could not dampen spirits. An overflow crowd of 10,000 to 12,000 was expected on a crisp autumn afternoon, with 2,300 tickets allotted to the Kansas side. Five trains were added to accommodate the anticipated crush, and when word spread that one of those specials was delayed, the teams agreed to push back the kickoff 20 minutes. Alas, Kansas brought a mere 200 fans, "counting deadheads and all," as the *Missourian* put it.

To no one's surprise, the game quickly turned into a defensive struggle. Brewer was concerned about the Jayhawkers' prowess with the drop-kick, and after a scoreless first half, Carl Delaney's 35-yard field goal gave Kansas a 3–0, third-quarter lead. Then, with five minutes left, the 8,000 students, alumni and fans who showed up to support the Tigers cheered heartily when captain Jimmy Shuck answered with a 23-yard drop-kick.

Fitting of a rivalry in which neither program has enjoyed a sizeable series lead, the game ended in a 3–3 tie. Word spread quickly. Both the *Tribune* and the *Missourian* published Extras, the latter generating three such editions in a 24-hour period. Western Union dispatched six press men from St. Louis to document the game, and they generated 34,000 words that were distributed to newspapers across the country. (By comparison, a four-page feature in *Sports Illustrated* might run 2,000 words.) There was a theme to the post-game analysis — players and coaches from both teams said their side should have won.

"All in all, it was as pretty a game as could be expected on a muddy field," the *Missourian* reported. "There was not a 'bonehead' play by either team. Every Tiger and every Jayhawker did his best, fought his hardest for his school. To an unprejudiced observer, anything but a tie score would have seemed undeserved."

In the aftermath, newspapers in Kansas City questioned the sustainability of an annual homecoming extravaganza. A *Kansas City Journal* editorial opined, "There is no question but that it is poor policy to play the game in the college towns from a financial standpoint, but the universities do not care about this. They want the return, as they term it, of the real college spirit."

While suggesting the game was boring compared to those contested in its town and that Thanksgiving was dull without the spectacle, *The Kansas City Star* wrote, "For 19 years, Kansas City enjoyed the noise of the collegians, the milling in the hotels and the celebration of the victors after the game. Today all is quiet — no bright colors, no cheering — not even a frat pin in sight."

In Columbia, the inaugural homecoming drew rave reviews. "It always is a great time Saturday when the 'eighty-sevens' and the 'ninety-fivers' and the 'ought-ones' get together on the campus," the *Missourian* wrote. "There was a flow of reminiscence and a rush of old memories and a carnival of handshaking such as was never seen here. Don't you think the campus a fitting place for it all?"

In fact, Missouri-Kansas was on campus to stay. The Jayhawkers hosted the Tigers for homecoming in 1912 — and won, 12–3, before a crowd of 9,000. In Columbia, the wheels were already in motion to capitalize on a new tradition.

"It won't do to break the continuity," the *Missourian* wrote. "Why not shove the Nebraska game a little farther down the season, and have our reunions here on years when Missouri plays Kansas at Lawrence? It doesn't do to forget the alumni. Sometimes we need them badly, particularly when a mill-tax campaign or other issue is at stake."

The series was interrupted by an influenza epidemic that canceled the 1918 Missouri season, but at 119 games, it remained the longest-running rivalry west of the Mississippi (and the second longest in the country after Minnesota-Wisconsin) when the Tigers left for the SEC after the 2011 season and the Jayhawks said they had no interest in continuing to knock heads. Neither program enjoyed more than a five-game winning

26

streak—Kansas from 1930–34, Missouri from 1938–42. The teams returned to Kansas City to play in 1944 and '45, and the Tigers won both meetings, by a combined score of 61–12.

In 1946, the teams went back to playing on campus. It also marked the return of Don Faurot to the Missouri sideline. Before leaving to fulfill a service commitment (during which he coached the Navy's Iowa Pre-Flight Seahawks and at the Naval Air Station Jacksonville), Faurot led the Tigers for eight seasons, and in 1941 he introduced the Split T formation and the option play to college football. A three-sport letterman at Missouri in the early 1920s, Faurot got the idea for the option while playing basketball. The team practiced a good number of two-on-one fast breaks, forcing the defender to make a decision. Faurot didn't see why the concept couldn't be adapted to football. The Tigers finished 8–2 in '41 and led the nation in rushing. Among the features of the Split T were wider splits among the offensive linemen, which effectively spread the defensive front and created wider running lanes.

In his book, *Football's Secrets of the Split T Formation*, Faurot wrote, "We needed the deception of the Split T together with its promise of more offensive punch to offset the superior manpower mustered by our opponents. If we couldn't beat them down to size, then we might bewilder them! It was worth a try."

John Kadlec was a two-way lineman who played and coached under Faurot and for 16 years was the radio analyst for Missouri football. "I'm not the only person who's said this," says Kadlec. "Don Faurot knew the game of offensive and defensive football better than any coach I've ever been associated with. He could communicate with his players. The players understood him, and he understood the players."

Faurot also took great satisfaction in beating Kansas. During his first tour, he never lost in eight meetings against the Jayhawks. He was the coach during the Tigers' five-game winning streak, and for his career he was 13–4–2 against Kansas. "On Sunday afternoon before that game," Kadlec says, "he started in on us about KU."

Faurot, who doubled as the school's athletic director, also had an eye for identifying coaching talent. When he stepped down after the 1956 season, he interviewed a pair of young assistants: Frank Broyles, the offensive coordinator at Georgia Tech; and Bob Devaney, who was on Duffy Daugherty's staff at Michigan State. Broyles was hired (Devaney landed the job at Wyoming and later resurrected the Nebraska program), but he stuck around for only one year before accepting an offer he couldn't refuse from Arkansas.

"A lot of people were disturbed Frank was here only one year," says Kadlec, "but Arkansas offered him double the amount of money he was making. We said we'd give him a fifteen hundred dollar raise, which would have taken him to 14–5 or 15 thousand. And he got 28 at Arkansas. Frank had four children. I didn't blame him one bit."

Looking back 55 years later, Kadlec wonders what might have happened had Missouri matched Arkansas' outlandish offer. "I really, really, really admired Frank Broyles," he says. "He was a heck of an offensive-minded coach, and he was a wonderful organizer. If he had stayed here—no offense to the coaches who followed him— I think he's the one guy who could've won a national championship at Missouri."

In 19 seasons with the Razorbacks, Broyles went 149–62–6, and he did win that national title—his undefeated 1964 squad was proclaimed as such by the Football Writers Association of America.

Faurot, it turns out, fared just fine with Broyles' successor. He looked southwest for a replacement and lured Dan Devine from Arizona State. When he accepted the job, Devine was still four days shy of his 33rd birthday, but he was one of the hottest young coaches in the country. In three seasons with the Sun Devils, he was 27–3–1, including a 10–0 mark in his final campaign.

Devine went 5–4–1 and 6–5 in his first two years in Columbia, so it came as no surprise that the Tigers were unranked at the start of the 1960 season. Nevertheless, Devine called the team one of his favorites, and as the *Columbia Missourian* put it, "There were no superstars, just a bunch of kids playing football because they liked it and because they made, as Devine once said, 'a heck of a football team.'" After an opening 20–0 victory over SMU, the Tigers entered the rankings at No. 16 and begin a steady climb. When they whipped Oklahoma, 41–19, for the first time in 24 years and handed the Sooners their first home defeat in Big Eight play since 1942, Missouri, at 9–0, moved to the top of the polls. Only a victory over Kansas stood between the Tigers and their first national championship.

At 6–2–1 and with their only losses to then-No. 2 Syracuse and then-No. 1 Iowa, the Jayhawks, led by the backfield trio of John Hadl, Bert Coan and Curtis McClinton, were a formidable foe. But with Mel West, Donnie Smith and Norris Stevenson (the first black scholarship football player in school history), Missouri had a potent ground game of its own. And the Tigers were playing in front of their home crowd, their smallest margin of victory in their first nine games had been 10 points and Oklahoma was the only team to score more than eight points against a suffocating defense. Plus, the all-time series record was deadlocked at 30–30–7, and for the first time in the history of the rivalry, the Tigers had a chance to move ahead. Oh, and it was homecoming. Scalpers were getting upward of $50 a ticket.

Yet before a record Memorial Stadium crowd of 43,000, the 10th-ranked Jayhawks stunned the Tigers, 23–7. Kansas employed a nine-man front that strung Missouri's power sweep to the sideline, held the Tigers without a first down until midway through the third quarter and limited them to 61 yards rushing. On the other side of the ball, Coan ripped off large chunks of yardage and scored two touchdowns. Devine called Hadl "a great athlete, probably the finest all-around football player I've seen in a long time." Meanwhile, the Tigers, who lost eight fumbles in their first nine games combined, fumbled three times. In becoming the third top-ranked team to fall in three weeks, following Minnesota and Iowa, Missouri basically coughed up its chance at a national championship. Devine took full responsibility.

The Missourian described the scene in the Kansas locker room "was almost like having New Year's Eve, a Polish wedding and a World Series no-hitter all rolled up into one gigantic, back-slapping victory orgy."

"I think I did a poor job of coaching this past week," he said. "I recognized Wednesday that pressure was building up inside these boys. We tried to combat it by kidding around and saying this was just another ballgame. But it didn't relax them, did it? We made more errors today than in the previous nine games. We don't normally fumble the ball and fumble punts, but we gave up the ball continually in our own territory."

But Devine was quick to add, "I don't want to take anything away from KU. They beat us with good, hard football. They were the best team on the field. They deserved to win."

The *Missourian* described the scene in the Kansas locker room "was almost like having New Year's Eve, a Polish wedding and a World Series no-hitter all rolled up into one gigantic, back-slapping victory orgy." Amid the bedlam, coach Jack Mitchell puffed on a victory cigar and proclaimed the triumph the most "satisfying" of his career.

The celebration was short-lived. A couple of weeks later, the Big Eight ruled Coan ineligible for accepting a plane ride when he was a TCU student in 1959 from KU alum Bud Adams (now the owner of the Tennessee Titans) to a college all-star game in Chicago. The Jayhawks, already on NCAA probation and ineligible for a bowl game because of their recruitment of Coan and three other transfers, were ordered to forfeit the Missouri game, and though the Tigers beat Navy in the Orange Bowl as President-elect John F. Kennedy looked on, the damage had been done. In those days, the national champion was crowned at the end of the regular season. Minnesota was so honored, while Missouri finished fifth.

The forfeit created confusion, because to this day, officials from the two rivals can't agree on the series record. The Tigers count the 1960 game as a victory. While noting in their media guide that the "series total reflects 1960 Kansas win as a Missouri win due to Kansas forfeit," the Jayhawks continue to put the game in their win column.

Even with the jarring defeat, the 1960 season would serve as a springboard to the most successful decade in Missouri football history. The Tigers went 77–22–6 in the '60s and were included in the same discussion as Alabama and Texas and Ohio State. The 1965 team was ranked sixth, the '68 squad finished ninth, and after another No. 6 ranking in 1969, the Touchdown Club of Columbus (Ohio) called the Tigers "the best major college football team playing the toughest schedule."

"Dan was a great motivator," says Kadlec. "He could turn that intensity button up, and by game time you were ready to play. And he never repeated himself. I never heard the same pep talk twice."

Bob Dudney remembers Devine as an intriguing individual with a Tom Landry-like stoicism. "You see stuff about Bear Bryant and people like that standing up in the tower," Dudney says. "They don't interact with the team too much. Devine was a little bit like that, but then he could approach you on a personal level and kind of surprise you."

It was at the end of the 1969 season that Missouri scored the most points in the history of its rivalry with KU. Legend has it that late in the 69–21 shellacking, Jayhawks coach Pepper Rodgers flashed the peace sign across the field to Devine, who responded with a one-finger salute. Devine denied he made the gesture, and years later, Rodgers admitted he had made up the story.

Perhaps he learned a thing or two from Don Fambrough. A star at Longview (Texas) High who played for the Longhorns under coach Dana X. Bible in 1941 and '42, Fambrough arrived in Lawrence in the summer of 1946 after serving in the Army for 3½ years. He was drawn to KU by Ray Evans, a star halfback for the Jayhawks who also happened to be Fambrough's commanding officer. Evans, who hailed from Wyandotte, Kan., talked of atrocities committed by Missourians against Kansans during the Civil War. Fambrough developed an immediate hatred for all things Missouri, and Evans suggested his new friend go to battle with him against the Tigers on the football field. There was one problem.

"In Texas, they'd tell you that if you ever left the state that you'd fall off," Fambrough recalled in 2010. "I swore by Mr. Bible. I said, 'Ray, I promised Mr. Bible that if I got out of the service I'd be back.' I was about 26 or 27 years old. I was married and had a boy. We swore by Mr. Bible."

The good news was that the new coach at Kansas was a Bible disciple named George Sauer, who had played for the coaching icon at Nebraska. "[Bible] said if I came here and played for one of his ex-players that I would have his blessing," Fambrough said.

He played two years for the Jayhawks as an offensive lineman, linebacker and kicker — his two extra points were the difference in a 20–19 victory over Missouri in 1946 — before being drafted by the San Francisco 49ers. He was offered $7,000 to ply his trade, but after much deliberation he decided to stay at Kansas as the freshman coach.

"I hadn't coached a day in my life," Fambrough said. But for the next 10 years he worked as an assistant at Kansas, East Texas State and Wichita State. He returned to the Jayhawks as an assistant in 1958, and in 1971 he was promoted to head coach, replacing Rodgers. Fambrough went 19–25–1 in four seasons before he was unceremoniously fired, but when the school was looking for a football coach again in 1979, he was curiously named to the search committee. He and his wife, Del, stayed up all night to fine-tune a presentation on the six coaching finalists (including Hadl and John Cooper), only to be informed by the athletic director and the chancellor at a meeting the next morning that a coach had already been found. As he watched in dismay as his long night's work was being flipped into a trash can, Fambrough asked, "Do you mind telling me who that is?" "Yeah," came the reply, "it's you."

Initially, an incensed Fambrough was reluctant to accept the job. "But when I calmed down," he said, "I wanted the job in the worst way. I had recruited all of those kids."

The reunion tour, however, was worse than the first go-around. Fambrough finished 17–24–4. In two terms, he went 4–4 against Missouri, and his last game was a 16–10 loss to the Tigers in Columbia. "The only record I can brag about is that I'm probably the only coach to get fired twice from the same school," Fambrough said with a chuckle. "But I'm still here. They couldn't run me off."

Then, turning serious, he added, "I coached here for years, and I graduated from here. This place is very special to me. It's not just a job."

Living in retirement at his modest home only a few football fields west of the KU campus, Fambrough continued to fuel the rivalry with Missouri. Not that he needed any reminders, but on his fireplace mantel were a handful of game balls — all of them from conquests of Missouri. As he sat in his living room on a chilly morning in November 2010, 88 years young, the memories were as vivid as ever. When the freshman teams played, he claimed, Faurot would fix the chains so that Missouri needed only eight yards for a first down. He told how Kansas coach J.V Sikes ordered his team bus be driven through a chain-link fence and parked behind the Kansas bench, with the engine running, after a surprise blizzard hit Columbia — the Missouri side had refused to loan the Jayhawks warm clothing.

And then there was his Civil War soliloquy. "I've made up so much about that war," the crusty coach said, "sometimes I believe it myself." During the week of the Missouri game, as late as 2009, he was invited to address the KU players. It was one of the highlights of Fambrough's year; he would pace nervously outside the locker room rehearsing his oration before reminding the Jayhawks this was the biggest game they would ever play in, that they needed to understand what was at stake, that they needed to know what heartless Missourians had done to the good people of Kansas. One year, he took it a bit too far.

"I had this wild-assed freshman who believed everything I said," recalled Fambrough, the excitement in his voice building. "When I got through telling everyone about Quantrill coming over to Lawrence and killing all the men and burning down the damn town, I said they later found out he was a Missouri alumnus. You would know that he had a history test a few weeks later, and one of the questions was, 'Who was Quantrill?' I'll be damned if he didn't write down that he is a Missouri alumnus."

Soon after, Fambrough got a call from the professor, who said, "Don, I'll make a deal with you. I'm going to let you coach football. You let me teach history."

Over the last 20 years of the 20th century, the rivalry wasn't without its history-making moments. In a 53–29 Kansas victory in 1991, the Jayhawks' "Tuxedo" Tony Sands ran for a then-NCAA record 396 yards. And seven years later, Devin West rushed for a school-record 319 yards in a 41–24 Missouri triumph. But for the most part the teams played uneventful games in stadiums that were often half-filled. The annual grudge match was a microcosm of both programs' bigger issue. Neither was any good at football.

Fambrough and his .428 winning percentage were gone after 1982, and over the next 19 years Kansas went through four coaches and endured 122 losses. The Jayhawks did have a year to remember in 1995, going 10–2

Then there was Fambrough's Civil War soliloquy. "I've made up so much about that war," the crusty coach said, "sometimes I believe it myself."

under Glen Mason and ranking ninth in the country, the program's highest finish since it ended the 1968 season No. 7. However, KU enjoyed only three other winning seasons during those 19 years, and never was the futility more evident than in 1986, when the Jayhawks squared off against Kansas State in a game that was billed as a matchup between the two worst programs in major college football. Fittingly, it ended in a 17–17 tie.

As bad football went, the Tigers were arguably running a close third. Powers oversaw six consecutive winning seasons, but after a 3–7–1 finish in 1984, he was shown the door. And thus the coaching carousel began. The Tigers took a flyer on Woody Widenhofer, a Mizzou alum and Pittsburgh Steelers assistant who had four Super Bowl rings to flash in front of recruits but no experience in closing the deal. In four seasons, Woody's Wagon won 12 games. Next came Bob Stull, whose staff included future NFL head coaches Andy Reid and Marty Mornhinweg. Those offensive-minded teams piled up yards and points, but they also had an aversion to playing defense, as evidenced by the school-record 403 points the Tigers surrendered en route to a 3–7–1 finish in 1991. In five years, Stull won 15 games. Finally there was Larry Smith, who ran the consecutive-season losing streak to 13 before he took the Tigers bowling in 1997 and '98, the latter under the watchful eye of new athletic director Mike Alden. When those bowl appearances were followed by two more losing seasons, Alden's patience had worn thin.

"It looked like we were going to be a good team," Alden says. "Maybe we were already over the hump. But then I looked at our facilities, our younger players and our recruiting base, and I just wasn't sure we were going to be able to sustain that."

It's no secret that football foots almost all of the athletic department bills at every major university. It was time for a change, time to energize what was left of a loyal fan base that in the previous 17 seasons had witnessed 122 defeats, 38 of them by 30 or more points. It was time to find a coach with a vision. But where?

Chapter 4

"Toledo? Pinkel?"

It was the night before the first Thanksgiving of the new
millenium, typically a festive time spent with family and friends. Yet
Mike Alden was on the clock to find a football coach, so his eyes were
fixated on the television. Over the last 72 hours, his odyssey had taken
him from Columbia to Tallahassee to Gainesville to Toledo to Kalamazoo
and back, and now his exhaustive search had attracted him to a Mid-
American Conference matchup between Toledo and Bowling Green, who
were squaring off in one of those made-for-ESPN mid-week
extravaganzas. Every time a camera panned the home team's sideline,
Alden was drawn to a solitary figure standing in front of the Toledo
bench. It was Gary Pinkel, the Rockets' 48-year-old coach.

"I remember it was cold and raining, and he was on the sideline with
that hood on," Alden says. "All I did was watch him — just his stoic
attitude, his jaw clenched, the way he focused on things. I'm thinking,
'I like this.' "

Four days earlier, Alden had handed Larry Smith his walking papers.
In seven years in Columbia, Smith went 33–46–1. There were the post-
season trips to the Holiday and Insight bowls, but those successes were
followed by 4–7 and 3–8 campaigns. It wasn't just that Smith's last two
teams lost 15 games, it was the way they lost them: 37–0 to Oklahoma;
51–14 to Texas A&M; 66–0 to Kansas State; 62–9 to Clemson; 38–17 to
Kansas. In one of the program's most inauspicious moments, during the
fourth quarter of the 1999 season finale at K-State, Smith's wife, Cheryl,
made her way to the sideline and marched up and down the Tigers' bench,
dropping expletives, berating players and accusing them of quitting on
her husband. Frankly, considering the game that became known as Rout 66
was preceded by the blowout loss to the Sooners and the spanking by the
Aggies, nobody would have blinked if Alden had dropped the axe on
Smith a season earlier.

"It was pretty amazing how they went from being pretty good in '97
and '98 to falling off the map," says Dave Matter, whose first year on the

beat for the *Columbia Daily Tribune* was also Smith's last as coach. "You can see why. They just didn't sustain the talent. I liked the coaches who were on the staff. They were good people who didn't seem to have a long-term plan."

In Alden's eyes, the problems ran even deeper. "Our facilities needed drastic improvement," he says. "From a recruiting standpoint, we needed to do a better job of locking down the borders in the state of Missouri because kids were flying out of here. We needed to have a more centralized theme and philosophy of what we were doing to train our kids. And then we needed to figure out what we needed to do to get the fan support at a higher level."

"I don't think anybody was doing cartwheels," DeArmond says of Pinkel's hiring. "One of the Toledo writers gave me a call and said, 'You're going to *hate* this guy. He's the biggest sourpuss in the history of the world.'"

On a short list of candidates that included Florida State offensive coordinator Mark Richt (who took the Georgia job), TCU's Dennis Franchione, Western Michigan's Gary Darnell, Purdue offensive coordinator Jim Chaney and Wisconsin defensive coordinator Kevin Cosgrove, Pinkel was attractive for a number of reasons. He had Midwestern roots—he grew up in Akron, Ohio, and played for Don James at Kent State—and Alden believed those sensibilities would play well with the Missouri fan base. The structure and discipline Pinkel advocated were exactly what the Tigers were lacking. He wasn't the type of coach who was going to jump from job to job or shop himself around; in fact, Pinkel had made it clear he wouldn't leave Toledo until the youngest of his three children had finished high school. "My goal was to have all three of my kids graduate from the same high school," he says. "And they did."

Perhaps most important, Pinkel was winning football games. In 10 seasons at Toledo, he was 73–37–3, and the team Alden studied on that dreary Wednesday night finished 10–1, its signature victory a 24–6 upset of Penn State in Happy Valley that gave Pinkel his third victory (in six opportunities) over a Big Ten school.

"I knew he was winning games, graduating kids and beating bigger teams on lesser resources," Alden says. "So I'm thinking, 'We've got lesser resources, we haven't won a lot of games, we need structure, we need somebody who fits with the culture of who we are, we need somebody who doesn't have a huge ego because I don't think Missourians would warm to that.' It wasn't one thing. It was a combination of all of those things."

At 7 a.m. on the day before the game against Bowling Green, at a Courtyard Marriott in Toledo, Pinkel met for three hours with Alden and his search committee. "Everything we thought about him was validated when we met that morning," Alden says.

The two talked again in Chicago on the day after Thanksgiving, and the following Monday, Alden flew to Dallas, where Pinkel was interviewing for the Arizona State job. The candidate was whisked on a private plane to Columbia and a meeting the next day with Chancellor Richard Wallace. On Wednesday, Alden closed the deal over the phone while sitting in a Pizzeria Uno in downtown Chicago.

On Thursday, Nov. 30, 2000, Pinkel was introduced as the 31st coach in the history of Missouri football. Alden could not have been more pleased. He had found the man to revitalize a program that, because it was the only NCAA Division I-A football school in the state and had two major metropolitan areas from which to draw recruits, for years had been called a sleeping giant. So how was the man charged with rousing the program from its slumber received at that introductory press conference?

"Let's just say it was lukewarm," Alden says. "We'd had two winning seasons in 15 or 16 years, we were averaging, though we said 50,000, about 40,000, and the first thing the vocal fans said was *Toledo*, with a question mark. *Toledo*, for Mizzou?"

Adds *The Kansas City Star*'s Mike DeArmond, "I don't think anybody was doing cartwheels. One of the Toledo writers gave me a call and said, 'You're going to *hate* this guy. He's the biggest sourpuss in the history of the world.'"

One of the first queries in the news conference came from DeArmond, j-school class of 1972. He wanted to know what made Pinkel think he wasn't going to fail. This, after all, was Mizzou, where so many coaches with big dreams had crashed head over heels. Though colleagues warned him he was walking into a job that had turned into a graveyard for coaches, Pinkel was still understandably stunned. He had succeeded at every level — as an honorable mention All-America tight end at Toledo, where he was teammates with Nick Saban and Jack Lambert; as the offensive coordinator under James at Washington, where he tutored future NFL quarterbacks Chris Chandler and Mark Brunell; as the coach at Toledo, where he succeeded Saban, who had heartily endorsed him for the job. Pinkel responded to DeArmond's question bluntly, saying he couldn't remember ever being asked how he *wasn't* going to fail.

"The media greeted him with skepticism because they said nobody else has done it before," Alden says. "The fan base is saying *Toledo?* And the second question is *Pinkel? Toledo? Pinkel?*"

The skepticism may have seemed unfair, but Pinkel soon understood the basis for it. David Yost, the quarterbacks coach and recruiting coordinator, was one of seven assistants Pinkel brought with him from Toledo. As the new coach made his way from the press conference to the athletic facility, he got a call from Yost, who was busily breaking down the Missouri roster. Yost, just 30, said he had good news and bad news, then asked his boss which he wanted to hear first. Pinkel replied that he wasn't in a joking mood, so Yost got to it: The Tigers had one scholarship cornerback on the roster, and he was scheduled for knee surgery the next day.

"It gave me chills," Pinkel says. "I thought, 'Welcome to Mizzou.' "

Excuse, however, isn't in Pinkel's vocabulary. For good reason. He grew up as the middle of three children, and both his older sister and younger brother were afflicted at an early age by spastic paraplegia, a rare disease that is characterized by weakness and stiffness in the legs. Both lost their ability to walk. Gary was the blessed child, and from the time he started to enjoy the active lifestyle of a typical adolescent, he never heard his brother or sister complain. Not once.

"I spent a couple of days with Gary that summer before he coached his first season," says Vahe Gregorian, a long-time sports reporter for the *St. Louis Post-Dispatch*, who in the spring of 2013 joined *The Star*. "I found him very personable one to one, but he hadn't really shown that publicly. I enjoyed the ride with him. He talked about things other than football.

"The thing that always stuck out to me was when he brought up his brother and sister. The illness skipped over him. I think that was a powerful driver for him and said a lot about who he became and the whole no-excuses context. That's often coach-speak, but for him you could trace where that came from."

Speaking at a high school football banquet in Jefferson City, Pinkel was especially candid. After describing the plight of his two siblings, he told the audience, "So I have a player who comes in and tells me how tough it was to get up. You know how well that goes over in my office? It doesn't go over real well."

Excuses? No thanks. Not even the reception he received from high school coaches around the state could discourage Pinkel. One school turned him away at the front door. Others talked about promises made by previous regimes that were never kept, how they had been hearing the same tired message for a couple of decades. Relationships didn't just need to be mended; they had to be rebuilt.

"It was very fragmented," Pinkel says. "I thought you said, 'I'm Gary Pinkel. We have a new program.' They'd been hearing that for 20 years, and nothing had changed. I vividly remember there was a lot of stuff in the state about Missouri at the time and that you inherit all of it. I thought you could draw a line in the sand and people would say, 'O.K. this guy's got a better reputation,' but that wasn't it.

"It was a reality shot. My whole thing with my staff was that everything we do in this state with high school coaches, we have to be honest. We have to communicate very well. When they ask you something, we get back to them. It's all about trust. We have to be very consistent in the pitch about what we're about at Missouri. And then treat people well."

> After describing the plight of his two siblings, Pinkel told the audience, "So I have a player who comes in and tells me how tough it was to get up. You know how well that goes over in my office? It doesn't go over real well."

The situation was particularly dire in St. Louis. Over the years came claims of racism. Talented black athletes would not even visit Missouri, opting to sign instead with Arkansas or Nebraska or any one of a number of Big Ten schools. "There was this racial overtone," says Matter. "For some reason Columbia wasn't seen as a good place for kids from the inner-city schools to go. I think it got lumped into being a Hickville, in the sticks, instead of a fairly progressive college town."

Gregorian, like Matter and DeArmond a j-school grad, says the problem dates almost a half-century. "The roots go back to how long it took Missouri to integrate — Norris Stevenson being the first black player in 1957," he says. "Bear in mind that was also a time when they were playing Dixie after every touchdown and Confederate flags were being waved in the stands. I got the impression it was not a friendly place. There were not a lot of social activities for African-Americans."

It didn't help that Pinkel's predecessors had been at best unorganized in the Gateway City. "They weren't very consistent," says Matter. "They had a different assistant work the area several years in a row. They didn't lay a foundation."

Consistency and organization have never been an issue for Pinkel, and he hit the ground running. Two days after his introductory news conference, he flew the assistants he brought with him from Toledo into St. Louis to attend a high school coaches clinic. The group worked the room, attired in their Mizzou gear. Then, about a week after signing day in February 2001, at the suggestion of Demetrious Johnson, who starred as a defensive back for the Tigers from 1979 to '82, Pinkel invited former players from the St. Louis area to the airport Marriott for a clear-the-air meeting. More than 100 attended, and for the better part of 2½ hours, Pinkel listened attentively as grievances were aired. Players spoke from the heart. They didn't have a lot of flattering things to say about the program.

"It was a bury-your-soul meeting," Pinkel says. "There was never any yelling, but guys were really honest about things. Some of the stuff offended other guys. You could see it in their body language. I told them I would be accountable for all the things they were upset about. That's when the healing started."

It was admittedly slow, almost as slow as the inroads the staff made early on in St. Louis. As his assistants worked tirelessly to establish relationships, Pinkel remembers telling them they would "not let recruiting in St. Louis dictate the success or failure of this program. The message to everybody else, in Kansas City or Texas or wherever: We will never change how hard we work [in St. Louis], but we're not going to let that town …"

He stops in mid-sentence, then adds, "I was just so frustrated. It was the climate. We had nothing to do with it, but that didn't matter."

Winning would have done wonders, but the 2001 opener showed how big a mountain Pinkel and his staff had to scale. The opponent was Bowling Green, and except for the new head coach (a guy named Urban Meyer), the Falcons sent essentially the same team to Columbia that Toledo manhandled, 51–17, in Pinkel's farewell. No worries, right? Well, the Falcons walked out of Faurot Field with a 20–13 victory. The Tigers turned the ball over three times and gained only 234 yards against a MAC team that hadn't experienced a winning season since 1994.

Dave Christensen, Missouri's offensive coordinator and line coach, was the assistant who drew the short straw of handling the post-game show on the Tigers' radio network. When he decided to move his wife and three young children to Columbia, Christensen didn't know much about the program, other than it competed in the Big 12. He couldn't remember if he had even set foot in the state. Now he was seeing how seriously fans of a BCS school took their football, even at a moribund program like Missouri's. Front and center at a Buffalo Wild Wings, Christensen was blistered by those in the audience as well as angry callers. There was a theme to the diatribes: This is what happens when you hire *Toledo* and *Pinkel*.

As he staggered out of the restaurant after being administered his second beat-down of the night, Christensen looked at his wife, Susie, and said, "I don't know if I've got this in me."

Christensen may have been looking for a sympathetic figure, but he wasn't going to find one in his significant other. "Dave," Susie said, "you better have it in you, because you moved your entire family out here to do this."

The highlight of an otherwise forgettable season was a 38–34 victory at Kansas, but by the time the season finale against Michigan State rolled around, Missouri was 4–6 and without a bowl bid for the third consecutive year. Scheduled for the third Saturday in September, the game had been postponed in the wake of the 9/11 terrorist attacks, and from the opening kickoff it was obvious that East Lansing was the last place the Tigers wanted to be. The Spartans racked up 639 yards of total offense, and the longest of their seven touchdown drives lasted 92 seconds. The final was 55–7. In a word, the Tigers quit. Outside the visitors' locker room, Alden found a shell-shocked Pinkel.

"Gary was so distraught," Alden says. "He was ashen. I remember him saying, 'Mike, I'm so embarrassed. You didn't bring me here to see this kind of stuff. I'm going to get this fixed.' "

But where to start? The last place one would have suspected was with a 6-foot-2, 190-pound quarterback from Youngstown, Ohio, named Brad Smith, who had drawn absolutely zero interest from other BCS programs. Pinkel had stumbled upon Smith's video when he was at Toledo. He was blown away by what he saw, figured the Rockets had absolutely no shot at landing such a talented kid and was stunned to learn that only Bowling

Green and Division I-AA Youngstown State were recruiting him. (That Smith was even able to run was amazing. Born with a form of club feet, he spent his early years in leg braces.) The Rockets were quick to offer a scholarship, and when Pinkel took the Mizzou job he invited Smith to join him.

If only it were that easy. Sherri Smith-Brogdon had moved Brad and his two siblings from Los Angeles to Youngstown when they were youngsters. She went to work as an administrative assistant at Mount Calvary Pentecostal Church. Brad was heavily involved in the church as well, singing in the choir, among other things. Before Smith was allowed to sign his letter of intent, Pinkel had to persuade officials at Mount Calvary that Missouri was the ideal fit for their young parishioner. Because Smith was considering a school that was 700 miles from home, a committee did a background check on Pinkel, then grilled him on everything from his coaching philosophy to player graduation rates at Missouri. The meeting, which included defensive coordinator Matt Eberflus, lasted two hours. When it was over, Bishop Norman Wagner gave his blessing for Smith to attend Mizzou. Pinkel recalls the clergyman telling him, "You have no idea what you've got here."

Before the eight-play, 77-yard touchdown drive was over, Yost turned to Christensen in the coaches' booth and exclaimed, "Coach, they can't tackle him!"

Frankly, other than having a raw talent who was more athlete than quarterback, the Missouri coaches could not have agreed more. While the highlight video was impressive, Smith had spent much of his high school career handing off. He had flashed his speed and elusiveness as a punt returner, but the coaching staff couldn't understand why no other BCS program was showing even remote interest. What were the Tigers seeing that so many others missed? That there was a debate whether to redshirt Smith spoke to the dearth of talent on the roster. But in the end the decision was made to use 2001 as a developmental season. Smith was suspect as a passer, and Yost didn't see him bolting for the NFL after three years. If he played another position, the thinking might have been different. But Smith was in Columbia to play quarterback, and Yost believed the first year would best be used coaching him up.

"I knew he was talented, but he wasn't ready," Yost says. "I hadn't trained a lot of quarterbacks, but I knew when they were ready. Could he have made some plays as a [true] freshman? No question. But would he have made more plays in his fifth year than he did in his first year? It was going to pay off."

The Tigers had an experienced quarterback in senior Kirk Farmer, who made 14 starts during the first three years of an injury-plagued career, and a higher-profile redshirt freshman in Sonny Riccio, a classic drop-back passer from Ellwood City, Pa. But as preseason practice dragged on in 2002, Smith kept making eye-popping plays. Missouri QBs are treated with kid gloves — they're impossible to miss in their green jerseys — and the staff was especially cautious with Smith. Christensen would blow his whistle before a defender could even breathe on the untapped talent. "You never knew what you had until you turned him loose," the coordinator says.

Two weeks before the season opener against Illinois in St. Louis, Pinkel announced he was turning Smith loose. The staff had discussed the QB situation daily. The competition had been close in the spring, but in two-a-days, Pinkel says, Smith was separating himself. Fans, of course, weren't privy to practice details, so the news was met with the same skepticism as *Toldeo* and *Pinkel*. The safe and sensible thing would have been to start Farmer, work Smith in for a series here and there, and let him get a feel for the college game. And while his gut told him one thing, even Pinkel had reservations. After the Tigers finished their walk-through on the eve of the game at the TWA Dome and boarded the buses for the short trip to the team hotel, Pinkel stayed back to do an interview with ABC. When he was done, he hopped in the car of Missouri sports information director Chad Moller, who after six years of overseeing basketball was in his maiden season with the football program.

"I could tell he was kind of fidgety, the day before a big game and all that," recalls Moller. "He was looking through his play charts. At some point, it got quiet. Then he looked over at me and said, 'Boy, I hope I made the right call here.'

"I said, 'Coach, I hope you did too.'"

Illinois won the toss and deferred. Who wouldn't? Let's see what the kid's got. Smith, it turned out, had more than the defending Big Ten champs could handle. On his third play, he completed a short pass for a first down. Then he ripped off a 20-yard run. He kept plays alive with his feet, completing four of five passes. In the blink of an eye it was 7–0, and before the eight-play, 77-yard touchdown drive was over, Yost turned to

Christensen in the coaches' booth and exclaimed, "Coach, they can't tackle him!"

By the end of the third quarter, Smith had ripped off five runs of at least 10 yards, including a 39-yard sprint during which he serpentined through the Illini defense. Early in the fourth quarter, he dropped a 25-yard sideline pass into the arms of blanketed wideout Justin Gage, prompting ESPN's Mike Tirico to excitedly ask analyst Irving Fryar a question to which both already knew the answer: "Are you liking what you're seeing?" Later, as he watched Smith bounce off of four tacklers on a 24-yard scoring dash, Tirico gushed: "Brad Smith—making plays, making touchdowns!" Then Tirico summed up college football's newest revelation with a simple exclamation: "Wow!" Missouri upset Illinois, 33–20. Smith finished with 152 yards passing, 138 yards rushing and no turnovers. The only thing more remarkable than his performance was the ease with which he operated.

"His ability to see and change directions—several times in that game, he would change his speed and completely fool the defense," says Mike Kelly, the radio voice of the Tigers since 1994. "They'd think they had a line on him, and then the next thing you know, boom, he's gone, or around the edge, 15 of 20 yards down the field."

Bishop Wagner was right.

"You talk to a kid and you ask [yourself], 'Does he have *it*?' " Pinkel says. "That sounds crazy, but you talk to a guy and [you have to] feel comfortable that he's got *it*. There's something in this guy. You can never have greatness in a quarterback unless you're mentally and physically tougher than nails. And you have to be a tenacious competitor. I don't care what skills you have.

"I remember telling my wife on the drive home, 'We've got a star here.' "

Smith had *it*, all right. In his fifth game, he came *this* close to single-handedly beating No. 3 Oklahoma, running for 213 yards and two touchdowns and passing for 187 yards and a score in a game the Sooners won, 31–24, on a fake field goal and two-point conversion with 6:33 left. The Tigers stumbled with seven-point losses at Iowa State and to Colorado (the latter in overtime), then won in double overtime at Texas A&M. With a 5–6 record, Mizzou held out faint hopes of a bowl bid, but in the season finale Kansas State prevailed, 38–0. While it wasn't Michigan State all over again, the game was testament to how much work lay ahead.

Smith finished with 2,338 yards passing and 1,029 yards rushing, becoming the second player in Division I-A history to record a 2,000/1,000 season. The foundation had been set, and Pinkel had a quarterback he could build around.

Like many in his profession, Pinkel is always looking forward, digging to find the recruit or the innovation or the tweak that will produce another victory, another step up the college football ladder. Yet almost eight years later, Pinkel couldn't help but reflect on what an under-the-radar athlete from Youngstown, Ohio, meant to Missouri football. "I always look back at the program as we struggled and we were building, and the big question is, 'What would you have done if Brad Smith had never been here?'" He pauses for several seconds. "I don't know."

The 2003 season was monumental for a couple of reasons: The Tigers beat Nebraska for the first time since the 1978 shocker in Lincoln—Smith ran for 123 yards and three touchdowns, passed for 180 yards and *caught* a 47-yard touchdown on a double pass in a 41–24 victory—and they went bowling for the first time under Pinkel, accepting a bid to the Independence Bowl. En route to an 8–5 finish, Smith produced more highlight-reel dashes. Against Texas Tech, he ran for 291 yards and five touchdowns, on a mere 19 carries. Against Iowa State, he rushed for 195 yards and a pair of scores.

As he broke down video week after week, Pinkel was at the same time amazed and perturbed. Yes, the kid was piling up yards and touchdowns (Smith's 1,406 rushing yards in 2003 were the fourth-most by a quarterback in Division I-A history, and he had a school-record 18 rushing TDs), but so effortless was his gait that Pinkel would grouse that Smith was loafing. Sitting alongside Pinkel, Yost would counter, "But Coach, nobody's catching him."

Pat Ivey, who played at Mizzou in the early 1990s and now oversees the athletic department's strength and conditioning program, says Smith's running style defies physics. "I remember telling NFL scouts that Brad's not going to look like he's accelerating," Ivey says. "Most of the time, you have to change your body angle to accelerate. You have to go from an

> "I always look back at the program as we struggled and we were building, and the big question is, 'What would you have done if Brad Smith had never been here?'" He pauses for several seconds. "I don't know."

upright position to a forward lean. But Brad could accelerate upright. He's the only player I have coached who could accelerate upright."

Ivey compares Smith's gait to that of wideout Jeremy Maclin, a burner who starred for two years at Missouri before being picked in the first round of the 2009 NFL draft by the Philadelphia Eagles. "Jeremy had a forward lean, and his hips would drop a little and then kind of rise," Ivey says. "Brad's hips were high and upright, and he could accelerate. Biomechanically, it doesn't make sense. But it works. It works well."

It worked so well that it made absolutely no sense what the coaches attempted to do with Smith in 2004: They tried to turn him into a pocket passer. The year had begun with big expectations. The Tigers were ranked 18th, and Smith was featured on the front page of *The New York Times* Sunday edition. The front page! The article branded the Tigers as contenders for the Big 12 title and Smith as a top candidate for the Heisman.

Missouri opened with a 52–20 victory over Arkansas State—Smith passed for 233 yards but carried only six times—and five nights later the Tigers hit the road to face Troy. Not *those* Trojans. Rather it was Troy of the Sun Belt Conference.

"On campus, you'd encounter people who'd say, 'Are you from Missou-rah?' 'You'd say, 'Yeah.' And they'd say, 'When you leavin'?' " recalls Kelly. "I guess that was their message for whoever dared venture into Troy, Ala. But talk about the perfect scenario for an upset: an evening game, the highest-profile opponent to ever visit that facility, a relatively new stadium and, oh, by the way, pretty good players on the other side, including a guy named DeMarcus Ware."

Nevertheless, it was tough to take Troy seriously. The Trojans were in their fourth year of Division I-A play. So small was the visitors' locker room in the 26,000-seat bandbox that Missouri players had their ankles taped in makeshift tents in the parking lot. Tight end Martin Rucker remembers several Texans joked that they had played in bigger stadiums in high school.

Early on, Missouri looked like the 18th-ranked team in the country and Troy looked like, well, a high school squad. Smith completed 13 of his first 14 passes, and just 7:32 into the game Missouri led 14–0. In the three-man ESPN2 booth, Lee Corso did have one nitpick. He wondered why the Tigers' star quarterback was holding on extra points, saying a defender could barrel in and break Smith's leg. Kirk Herbstreit chuckled. "I've had it happen before, sweetheart," Corso replied, prompting Tirico to alert Corso that he might come back to him later to finish the story. Before Tirico could complete his sentence, Herbstreit jumped in. "We may need it," he said.

Could anybody blame the crew for getting its filler material ready? Things were equally lopsided when the Missouri defense was on the field. In the first 20 minutes, Troy had minus five yards of offense and no first downs. But, just like that, the defense settled in, and the home team channeled its namesake on the West Coast. The Trojans got on the board with a halfback pass, and on their next possession came the game's signature play. DeWhitt Betterson fumbled on a run up the middle, and left guard Junior Louissaint snatched the ball out of the air and rumbled 63 yards for a touchdown. Much had been made of Missouri's team speed, yet there was the 277-pound Louissaint out-plodding 11 Tigers down the middle of the field. "It was a play-by-play guy's nightmare," Kelly says with a laugh, "because he had a French name that I had no idea how to pronounce."

Missouri's nightmare was only beginning. Troy took a 17–14 lead into halftime, tacked on another touchdown midway through the fourth quarter and celebrated a 24–14 victory. "We don't have to beat them 365 days," Trojans coach Larry Blakeney said afterward. "We just have to beat them for one 60-minute segment of history. For that one 60 minutes, Troy was better than Missouri."

Let that sink in.

Though Mizzou rebounded to win its next three games, a lot of teams proved to be better than the Tigers in 2004. They slugged it out with Texas in Austin but lost, 28–20. At homecoming against Oklahoma State, they blew a 17–0, second-quarter lead and lost, 20–17. They lost at Nebraska, 24–3. They coughed up a 21–0, second-quarter advantage at home to Kansas State and fell, 35–24. They lost at home to underdog Kansas, 31–14, for their fifth consecutive defeat.

It was after the loss to Oklahoma State that the wheels started to come off. During a post-game interview, junior tailback Damien Nash questioned the play-calling. Pinkel suspended Nash, and the staff decided to burn the redshirt of Tony Temple, a freshman from Rockhurst High in Kansas City, Mo. Temple was Pinkel's most high-profile recruit to date— Mizzou beat out Notre Dame and Florida State, among others—but he was slow to pick up the offense after an assortment of leg injuries limited him during pre-season camp.

The Tigers limped into Lincoln losers of two straight, and during a season filled with disappointment, nothing spoke more to their futility than what happened before and during the game against the Cornhuskers. First, the Friday afternoon charter slid off the tarmac while taxiing at Columbia Regional Airport. No one was injured, but when another plane couldn't be procured immediately, Pinkel opted to have the team fly out on Saturday morning for the 11:10 a.m. kickoff. The players reconvened at 6 a.m., and 2½ hours later they conducted their pre-game walkthrough in a parking garage at the Lincoln airport.

Pinkel, who at Toledo never lost more than three consecutive games, minces no words. "It was my worst year as a head football coach, my worst year of coaching," he says.

Temple's season ended after a six-carry, 13-yard afternoon—he rolled an ankle and missed the last three games—and on a day when winds gusted to 25 mph, Smith threw 56 passes, misfiring on 32 of them. He carried 21 times for 25 yards. Never was the frustration more evident than when he sailed a pass a story or two over the head of Rucker, who was standing alone in the front right corner of the end zone. The tight end flung his arms in the air.

"I wasn't mad at Brad," Rucker says. "He was scrambling, and I broke to get away from my guy. When he threw it and it went so far over my head, I was like, 'My gosh, can *anything* go right?' "

Rucker's body language said otherwise, but who could blame him? The experiment to turn Smith into a pocket passer was failing miserably. After running for 2,425 yards in his first two seasons, Smith netted only 553 yards as a junior. The coaching staff had essentially taken away the most-feared weapon of one of the game's most electric players: his legs.

"I think Pinkel got more concerned with making [Smith] an NFL quarterback than winning," an unnamed Big 12 coach told Bruce Feldman for an *ESPN the Magazine* article in 2005. "He was the most dangerous runner in our league, tougher to handle than Vince Young [of Texas] and Reggie McNeal [of Texas A&M], and suddenly he got so stiff. You'd watch film and go, 'What the hell are they doing with him?' It was like you could hear the gears grinding in his head."

Though they earned some satisfaction with a 17–14 overtime victory at Iowa State that denied the Cyclones the opportunity to play for the Big

12 championship, the Tigers finished 5–6. That meant no 12th game, none of the invaluable 15 extra practices that are awarded to bowl teams and plenty of time for self-examination on a season gone horribly wrong.

Looking back, Pinkel, who at Toledo never lost more than three consecutive games, minces no words. "It was my worst year as a head football coach, my worst year of coaching," he says. "We had better players. We should have gone to a bowl that year. The infrastructure was such that we had a lot of problems I didn't realize. We weren't a close team. What happens to teams that aren't real close and don't have good leadership is that when adversity hits, it all comes out. You've seen it in sports for years, teams that can't deal with that stuff. That's what happened to us. I'm responsible for that."

Christensen remembers a December afternoon spent at home in the basement watching bowl games with his wife. As he drained the batteries in the remote, he was drawn to the games involving up-tempo offenses that were spreading the defenses from sideline to sideline and creating mismatches all over the field. That's when it hit him.

"I looked at Susie and said, 'We've got to change our offense,' " Christensen recalls. "'We've got to go to a spread, fast-paced scheme because we can't get the guys to compete with the best players. If we could get enough players to use space to our advantage, we could do some things. But I don't know if I want to tell Gary that. Or if he's going to want to hear it.' "

Again, Susie Christensen was quick with the comeback. "Well, if you don't do something, you're going to get fired," she said. "What do you have to lose?"

Chapter 5

Zo and Ruck (or T)

Lorenzo Williams always wanted to be a Sooner. He knew it when he was tearing it up as a running back on the Pop Warner fields of Central Oklahoma, and that desire only intensified during his days as a star linebacker at Midwest City High. An all-state selection as a senior in 2002 and the ninth-ranked prospect in the state of Oklahoma, he certainly fit the profile. Zo knew it. His parents did too. He was meant to wear the crimson and cream.

"Everybody wanted to be a Sooner," Williams says matter-of-factly. "I just knew I was going to OU."

Bob Stoops and the Oklahoma coaching staff knew all about Williams. Then again, considering that Midwest City High School Stadium, home of the Bombers, was just 19 miles up State Highway 77 from Norman, it would have been difficult to miss him. It didn't hurt that Williams' primary recruiter, defensive line coach Jackie Shipp, was a good friend of Lorenzo's parents. Shipp and Lorenzo's father grew up together, then competed as rivals at Oklahoma and Oklahoma State, respectively. The Cowboys were recruiting Williams hard, but he was already making plans to spend the next big phase of his life in Norman.

If he had come along in, say 1999, Williams most definitely would have been a must-have commitment for Stoops. But timing is everything. The Sooners were two years removed from a national championship, and they had won 36 of their last 40 games. The Oklahoma mystique, so strong during the days when Bud Wilkinson and Chuck Fairbanks and Barry Switzer paced the sideline, was back. Stoops could be more selective in recruiting. For the last of the 23 scholarships they had available in 2003, the Sooners, Williams says, debated between him and Dane Zaslaw, a linebacker from Edmond, Okla. According to Rivals, only one linebacker in the state was rated ahead of Williams. Of course it was Zaslaw, who also happened to be the No. 11-ranked inside backer in the country. (In the inexact science of college football recruiting rankings, Williams was listed 47th, 13 spots ahead of a prospect from

Hollow Rock, Tenn., named Patrick Willis, who would develop into an All-American at Ole Miss and an All-Pro for the San Francisco 49ers.) Wanting to give Williams time to explore his options, Shipp called to break the news. OU would land a Darien Williams and a John Williams, but there would be no Lorenzo Williams among the school's list of recruits who signed letters of intent on the first Wednesday of February in 2003.

Williams was crushed, but he had a backup plan. If the school he so dearly wanted to play for wouldn't have him, he'd head directly to the program at which he could "kick OU's butt every year," as he puts it. Williams scheduled an official visit to Oklahoma State, and on the first weekend of December 2002 he made the 67-mile trip up I-35 North. The Cowboys were on the rise, even if they were coming off a 49–17 defeat to Oklahoma. Coach Les Miles was wrapping up his second year in Stillwater, and OSU had just accepted its first bowl invitation since 1997. Offensive coordinator Mike Gundy, Williams' primary recruiter, was from Midwest City. Lorenzo felt wanted.

"We stopped and asked somebody: How do you get to Mizzou?" says Williams. "A lady at a convenience store said, 'You are a *long* way from where you need to go.'"

He committed on the spot, only to return from Stillwater to field a phone call from an old friend. The familiar voice on the other end of the line was Tony Palmer, who was two years ahead of Williams at Midwest City. An offensive lineman, Palmer encouraged his former Bombers teammate to visit Missouri; he said the Tigers were worth a look because they were building something special. Williams didn't know much about Mizzou, but Smith's coming-out party against Oklahoma that fall was still fresh on his mind. So the next weekend, he and his mother jumped in the car and motored across I-44 East.

After crossing the border into Missouri, they pulled into Springfield. It had not been an especially long trip — 286 miles — but as they drove around town, Mother and Son were lost and confused. "We were thinking, 'What's with all of these Bears? I don't think we're in the right spot,' " Zo recalls saying. "We stopped and asked somebody: How do you get to Mizzou? A lady at a convenience store said, 'You are a *long* way from where you need to go.' "

In fact, Lorenzo and LaRhonda were parked within the city limits of the Division I-AA Southwest Missouri State Bears. They were still 168 miles from where they needed to be. They got back in the car and continued up I-44 to Lebanon and past the Walnut Bowl Capital of the World, then traversed along the mostly two-lane highways through Osage Beach, over the Lake of the Ozarks and past the state capital of Jefferson City into Columbia. It is a scenic drive, but bottleneck traffic can also make it a bit maddening. Somewhere along the way, LaRhonda turned to Lorenzo and said, "If I had known it was this far, we would not have driven up here."

The 454-mile odyssey, it turned out, proved to be worth every last drop of $1.53-a-gallon gas. Upon arriving in Columbia, Williams was mightily impressed. "It reminded me a lot of Midwest City," he says.

He connected with some of the other recruits who were in town for the weekend: wideouts Brad Ekwerekwu and Jason Ray; running backs Damien Nash and Marcus Woods; and offensive linemen Tyler Luellen and Adam Spieker. Williams was already a friendly rival with Ray, who was the 10th-ranked player in Oklahoma and had starred at Broken Arrow High, outside Tulsa. As they are wont to do, the recruits took down each other's phone numbers and promised to stay in touch. Williams didn't leave town without one final reflection: "I remember thinking I could really start something here."

On the night before signing day, Williams committed to the Tigers. Early on the morning of Feb. 4, 2003, he faxed his letter of intent to the Missouri football office. So did Ray and the five other players with whom Williams had connected during his visit. The Missouri class of 2003 included 23 players from nine states (but interestingly no quarterback). The most pleasant surprise was a rail-thin receiver from St. Joseph, Mo.

Martin Rucker always wanted to be a Cornhusker. No surprise there. He had been raised a Nebraska fan; his older brother, Mike, was an All-America defensive tackle for the Cornhuskers and was now starring in the NFL for the Carolina Panthers. Martin, decked out in red, was at Faurot Field on that memorable November afternoon in 1997 when Larry Smith got a tear in his eye and the Tigers came within an illegally kicked ball of knocking off No. 1 Nebraska in the overtime classic that became known as the Flea-Kicker.

"I really wanted to go to Nebraska," Rucker says. "*Really* bad. It was just the tradition. They were winning championships. I was traveling all over the place watching them play. It was a big deal. When I got the offer from them, I said, 'This is it. I don't care if I get another offer.' "

Rucker, of course, got other offers. He was the 12th-ranked recruit in the state, the 28th-rated tight end in the nation. Kansas showed interest and was the major-college campus closest to his hometown, but he wasn't crazy about Lawrence or the program. In fact, he was so uninterested that on his one and only visit, he joined the throng of fans who made a habit of flocking to the exits at halftime of football games. The finalists were Missouri and Nebraska. On the weekend Williams was in Stillwater, Rucker made the three-hour drive southeast to Columbia. As Williams was on his round-about trip to Columbia, Rucker was in Lincoln, a couple hours north of St. Joe. In recruiting, the coaching staff that has the last word often wins, but Rucker kept an open mind. In the end, in what was one of Pinkel's early recruiting coups, Rucker pledged to the Tigers.

"It came down to the visits," he says. "Nebraska, it was like a machine. Some guys make it, some guys don't. It doesn't matter. They win. At Mizzou, they were building something. It was more of a family. That's what Coach Pinkel is all about."

There was more to it than that. Like Williams, Rucker saw an opportunity to be a part of something special, had a vision of where he could lead the program. Plus, he felt an obligation to the flagship university in the state he called home.

"When I went on my visit, everything felt right," Rucker says. "There are so many Mizzou fans in this state. This is your home state. All they want is a good team to cheer for. I got to thinking, 'Wouldn't it be awesome? I could be the guy who went to Missouri and changed everything, changed the entire mind-set of the state.' You know, they used to be good. I wanted to be part of something that could restore the program to what it was."

Ruck, who because he shared the same first name as his father also became known as T, and Zo would redshirt in 2003. Neither was anywhere near big enough to handle the demands of Big 12 football. Rucker reported for fall camp weighing a gangly 208 pounds; Williams dipped to 224 pounds after he came down with tonsillitis. Even as a sideline spectator, Rucker took particular delight in Mizzou's first victory over Nebraska in 25 years, and as their freshman year dragged on, the players' bond drew extremely close. They lived with wideout Greg Bracey and offensive lineman Monte Wyrick, and their dorm room became the freshman hangout. Rucker and Williams would talk late into the night about their shared vision of turning around Missouri's football fortunes, even if they weren't exactly on the same page. Williams knew next to nothing about the years and years of futility, about the Fifth Down Game or the Flea-Kicker — remember, this is the guy who thought the campus was in Springfield — but Rucker was quick with a history lesson.

"The one thing Ruck said was, 'If we've been bad this long, it will be real easy to put our names on the program,'" Williams recalls.

Adds Ray, another out-of-state redshirt: "Ruck did have to school some of us. You're indoctrinated into it pretty quickly."

If there was a perfect year for a turnaround at Mizzou, 2004 was it. Williams had been moved from linebacker to defensive end — "a whole new experience," he says — and he was up to 260 pounds. Rucker, slowed during spring ball by a torn labrum, had jumped to 228 pounds and was in a heated battle with Victor Sesay for the tight end job. (A junior college transfer, Sesay caught the go-ahead touchdown pass on a fake field goal in the 2003 upset of Nebraska.) During the last scrimmage of fall camp, the two traded out plays under the coaching staff's watchful eye. Rucker remembers it being an especially stifling day; the heat seeped out of the artificial turf at Faurot. He's not sure how he kept going, but he did enough to move to the top of the depth chart.

"The one thing about our class is that we never had a feeling we made the wrong decision," says Williams. "Everyone thought we would be the ones to change Mizzou. We talked about it every day in the dorms."

"That scrimmage prepared me for the rest of my career," says Ruck. Of the heat that day, he says, "It doesn't matter. You just keep going."

He kept going, all right. On the first drive of the season opener against Arkansas State, on the 10th play of his college career, Rucker snagged a 24-yard touchdown pass. He remembers the play vividly. He also remembers the first thought that crossed his mind as Smith zipped a dart in his direction.

"It was like a dream," Rucker says. "The first pass comes to me. *Catch it!* That's the first thought. You see the ball coming. *Catch it!* I caught the ball, turned around, ran for a touchdown. Nothing could have been better. This is the way it was supposed to happen. I'm supposed to be here, and this is what I'm supposed to be doing."

Rucker's first catch was also his last in a 52–20 victory. Williams chipped in with a solo tackle, and the Tigers were on their way. Or were they? Next came the trip to Troy—Rucker says Pinkel was "smokin' hot" on the charter home—the dissension, the five-game losing streak. It wasn't exactly what Rucker and Williams envisioned during those dorm-room discussions. But they remained unfazed.

"The one thing about our class is that we never had a feeling we made the wrong decision," Williams says. "Everyone in my class thought we would be the ones to change Mizzou. We talked about it every day in the dorms. Mizzou hasn't been good, but we were going to make it good. Even when we went through that low point, a lot of us weren't playing."

One of the few freshmen who was contributing, Rucker finished the season with 19 receptions for 263 yards and four touchdowns. Two of those scores came in a 36–10 victory at Baylor, but the much-anticipated trip to Lincoln was deflating, to say the least. The plane went off the runway, the walk-through was staged in the parking garage, the sure-fire touchdown pass sailed over his head. This *wasn't* the way they did things at Nebraska. The following week's home loss to Kansas State was especially stinging. With a 21–0, second-quarter lead, the Tigers appeared on their way to snapping their 11-game skid in the series, but the Wildcats rallied for a 35–24 victory. This *wasn't* the way it was supposed to happen. Mizzou football was at a crossroads. Rucker knew it. Williams knew it. Pinkel knew it. Christensen knew it.

"There was nothing else you could do," Rucker says. "You could either go one way or the other."

Chapter 6

The Missouri Spread

It wasn't simply the win-loss record that led Pinkel to call 2004 his worst season as a football coach. The issues ran significantly deeper, and one charge was so disturbing it made the five-game losing streak seem trivial. The indictment: The head coach didn't know his players. Sure, he knew their names and their hometowns and maybe even their majors, but he made no attempt to get to *know* them. Just as troubling, the players didn't know their coach either. So even as he was having the same thoughts about shaking up the offense as the man he had charged with coordinating it, Pinkel first had to do some soul-searching.

The news bulletin was delivered by one of his players. Derrick Ming, a linebacker from St. Louis with a year of eligibility left, told Pinkel that one of the best relationships he enjoyed was with his high school coach, but that he and a lot of teammates didn't feel any kind of connection with the man who had recruited them. So in early 2005, Pinkel arranged a meeting with Ming and about a half-dozen other soon-to-be seniors. "We did a lot of things that had a huge impact on the success of the program," Pinkel says. "My thing was to turn a negative into a positive."

He vowed to make himself more accessible and approachable, to be more forthcoming. He established a players council that was designed to address team issues and concerns, further opening the lines of communication. He had weeded out most of the bad apples—"When we got here [in 2003], the program was in shambles as far as attitude," says Rucker—and he turned over ownership of the team to the players and made them more accountable.

In 2004, quarterback Chase Patton says the locker room was rife with a players-versus-coaches mentality. Team chemistry? There wasn't any. The transfer of title could not have come at a better time. "If you weren't on the bandwagon, weren't on the train, you were going to get thrown off by the players," Patton says, "whereas before the coaches were the ones who were having to do all of the discipline."

For Pinkel, the catchword of the offseason was *communication*. He demanded unfiltered dialogue with his players. "They've got to know the truth, and they've got to know about it before anybody else does," he says. "We had a communication thing going on. They'd never get blindsided about anything. Nothing."

Whether it was good news or bad, the players would be first to learn about developments in the program. There would be no discovering about depth-chart changes or injury updates or player arrests in the *Tribune* or the *Missourian*. Pinkel would talk to his players about their life outside of — and after — football. Most important, the coach was going to make damn sure his players knew who *he* was.

"Some of the players will talk about the kinder, gentler Gary Pinkel," Moller says. "I see that as the start of it."

"For him to open himself up, that's a major shift," says Alden. "And to tell his coaches: 'Guys, we've got to open ourselves up more. If we expect our kids to respond to us, we have to open ourselves up.' "

Pinkel also had issues with the media. The sourpuss who arrived in Columbia in late 2000 had taken things to another level. *Surly* was the adjective most often thrown around. On several occasions during the 2004 season, Pinkel engaged in uncomfortable interactions with reporters, whether it was during his post-game media scrums or his early-week press conferences, when scribes turn into Monday morning quarterbacks. There was nothing disrespectful in Pinkel's words, but the tone of his voice and his terse responses were a red flag to Moller.

"He built a reputation through his first four seasons of not being real media-friendly and having this persona you don't like your coach to have," says Moller. "I knew it was my job to sit down with Coach and say, 'There's this perception, and maybe there are things we can do to change it.' To his credit he beat me to it. He called me in shortly after the season was over, and he said in his own analysis of dealing with the media and our public face, there were a couple of times this year where he didn't handle things the right way."

Pinkel apologized to Moller for putting him in awkward situations and announced that Mr. Surly was leaving the building. He pledged to have great relations with the media regardless of what happened on the field. He said his program would do things the right way — win or lose.

"Some of the players will talk about the kinder, gentler Gary Pinkel," Moller says. "I see that as the start of it."

Kinder and gentler also meant Pinkel was more energized and refocused. He zeroed in on the offense. The Tigers averaged only 23 points a game in 2004, a touchdown less than the previous year, and though nobody in the program wanted to admit it, the Brad Smith experiment had failed miserably. His completion percentage— 51.8 —pretty much said it all. With Smith's senior season looming, it was time to shake things up.

"I felt we had to do something to give ourselves an edge," Pinkel says. "I'm watching Mike Leach at Texas Tech going to bowl game after bowl game after bowl game. He's doing that because his offense is so far ahead of everybody else's."

So Pinkel worked the phones, calling around the country to friends and colleagues who were earning their keep on the defensive side of the ball. He asked his counterparts which offense they least liked to defend. "Every one of them said the spread," Pinkel recalls. "They hated it."

Alden remembers the day that Pinkel told him he was overhauling the offense. It was early one winter morning when the athletic director stuck his head in the coach's office at the Tom Taylor Building.

"You know how he talks—really fast, especially when he's excited about something," says Alden, who then breaks into a poor-man's Pinkel impersonation: "Mike, I've looked at this, really mulled it over. This is *hugely* important. We're going to have to change our offense. This is *huge* for me. I've never done anything like this, but by gosh, we're going to have to make a shift. If we're going to compete, we're going to have to do this.

"He kept saying, 'This is *huge* for me. I've never done stuff like this. This is so different for me.' I said, 'You know what you're doing. If there's anybody who knows about offense, it's you.' That's the thing about Gary: He had analyzed every statistic. When he made the decision to change the offense, he said he had to revamp it completely. He kept saying, 'This is a career decision.' "

Of course, the wheels were already spinning in Christensen's head, from that afternoon spent watching bowl games in his basement. "Credit to him," he says of Pinkel, "because it's tough to change. We went to something drastically different from anything we'd ever done."

The spread is as simple as its name implies: Stretch the defense from sideline to sideline, exploit one-on-one mismatches, attack with quick passes, create gaping running lanes with wider line splits. Almost every snap—even from the opponent's one-yard line—is taken out of the shotgun. Texas Tech wasn't the only program in the country employing the offense (in 2003, Urban Meyer parlayed his success at Bowling Green into the Utah job), but the Red Raiders happened to be running it as well as, if not better than, anyone. En route to an 8–4 finish in 2004 and its fifth consecutive bowl appearance, Tech *averaged* more than 54 pass attempts a game (and never threw fewer than 39); twice the Raiders scored 70 points, against TCU and Nebraska. What quarterback or wide receiver in his right mind wouldn't want to play in a video-game offense like that? As Christensen puts it, a program such as Missouri couldn't compete with the perennial powers for all of the top talent, but the Tigers believed they could attract enough playmakers to use space on the field to their advantage.

As is the case with any offense, the spread has as many systems as Ben and Jerry's has flavors, so the Missouri coaches began sampling the variations being used around the country. They settled on three finalists: the Clemson spread, which was being operated by quarterback Woody Danzler; the Meyer-Bowling Green model; and the Toledo offense. Toledo! There was debate and disagreement over which made most sense. "And that's a good thing," says Pinkel.

Yost preferred the Toledo spread, because it was built around a naked bootleg that had made Smith so dangerous. He had reservations about Bowling Green and its five-wide look. That set, he reasoned, screamed "Pass!" and the Tigers had been down that road. Smith may have had only one year of eligibility left, but Yost thought, "We need to be successful with Brad." After all, there was an urgency to capitalize on the momentum Smith had generated.

Yet the more Yost looked at the Bowling Green spread, the more he liked it. And the more sense it made. "You spread people out to give yourself running lanes, and you give yourself easy completions and throws," he says. "And we were able to find within that what Brad was good at. It fit him well."

Stories abound about coaching staffs that spend time in the offseason roaming from campus to campus for clues about the way their colleagues do their jobs. It is one of the stranger customs in the college game—even in *Football: Secrets of the Split T Formation*, Don Faurot included a chapter on how to defend his innovation—but the sharing of trade secrets is an accepted practice. However, when Pinkel and his staff settled on the Bowling Green spread, they didn't travel to Ohio. Rather, Christensen suggested that the program pay Falcons coach Gregg Brandon and his offensive aides to visit Columbia and school the Missouri staff on every last detail of their attack.

The two staffs convened at 8 a.m. The Bowling Green coaches scribbled a play on the board, then explained the thinking behind it. The Missouri coaches did a lot of listening and note-taking. This went on for four days. Christensen, Yost and the offensive assistants then went about the gargantuan task of rewriting the playbook, spending weeks working on terminology, molding the Falcons' model to suit their personnel, taking some elements from the Utah and Texas Tech spreads, adding some of their own wrinkles, including line splits wide enough to drive a truck through. (Somewhere, Faurot was smiling.) Put all of those elements together and, says Christensen, "That's how it became known as the Missouri Spread."

"There was not one word of terminology that was a carryover," he adds. "We started from absolutely ground zero. The great thing is we had a staff that was very willing, and we had a bunch of players who were very willing. Everybody had the same excitement going into it."

One of the most significant benefits of the spread was the effect it would have on recruiting. While there were still holes in the fences, the Tigers were starting to lock down the borders. Patton, Temple and linebacker Van Alexander were among the quintet of four-star, in-state recruits signed in the Class of 2004. Mizzou was also making inroads in St. Louis.

Bob Bunton, the coach at Parkway North High, noticed the change in attitude and organization under Pinkel almost immediately. Assessing the problems of previous regimes, Bunton says, "I don't think Mizzou got into enough schools, to be honest. If you had a kid who was very good, you might see someone walk in."

That all changed with Pinkel, who assigned cornerbacks coach Cornell Ford to work the St. Louis area. Coaches could always count on Ford to pay a visit, even if it was just to say hello.

"Cornell still comes by," says Bunton. "And I tell him, 'Cornell, we don't have a D-I kid, and we probably won't for two or three years.' He still comes by. I hear that from a lot of coaches in the area. Missouri is in your school whether you have talent or not. It makes you feel good. It's not like we're a garbage program because we don't have a Division I recruit. You respect that. And I don't think we saw enough of that prior to Coach Pinkel and his staff coming in."

The '05 recruiting class served as proof that the Tigers were making headway elsewhere as well. As was the case when he worked for Don James at Washington, Pinkel knew there wasn't enough talent in his home state to sustain the program. And just as James identified California as a secondary market for players, Missouri would flood Texas with resources.

It is a numbers game. "I can't think of a handful of kids in southern California that we beat USC and UCLA on," Pinkel says of the 12 years he spent with the Huskies. "But there were a lot of kids down there, and we evaluated well."

Texas, with its 1,700 high schools, would become to Missouri what California was to Washington. Five coaches, half of the staff, were assigned to the state. Major metropolitan areas such as Houston and Dallas were obvious hotbeds, but small schools in the dusty, back-roads environs of East and West Texas had to be scoured as well. Looking back at the early years, Matter remembers

Daniel didn't come to Columbia to make Missouri respectable; he came to win championships. "He talked with us about bringing Mizzou to where we wanted it to be," says Rucker. "When he was a _freshman_."

Pinkel's being asked what the key was to finding all these players. "Garmin," the coach replied. "We all have Garmin."

Says Pinkel, "Texas is going to take who they want, Oklahoma is going to take who they want, but there are a lot of kids down there. You can bring great talent out of there."

That there were no four-star signees in the 2005 class speaks to what a crapshoot recruiting can be. Evander (Ziggy) Hood was a three-star defensive lineman out of Palo Duro High in Amarillo, Texas, who had offers from only two other BCS schools—Arizona State and Baylor. He didn't even merit a ranking in the state top 100, yet five years later, Hood was a first-round draft pick of the Pittsburgh Steelers.

The gem of the class was another Texan: Chase Daniel was the sixth-ranked dual-threat quarterback in the country but only a three-star recruit in the eyes of Rivals. That's partly because there was no category on the evaluation form for winning. In two seasons directing a spread attack at Southlake Carroll High, Daniel won a state championship and lost only once in 32 starts—a one-point defeat in the title game at the end of his junior season. He was a cocksure, tough-as-nails competitor who took only one official recruiting visit (to Columbia) and committed to the

Tigers during the summer before his senior year. Not even the Troy upset or the five-game skid in 2004 gave him second thoughts.

"Coach Steck [linebackers coach Dave Steckel] and Coach Pinkel and Coach Yost sold me on the university," says Daniel. "I loved it."

He saw the program as a perfect fit—and that was before Pinkel made the career-defining decision to install the spread. The early commitment was all part of the plan; Daniel was bent on enjoying his final year of high school. "I wanted to get it out of the way," he says. "We had some unfinished business [at Southlake Carroll]. We lost the year before in the state finals, and I wanted to be focused on my senior year."

Daniel even refused to waiver when the Texas Longhorns made an 11th-hour run at him after Ryan Perrilloux, the top-rated dual-threat QB, had a change of heart and announced he would attend LSU. Like Williams always wanted to be a Sooner and Rucker always wanted to be a Cornhusker, Daniel always wanted to be a Longhorn—his high-school coach, Todd Dodge, played there, and his sister was a student in Austin. Yet when the Texas coaching staff reached out to Dodge to gauge Daniel's interest, he didn't even consult his star.

"He was like a second dad to me, and still is to this day," Daniel says. "We talked a lot. He knew exactly what I was thinking."

Daniel, who also had offers from Texas A&M, Oklahoma State, Stanford and Maryland, may have been only a three-star recruit, but in terms of confidence, his rating was off the charts. He didn't come to Columbia to make Missouri respectable; he came to win championships. "He talked with us about bringing Mizzou to where we wanted it to be," says Rucker. "When he was a *freshman*. He was impressive. Not only that, he also worked. He was there all summer. He understood what it meant to be a Tiger, wanted to be a Tiger, wanted to get where we wanted to get."

When he heard of Daniel's commitment, Patton thought little of it. Sure, he did the obligatory Google search of the new guy on the roster, but he also understood the recruiting process. If the Tigers expected to be a player on the national stage, they had to go after the best. "I looked him up because I was interested to see what we were getting. Oh, another quarterback," Patton remembers thinking. "We try to get one every year. Even if you get a good quarterback one year, the goal is to get an even better one the next year. That's just the way you do it."

Yet from the time Daniel stepped on campus in the summer of 2005, it was obvious that Mizzou wasn't getting just another quarterback. Yost and Christensen marveled at how ridiculously polished and savvy Daniel was. He was a football junkie, a student of the game, an intelligent kid, a leader with great charisma. It wasn't long before Pinkel was throwing around the *it* word again.

"He had been trained to be a college quarterback," says Yost. "Coach Dodge did an unbelievable job with him. He had so much background as a thrower in a spread-type offense. Being in the spread, it's not only how many times you throw the ball in a game. It's also, 'Are you a throwing team? Do you throw the ball in Monday practice, Tuesday practice, Wednesday practice? And then what do you do in the summer?' In the state of Texas, you play seven-on-seven, and you're at a high-level high school like he was and you've been trained as a quarterback, and he's thrown 100,000 passes in his career and he's such a smart and competitive guy. He had such a bank of philosophy and an understanding of the concepts."

Almost immediately, Patton began to second-guess his decision to redshirt in 2004. He had played quarterback for only three years in high school and spending a season learning under Smith seemed like the right call. Now, however, he was wrestling with a new offense and new terminology while facing competition from a confident freshman who was already schooled in the spread. "To be perfectly honest, you sit there and wonder, 'What's that all about?' " Patton says. "It's the same offense he ran in high school."

Actually, it was not a dead ringer for the Southlake Carroll attack. Nor did the coaching staff fly in Dodge to teach them the offense. There were similarities between the two schemes, but the Dragons modeled theirs more after Leach's offense at Texas Tech, which liked to position a running back next to the quarterback. At Southlake Carroll, Daniel was a running threat; he points out he carried about 250 times in both his junior and senior seasons. Mizzou, however, wanted to ride Daniel's arm. "We went empty all the time," says Yost, referring to the five-receiver sets. "We decided that's what we wanted to be."

Even as the summer dragged on, the excitement was building. Pinkel had delivered his strongest recruiting class to date. Smith was preparing for his senior season, his heir apparent was already taking charge and the Tigers were just weeks away from rolling out the Missouri Spread. Imagine Rucker's delight.

"They brought in the spread offense, and I'm a receiver *and* a tight end," he remembers thinking. "It doesn't get any better than this."

Chapter 7

A.O.

If there is a slow time for college football coaches, it is typically the four weeks from the middle of June to the middle of July. NCAA rules stipulate next to no contact with the players, but the strength and conditioning staff is allowed to oversee training sessions in shorts and T-shirts. These are called voluntary workouts, but for a player who has designs on a successful college career, they are pretty much mandatory. It is also a time when bonds are cemented and team chemistry is developed.

The Missouri players split into three groups for their conditioning drills, and early on the afternoon of July 12, a dozen Tigers walked into Faurot Field to unseasonably cool temperatures. "It was a perfect 75 degree day," says Williams, who was on the move again, to defensive tackle, and as a redshirt sophomore was already developing into a team leader. "We work hard, but it wasn't the hardest workout we've ever done."

Under Ivey's direction, the 60-minute session was winding down when Williams noticed that Aaron O'Neal, a 19-year-old middle linebacker from Parkway North High in St. Louis, was struggling to complete his runs. That was a surprise to Williams, who says he couldn't remember O'Neal ever taking a drill off. O'Neal said he hadn't eaten breakfast or lunch. Williams and other players urged him to keep pushing. It would be one of those team-bonding experiences, a moment Williams, O'Neal and the 10 other Tigers who participated in the session would reminisce about when they were hoisting championship hardware. Williams approached O'Neal.

"I was like, 'What's going on with you,' " Williams says, his vibrant voice turning to a faint whisper. "He looked me right in the eye, and his eyes were glossed over, and he said, 'Man, I can't see.' What do you mean you can't see? He said, 'Man, I can't see you.' Then he looked right over my head, because he was a couple of inches taller than me, and said, 'Zo, I'm hurting, man.' "

O'Neal still had one run to complete, and Williams encouraged him to dig deep. "I said, 'Let's make this last run. I'll make it with you,'" Zo recalls. "He ran that last one, and he kind of fell out."

According to a timeline released by the university, O'Neal collapsed at 2:39 p.m. Four minutes later, he was helped off the field. He was in the locker room at Faurot for 12 minutes before being moved to a university pickup truck. University Hospital was just down the street, but instead the vehicle took O'Neal in the other direction—across Providence Road to the locker room at the Tom Taylor Building. It was now 3:03 p.m. He was stretched out on the floor, his breathing labored, and five minutes later a 911 call was made.

"It's not unusual to see guys laid out on the floor of the locker room after a workout," Williams says, "but he was in there a little too long."

Driving by after lunch, Mike Kelly noticed a fleet of police cars parked outside the Taylor Building, lights flashing. "I said to somebody, 'That's never good.'"

Paramedics were on the scene at 3:14, and O'Neal was rushed down Stadium Drive to University Hospital. He arrived 16 minutes later. At 4:05 p.m., Aaron O'Neal was pronounced dead. The medical examiner ruled the cause of death as viral meningitis. Swelling on O'Neal's brain pushed on his spinal cord, causing his cardiovascular system to shut down.

Word spread quickly of an unidentified player death, but the reports were coming from sources outside the program. Williams was in his apartment playing video games with defensive end Xzavie Jackson when he got a call from his hysterical mother. "She was screaming," Williams says. The two had talked that morning, and Zo had mentioned he would be working out that afternoon. Now LaRhonda had heard on TV that a Missouri football player had died, and she was positive it was her son. A couple of frantic female classmates called as well. "Nobody's dead," Williams told them. "I don't know what you're talking about."

This being their slow time, many of the Missouri coaches and administrators were scattered around the country. Pinkel was in Las Vegas. Christensen and his family had been visiting relatives in the Pacific Northwest and were preparing to board a flight home. Alden was vacationing on the San Juan Islands off the coast of Washington.

Pinkel had already coped with tragedy in 2005. On the Wednesday in February the Tigers unveiled their gem of a recruiting class, he was in Akron, making funeral arrangements for his brother, Greg. Now on a July afternoon, Gary and his then-wife, Vicki, were kicking back with another couple some 1,500 miles from home. He promised to leave his cell phone in the hotel room that day, only to return mid-afternoon to find it blinking madly with more than a dozen messages. Even before he called Columbia, Pinkel knew something had gone horribly wrong.

"I hung up the phone, looked at my wife and said, 'I don't know if I'm going to be able to overcome this,' " he recalls, his voice shaking.

In St. Louis, Bob Bunton, O'Neal's high school coach, was watching TV in his family room when his son Bo walked in and told him rumors were circulating that Aaron had died. "I said, 'That's ridiculous,' " recalls Bunton. He turned back to the TV.

Not 15 minutes later, Bo interrupted his father again and told him he was hearing more and more chatter. Bunton grew more concerned, so he decided to go straight to the source to put the rumor to rest. He called O'Neal's cell phone. There was no answer, only O'Neal's familiar tone on his voice mail.

> **"I will never forget Cornell's words," Bunton says. "I said, 'Coach, I'm hearing some strange things that Aaron passed away today.' And he says, 'Coach, we lost him.' I did not fathom what he had said. I said, 'What do you mean, we lost him?'"**

"I really started to panic," Bunton says, "so I called Coach Ford."

O'Neal's primary recruiter, Ford was on vacation as well, visiting family in Ohio.

"I will never forget Cornell's words," Bunton says. "I said, 'Coach, I'm hearing some strange things that Aaron passed away today.' And he says, 'Coach, we lost him.' I did not fathom what he had said. I said, 'What do you mean, we lost him?' He said, 'Coach, he died in a workout today.' "

The news was slow to be released because school officials first needed to notify the family. After contact was made with O'Neal's father, Lonnie, the players were summoned to an emergency meeting. Williams and Jackson walked into the Taylor Building together. "Xzavie looked at me and I looked at him and said, 'No way,' " Williams says. "And he's like, 'Man, there's just no way.' I didn't know what they were going to tell us, but that couldn't be it."

Before a hushed room, one assistant after another stood before the players, unable to speak. Finally, Yost got the words out. "It was one of those things you hear about on ESPN," Rucker says, "but it doesn't happen at *your* school."

Because Williams was at the workout and already developing into a spokesman, the coaches asked him to talk on behalf of the players. "He was the most genuine, eloquent, heart-felt voice they had," says Matter.

After the meeting ended, Williams didn't leave the facility for almost six hours. He and the others who participated in the workout immediately began questioning and blaming themselves. "What did we do wrong?" Williams remembers asking. "How could we not have known? I just kept going over that conversation in my head. *Man, I can't see.* I should have just stopped him right there and said, 'Coach, can we sit him down?' I could have stopped it. I could have made a difference. But I didn't. I was trying to be that guy, trying to be that leader, trying to step up."

Three days later, O'Neal was laid to rest in St. Louis. The Missouri coaches and players attended the funeral, and upon returning to Columbia the reflection began. O'Neal was a popular player, but many of his teammates knew little about him. "He was in my [recruiting] class," says Patton. "He was an amazing person—the hardest worker on the team, by far."

Adds Ray, "I was in a class with him. He sat near the front. I remember him in the locker room. He was always wearing a hat."

And a smile. That's because A.O., as he was known around the program, always wanted to be a Tiger.

"When he was a freshman in our program, he was a college football nut," says Bunton. "He wanted to go to Miami. That's when the Hurricanes were pretty good. As a junior, he was starting to get a little attention. And he started going to Mizzou games. Any weekend he could get away, he would go with friends, and I would start to hear a little more: 'Hey, Coach, I'd kind of like to play for the Tigers.' It became a goal of his to play football at Mizzou."

So respected was O'Neal among the Parkway North coaches that in March 2005, the staff used a day of spring break to pile into Bunton's van and make the 120-mile drive to Columbia. A running back in high school, O'Neal was the first Viking in several years to sign with a Division I-A program, and the coaches were eager to watch their star participate in spring practice.

"We looked kind of geeky," says Bunton, who brought two of his four sons along for the trip. "We were all right there in his linebacker drills, about eight yards away. We probably drove him crazy. It was a thrill. Boy, he had gotten bigger. He was becoming a little more physical.

"As a coach, it's what you want. You want your kids to succeed. He was doing well in school, and he was fitting right in. We had a great day. We talked about him all the way home, like he was our own son. We were just tickled for him. Sadly, that was the last time we saw him in a football uniform."

Bunton, however, remembers O'Neal as much more than a talented football player. "I'm sitting here with tears in my eyes, goose bumps," he says. "That's the way Aaron was. You wouldn't look at Aaron O'Neal and say, 'Oh, there's a jock.'

"People would say, 'Describe Aaron O'Neal,' and I'd say, 'Aaron O'Neal is a beautiful kid. There isn't a mean bone in his body.' He said very little, but what an example he was to a lot of people."

A.O. most certainly made an impact on free safety William Moore. The two were in the same recruiting class, and almost immediately upon arriving on campus in the summer of 2004, the youngster from big-city St. Louis and the kid from the Missouri Bootheel hamlet of Hayti hit it off. They weren't roommates, but considering the amount of time the two spent in each other's dorm room, they might as well have been. As redshirts playing on the scout team, they talked about how they one day were going to be difference-makers; they saw themselves as the future of Missouri football.

"He was humble," says Moore. "It was a blessing just to spend that time with him. The guy really loved Mizzou."

He also quickly grasped the significance of the rivalry with KU. Though he knew he would redshirt, O'Neal dressed for all of the home games in 2004, so he was in uniform for the season finale against the Jayhawks. Bunton was there too. He had his eyes trained on A.O., and he remembers how incensed the true freshman became after watching KU players stomp on the "M" at midfield during pre-game drills. "He was pumped," says Bunton.

It was the last time O'Neal put on a Mizzou game uniform.

Moore and O'Neal shared a summer-school class in '05, but on the morning of July 12, Moore says his sidekick told him he wouldn't be attending that afternoon. A.O. was looking forward to participating in conditioning drills with his fellow Tigers. After all, a teenager was just 53 days from realizing his dream of playing D–I football.

"That was the last time I talked to him," says Moore, a Pro Bowl safety with the Atlanta Falcons who keeps his friend's memory alive by wearing his jersey number. "I continue to rock the No. 25 for A.O. in Atlanta."

In the wake of O'Neal's death, the finger-pointing followed, and the trust that Pinkel had worked so tirelessly to establish was tested. The players had put themselves in the hands of the coaches and the training staff. Now one of their own had died. Who would have *their* backs? Who could guarantee this wouldn't happen again? There was talk of defections and transfers.

"That whole next year everybody was looking for somebody to hold onto, somebody to be a leader, somebody to step up," Williams says. "I had a hard time telling anybody to do anything."

"All the things we did when we hit that adversity, it all came together —how we communicate with each other, how we care about each other, all the things we did in meetings and building relationships," Pinkel says.

No doubt, the coaching staff could not have handled such a crisis in 2004.

"That was a surreal experience that everyone lived through together, all throughout the football program, the athletic department and the university," says Moller. "I give Gary and everyone credit. All you can do in a situation like that is try to do the right things and try to make something good out of it. I think he did—with the relationships the coaches had with the kids. The improvement of those relationships really helped those teams down the road from a chemistry standpoint."

Ivey approached Pinkel and requested a meeting with the seniors. Still in his suit from the funeral, he addressed the players in the same locker room where A.O. had taken some of his last breaths. "I told Coach Pinkel there was no way I could step back in front of the team without first meeting with the seniors," Ivey says. "I laid it all out there. I knew I needed their trust in what we were doing, and I wanted them to know I was in it with them and that they were my No. 1 priority. I had their trust after that meeting."

Most of it, anyway. Williams, for one, went into seclusion, hiding out in a friend's apartment for five days. As the players convened for the start of fall practice in early August, the investigation into O'Neal's death was in full gear. When the players weren't being questioned by medical examiners, they were bombarded with queries from the media. On the practice field, the outgoing Williams was afraid to open his mouth. "That whole next year everybody was looking for somebody to hold onto, somebody to be a leader, somebody to step up," he says. "I had a hard time telling anybody to do anything."

The Tigers dedicated their season to O'Neal, and they wore No. 25 decals on their helmets. "A.O. 25" was stenciled on the banks behind both benches at Faurot. Competition can be therapeutic for a team, and for the 2005 Missouri Tigers, the football was especially cathartic. It was also Smith's senior season. There was much anticipation about the Missouri Spread, and the Tigers were determined to prove that 2004 was an aberration. They were playing with heavy hearts, but they were also playing for A.O.

As expected, Missouri opened with a walkover against Arkansas State at Arrowhead Stadium, home of the Kansas City Chiefs. In a 44–17 victory, the Tigers piled up 317 yards on the ground and another 340 through the air. The no-huddle offense got off 89 snaps. Asked to make mostly short throws, Smith was his old self. He passed for 317 yards and four touchdowns—the combined yardage for those scores was 28 yards—but the most encouraging statistic was his rushing total: 92 yards. Brad was free again.

As had been the plan going in, Daniel was thrown into the fire. He had won the backup job in pre-season camp, and the decision to burn the redshirt was an easy one.

"I fought my butt off in camp, had four good scrimmages, played well, knew the offense backwards and forwards already, because I studied it," Daniel says. "I remember the day Coach Pinkel called me into his office and said, 'Hey, we want you to be the backup. We want to burn your redshirt, I want you to call your family and see what they think about it and get back to me.' I called, talked to my dad, and they were so excited. Of course, I was going to take it. I wanted to play."

He took the first snap of his college career in the third quarter at Arrowhead—a three-yard completion to wideout Arnold Britt—and as the season unfolded, Daniel got a series at the start of the second period. The thinking was that giving the true freshman even a little experience would help smooth the transition in 2006, but there was more to it than that.

"He got a series because Chase offered something different than Brad," says Yost. "We weren't going to run Chase. There was no reason to. At the time, Brad was the best running quarterback in the history of college football. We'll run the heck out of him. When Chase came in, we said we're going to throw the football. You don't buy a Ferrari and drive your other car as fast as you can. You buy your Ferrari to drive fast, and you buy the other one to tow your truck."

Against Arkansas State, Daniel was more sub-compact than sports car: four of 11 for 23 yards and six carries for 22 yards. The Missouri Spread, however, got off to a flying start—even if the opponent was an overmatched outfit from the Sun Belt Conference. Among those in the crowd of 32,906 were Pat Neylon, the pride of St. Joseph, Mo., and his wife, Karen. Both are proud Mizzou alums, and Neys is a fellow Delta Sig and best friend from college. Asked what he thought of the five-wide sets, the ridiculous line splits, the shotgun formation and the no-huddle hysteria, Neys reported, "It's certainly different."

The results, however, were much the same. Though they got off 105 snaps in the home opener against New Mexico on a night they dedicated to A.O., the Tigers lost, 45–35. Two weeks later came a 51–20 defeat to eventual national champion Texas. In typical fashion, Missouri was hanging around at 21–13 near the end of the first half when, on third-and-30, Vince Young scrambled for 33 yards, setting up a field goal. Ballgame. Same ol' Mizzou. As homecoming approached, the Tigers were at a crossroads. The loss to the Longhorns aside, they were averaging 552 yards and 42 points a game, but they had only a 3–2 record to show for their eye-popping statistics.

Every school has an annual migraine opponent, and for Missouri (before leaving for the SEC in late 2011), that program was Iowa State. The Tigers own a 61–34–9 series edge, but no matter the year, no matter the records, the Cyclones always had a way of making things tough. It was no different in 2005, even after Missouri jumped ahead on a pair of defensive touchdowns. The visitors scored 24 unanswered points, sending some 10,000 fans in the crowd of 55,016 at Faurot Field to the exits. With 39 yards rushing and 45 yards passing, Smith was in the midst of one of his worst days as a Tiger when he was sidelined by a fourth-quarter concussion.

"I remember being down on the field and being really depressed, thinking, 'Man, it's not supposed to be this way,' " Moller says. "It was homecoming."

If only Moller could have consulted Daniel. "Warming up that day, I remember thinking, 'Man, I'm throwing great,' " he says. In his second-quarter series, Daniel engineered a 13-play, 62-yard drive, completing four of six passes for 39 yards along the way, but the Tigers stalled and Adam Crossett missed a 36-yard field goal. Daniel was itching for another opportunity.

It came with under nine minutes left. Missouri trailed 24–14 and was facing a third-and-10 at its 25-yard line when Daniel trotted back onto the field. Good luck, kid. His first pass was a 13-yard completion to wideout Brad Ekwerekwu, but the next three plays netted only three yards so Pinkel reluctantly sent out the punt team. The decision was met with a smattering of boos, and the coach had a change of heart. Daniel zipped a 25-yard pass to tight end Chase Coffman, another true freshman, and nine plays later the Tigers pulled to 24–17.

"I remember him being calm and cool, and I remember thinking, 'I know he can do this,' " Rucker says. "But now we'll see what he's *going* to do."

> **"When Chase came in, we said we're going to throw the football," says Yost. "You don't buy a Ferrari and drive your other car as fast as you can. You buy your Ferrari to drive fast, and you buy the other one to tow your truck."**

What Daniel did next was lead the Tigers 87 yards in 11 plays in a swift 2:12, the last four yards coming on a perfectly placed fade pass to wideout Sean Coffey with 20 seconds left. The visitors missed their field goal in overtime, the home team made its, and the Tigers had an improbable 27–24 victory.

"When Brad got hurt, the air went out of the stadium," Kelly says. "Chase arrived with so much fanfare that, 'O.K., here's your time.' The place exploded and you're like, 'Wow, this guy is pretty good.' "

Ferrari good. Daniel finished 16 of 23 for 185 yards and the TD pass to Coffey. "Sometimes I didn't have an idea where the ball was going," a modest Daniel said afterward. He also said all the right things, extinguishing any talk of a quarterback controversy.

"He had a level of maturity you just don't see in young people," says Kelly.

Patton? "That was the biggest downer of my career," he admits. "I'm like, 'This is not going well at all.' I was genuinely happy for [Daniel], but it was also obvious he was doing big things and the coaches were going to be excited about what he did."

Naturally, Smith returned the following week against Nebraska, and naturally, he had a game to remember. He ran 28 times for 246 yards and three touchdowns and passed for 234 yards and another score. His most memorable play: a 79-yard touchdown sprint late in the first quarter. The Tigers spread the field from sideline to sideline in a five-wide set, and the Cornhuskers responded by basically splitting their defensive linemen from hash mark to hash mark and leaving nary a linebacker or a safety in the middle of the field. Without making so much as a head fake, Smith was home free by the time his right foot hit his own 25-yard line. He finished with a school-record 480 yards of total offense, and Missouri had its second consecutive home victory over the Cornhuskers — by the same 41–24 score.

It's not as if a soft-spoken quarterback who was making his 43rd consecutive start had anything to prove, but Yost believes Smith was sending a message to anyone who dared suggest the wrong guy was taking snaps. "I'm telling you, Brad would never say it," Yost says, "but he heard all that stuff and he wanted to prove to everybody, *I'm the starting quarterback.*"

Continuing a late-season swoon that had become a troubling pattern under Pinkel, the Tigers lost three of their last four games. But a victory over Baylor in Smith's home finale got Missouri bowl-eligible. Nobody can say how the season would have played out, but what if Pinkel had sent out the punt team against Iowa State? What if Daniel hadn't rescued the Tigers? What would a second consecutive 5–6 season have meant? Pinkel was already facing heat after the disaster that was 2004, and a second consecutive bowl shutout would have turned up the temperature. There were rumblings that the staff had reached its ceiling.

Alden steadfastly insists that Pinkel had the full support of the administration. He references a conversation with Chancellor Wallace. "I remember telling Dr. Wallace the reason Missouri has gotten to where Missouri has in football is because of what Missouri has always done," Alden says. "They try and bring somebody in here, they think they ought to have success right away, and they turn around and fire him. It's been a revolving door. I said, 'Boss, we've got to ride this horse, and we've got to ride him through the ups and downs.' So when the negative nellies got out there again, I went back to Dr. Wallace and I said, 'Remember, we talked about this. We're going to have to stay the course. I have no idea where it's going to end, but we can't allow this type of negativism on the outside to affect what we're doing.' "

Kelly agrees: "The one thing about Mike is that he was very forthright and never waivered in his support for Gary. Never did I sense he was in trouble that year."

At least one beat writer isn't so sure. "I don't know there were a lot of people who said, 'Yeah, we believe in him,' " says DeArmond, who at *The Star* had been on the beat long enough to report on two firings. "There were the people who wanted him gone, but there were the people who said, 'You can't keep doing this shit.' "

For the second time in three years, the post-season destination was the Independence Bowl, and early on the Tigers looked as if they were less than thrilled about being back in Shreveport. South Carolina jumped to a 21–0 lead before the first quarter was barely half over. As the second quarter began, ESPN analyst Mike Gottfried said the Tigers needed one big play to turn things around, eliciting a chuckle from play-by-play man Sean McDonough, who said, "Mike Gottfried [is] going for employee of the month at ESPN." Cornerback Marcus King delivered the momentum-turning play when he returned an interception 99 yards for a touchdown, prompting fellow analyst Craig James to ask: "Well, you think that will be enough to wake them up over there?" Yet when the Gamecocks marched back down the field for a 28–7 lead, James changed his tune, rightfully questioning the Tigers' effort on defense. "The game's not over, Craig," Gottfried said. "There's still 4:28 to go in the half." James cackled. Even after Mizzou scored 20 seconds before halftime to make the deficit a manageable 14 points, James rolled his eyes at the prospect of a comeback, calling the offensive and defensive lines that played in the first half "imposters" and saying the Tigers stood no chance if they didn't get more physical.

Well, in the second half, Mizzou got more physical — and made a prophet of Gottfried and a fool of James. That's because in his final college game, the kid from Youngstown, Ohio, put the Tigers on his back one last time. After going to the sideline early in the third quarter for a quick tape job on a sprained right ankle, Smith returned as Superman. In the second half alone, bum ankle and all, he ran for 124 yards and three touchdowns while passing for another 134 yards. All told, he rushed for 150 yards, passed for 282 yards and a TD and led Missouri to its biggest comeback in school history. Fittingly, Smith set up his own game-winning touchdown run with a 59-yard dash, an improvisational play during which he started left, zigged back to the right, then zipped down the middle of the field. Aside from an overtime victory over Middle Tennessee State and the rally against Nebraska in 2003 (when the go-ahead touchdown pass came courtesy of Sonny Riccio on the fake field goal), it was the only other fourth-quarter comeback in Smith's career. As the clock wound down in a 38-31 Mizzou win, James turned to Gottfried and said in a bemused tone, "You were right! You know what, when you said be patient, that this thing had a chance to turn around. You know, you did it."

"I think you could go into any house in Big 12 country and say, 'We're from Mizzou,' and they'd say, 'That's where Brad Smith is from,'" Pinkel says.

Replied Gottfried, "As long as you have Brad Smith on your football team, you have a chance."

Missouri's last six plays were Smith runs (in the second half, the Tigers got off 50 snaps and never punted), and after the clock hit zero and a beaming Smith did a hasty ESPN interview and was subsequently mobbed by his teammates, the Tigers accepted the Independence Bowl trophy. At the 25-yard line.

"There's nothing you can do to be prepared for something like that," Ivey says of the O'Neal tragedy. "It was a defining moment for our program—what we were going to do and who we were about. We knew that winning football games was important, but I think it helped us focus and start looking inward. We analyzed what we were doing. Our players were hurting. Our program was hurting. We were all hurting, and we had to be there for each other. Around that time, we stopped saying we were a team and started saying we were a family."

Brad Smith left the Missouri family as the only quarterback in NCAA history to pass for 8,000 yards and rush for 4,000 yards in a career. Only one other quarterback—Clemson's Danzler—had passed for 2,000 yards and rushed for 1,000 yards in a season. Smith did it twice. His list of school, Big 12 and NCAA records are too numerous to note (69, according to the Mizzou football media guide), but he finished as the leading rusher among quarterbacks in Division I-A history and his 13,088 total yards nearly doubled the previous school record.

"You could write a book on Brad Smith," says Kadlec, who retired from the broadcast booth in 2011. "First of all, as a person, Brad Smith is one of the most outstanding young men I have met. If he would have had a supporting cast, he was such a force we might have gone undefeated. His best play was when a lineman would miss his block, and he'd just take off."

Pinkel reflects not only on the Houdini acts Smith pulled off on the football field but also on the impact he made in the living rooms of recruits and their parents in Missouri and Texas and Oklahoma. "I think you could go into any house in Big 12 country and say, 'We're from Mizzou,' and they'd say, 'That's where Brad Smith is from.' "

The comeback victory gave Missouri a wave of momentum heading into 2006, but it was significant for another reason. Had the Tigers packed it in at halftime, had they allowed themselves to be the punch line of more jokes from James, Smith would have finished his career with another frustrating loss and a final could-have-been opportunity. But by virtue of that one scintillating second-half surge, he walked off a college football field for the last time with a 25–23 career record.

Brad Smith left Mizzou a winner.

Chapter 8
"I Should Have Won an Emmy"

The Ryder rental truck bounced westward along I-70, just north of Oxford, Ohio (and the Cradle of Coaches), through Indiana and Illinois, by Columbia, within spitting distance of Arrowhead Stadium, across the Missouri River into Kansas and past Lawrence. It was the spring of 1991. When he pulled into Manhattan, Kan., Mark Mangino had his wife, Mary Jane, the couple's two young children, a 1988 Buick LeSabre and the rest of the family's life possessions in tow. And $500 in his pocket.

And Mark Mangino was ecstatic. He was chasing a lifelong dream—the dream of being a college football coach.

He had been down this road before. During his early years living in the western Pennsylvania hamlet of New Castle, Mangino moonlighted as an assistant in the high school ranks. In the mid-1980s, he decided he wanted to make a career of coaching, so he went back to school to get his degree, enrolling across the border at Youngstown State. With a wife and two toddlers to support, he kept the night job — working in emergency services for the Pennsylvania Turnpike.

"I was lucky enough that some of the coaches at Youngstown knew I was on campus," Mangino says. "They offered me the chance to be a part-time assistant, and they paid for my education. The head coach was Bill Narduzzi. He gave me that first opportunity."

In 1986, Narduzzi was succeeded by Jim Tressel, who would coach the Penguins for 15 seasons before taking over at Ohio State. Tressel remembers Mangino as a tireless worker who was determined to become a success on the sideline.

"He was unlike anyone I ever had," Tressel told reporters in November 2007. "He worked on the Pennsylvania Turnpike from midnight to 8 a.m. And he was finishing his degree, so he was going to school in the morning and early afternoon. He worked with us from about 2 p.m. until 10 or 11 p.m., then he'd drive back to the turnpike to go to work. I knew right then he was going to be something special. I don't know when he slept."

Degree in hand and with two years of coaching experience under his belt at Youngstown State, Mangino was eager for more responsibility, so he moved back across the border and became the offensive coordinator at Division II Geneva College in Beaver Falls. He was with the Golden Tornadoes for two years, but after taking the head position at Ellwood City High, he needed only a year to realize the prep game wasn't for him. His career seemed to have hit a dead end; maybe it was time to consider another line of work.

I said, 'Coach, I'm *broke*.' He said, 'Can you hang in there a little longer?' I said, 'I don't know. I'm trying, but I'm pretty close to having to pack up and head out of town.'"

That's when Mangino made the call that would change his life forever. He phoned former high school teammate John Latina, who was the offensive line coach and running game coordinator for Bill Snyder at Kansas State. "I told John I really wanted to get back into college coaching, even if I had to come in as a GA," Mangino says. Latina put in a good word for his good friend, and Mangino had a job. He was 35, quite possibly the oldest graduate assistant in the history of college football.

Snyder was in Year Three of what many still call the greatest reclamation project in college football history. When he was hired on Nov. 24, 1988, the Wildcats had lost 26 of their previous 27 games (the lone "highlight" being the '86 tie against Kansas). A *Sports Illustrated* article billed K-State as Futility U, and with good reason. The Wildcats' 510 losses were the most in major-college football, they had enjoyed only four winning seasons in the previous 44 years and they had been to exactly one bowl game in their 93-year history. That didn't matter to Mangino; Kansas State was his ticket to the big time, even if he was starting at rock bottom, both in terms of the program and the job title.

There were obstacles. The Manginos rolled into Manhattan in the midst of the first Gulf War, and troops returning to Fort Riley had snatched up every last dwelling in the Little Apple. The Latinas turned their garage into a makeshift storage unit and kindly opened their home to Mangino and his family. They stayed for more than a month before finding a cramped, two-bedroom condo.

Not that Mangino could have afforded anything more. Considering what he was taking home, he may as well have been living in the *Big Apple*. "I was making graduate assistant money, so we didn't have much," Mangino says. "My wife, trying to keep things afloat, got a credit card. I didn't know about it. She bought the kids Christmas gifts and school clothes. We didn't have any money. I was clearing maybe 750 bucks a month."

Undaunted, Mangino forged on. "I said I'll give it my all," he says. "If I fall on my face, you can't feel bad about giving it your best."

In his first season, Kansas State finished 7–4. In those days, bowl bids weren't handed out like Halloween candy, but even though the Wildcats rang in the new year at home, there was plenty of reason to celebrate. It was the program's first winning season since 1982. Nevertheless, those victories weren't putting money in a certain GA's bank account. Mangino could have used a bowl bonus, and in early 1992, he sheepishly walked into Snyder's office. He told his boss how much he loved K-State and Manhattan and how much he loved coaching for him. But he also told Snyder he was broke, that he no longer could put bread on the table with the check he was taking home.

"He sat there and scratched his head and said, 'How broke?' " Mangino recalls. "And I said, 'Coach, I'm *broke*.' He said, 'Can you hang in there a little longer?' I said, 'I don't know. I'm trying, but I'm pretty close to having to pack up and head out of town.' "

And this, according to Mangino, is what Snyder told his GA: "He said, 'Mark, I can't make promises I can't keep. But trust me. Just stay here a little while longer. Just find a way to do it. It's easy for me to say, but just hang in there. Something good will happen for you.' "

Still broke but at least feeling somewhat reassured, Mangino went home that night and told Mary Jane, his high school sweetheart, "Let's hang in there. We've come so far. Let's dig in."

Four months later, Snyder came through with a full-time position. Mangino was appointed recruiting coordinator, and his salary ballooned to $30,000. When the NCAA in 1993 stopped classifying the position as a full-time role, Mangino added the title of assistant offensive line coach. He joined an all-star staff that would include Bob and Mike Stoops, Jim Leavitt and Brent Venables.

"We were young, and we didn't know any better," Mangino says. "All we wanted to do was coach football. It was a staff with tremendous enthusiasm. Working a long day was no big deal. Being on the practice field was no big deal. It could be a hundred degrees or 20 below—the enthusiasm was the same."

For a guy who as a student at Youngstown State didn't know what sleep was, Mangino must have felt like he was on vacation. It helped that the Wildcats were winning. In 1993, they finished 9–2–1 and whipped Wyoming, 52–17, in the Copper Bowl. It was the first bowl victory in program history and the first of nine consecutive winning seasons for Snyder, who during the span never won fewer than nine games and five times won 10 or more. In 1998, K-State ascended to No. 2 in the polls; only a double-overtime loss to Texas A&M in the Big 12 championship game in which they blew a 15-point, fourth-quarter lead kept the Wildcats from playing Tennessee for the national title.

With success comes opportunity, and in December 1998, Bob Stoops accepted the head-coaching position at Oklahoma. Proud owners of six national championships, the Sooners were one of the most storied programs in college football, but they hadn't had a winning season since 1993 and most recently had been 12–22 in three seasons under John Blake.

New athletic director Joe Castiglione, who had come over from Missouri, was looking for a young, vibrant coach to energize the program, and the 38-year-old Stoops fit the profile. He had left Manhattan after the '96 season to become the defensive coordinator at Florida and was fresh off a national championship with the Gators. Stoops, who hailed from Youngstown but didn't know of Mangino until their paths crossed in Manhattan, raided Snyder's staff, adding his brother Mike and Venables as defensive assistants. He offered Mangino the offensive coordinator's position.

"Bob was a great friend," says Mangino, who by this time had added the titles of assistant head coach and run game coordinator at K-State. "I had great respect for Coach Snyder, but I had been there eight years. At that point, that had been the longest tenure on his staff. I really enjoyed Manhattan and Kansas State, but I thought it was time to take on a new challenge. In the grand scheme of things, Oklahoma was a traditional football power. At least, I grew up in an era when it was."

If only it were that simple. Samantha Mangino was in the middle of her junior year of high school. She was an honors student and a cheerleader. Not unlike the dilemma faced by countless other college assistants, Mangino was reluctant to pick up and move his family—even if the school holding on Line One was Oklahoma.

"I told Bob I didn't think I could go because of Samantha," Mangino says. "He waited two weeks. I called and said, 'Did you hire anybody?' He said, 'No, I'm waiting on you.'"

That's when Mary Jane intervened. She knew how much her husband wanted the job with the Sooners and what it could mean to the family's future, so she made a deal with him. He would find an apartment in Norman. She would stay behind and get Samantha through high school, at which time she and son Tommy would relocate.

Promises, promises. Mangino moved to Norman, all right, but he never went apartment hunting. Upon hearing of his housing quandary, a student secretary in the football office offered him a dilapidated couch from her sorority that had been tagged for the dumpster. And for the next eight months, Mangino, the man known as Little Bear, slept in his office at the Barry Switzer Center. Only when he grew weary of the cleaning lady's daily 5:30 a.m. wake-up call did he pony up for an apartment on the east side of town.

Displaying the same enthusiasm they had exhibited during those early years in Manhattan, the Stoops Gang was an immediate hit in Norman. In 1999, the Sooners went 7–5 and to their first bowl game in five years. Family night became a Wednesday ritual for the coaches— wives and kids would descend upon the football complex for a night of fellowship. Coaching had turned into a job and then some under Snyder, who put in 18-hour days and expected a similar commitment from his staff. Work was fun again.

"With Coach Snyder, it was an employee-management relationship," Mangino says. "Bob being a friend, it was different."

Mary Jane and Tommy moved to Norman in 2000 (Samantha enrolled at Kansas), in time to witness one of the most surprising seasons in Oklahoma history. Ranked 19th at the start of the year, the Sooners put the college football world on alert with a 63–14 trouncing of Texas in the annual bloodbath in the Cotton Bowl, and in a much-ballyhooed return to Manhattan, Stoops and Co. beat second-ranked Kansas State, 41–31. Oklahoma completed the trifecta and jumped to the top of the polls with a 31–14 triumph over Nebraska, won the rematch with K-State in the Big 12 championship game and beat Florida State, 13–2, in the Orange Bowl for its 13th straight victory and the program's seventh national title.

After coordinating an offense that averaged 37 points a game, Mangino was fitted for a national championship ring and collected the Frank Broyles Award as the game's top assistant. He was light years from that candid conversation in Snyder's office, an eternity from those days of calling plays for the Golden Tornadoes.

Naturally, the phone started ringing. Just as Stoops had parlayed his success coordinating defenses in Manhattan and Gainesville, Mangino was a hot commodity. "I had some headhunters who contacted me right after the 2000 season," he says. "No disrespect, they weren't any programs I wanted to tackle. My wife took such a liking to Norman that we thought we'd settle there for a while and then maybe five, six, seven, eight years down the road look for a head-coaching position."

"There were a lot of times you would go into a school and the coach would say, 'Well, I've got five guys who can play for you,'" Mangino recalls. "And they've got three other guys they won't let you talk to because they don't think your program's good enough."

How time flies. Those six or seven or eight years turned into 12 months. Ranked third in the country at the start of the 2001 season, Oklahoma ran its winning streak to 20 games before falling at Nebraska, and after an 11–2 finish, Mangino got the itch. "You've got to seize the moment," he says. "Championships are hard to come by."

Looking for a replacement for the fired Terry Allen, who had presided over six consecutive losing seasons, the folks at Kansas were among those who came calling. Urban Meyer's name had been bandied about, and athletic director Al Bohl flirted with Alabama coach Dennis Franchione, who was quietly looking to sneak out of Tuscaloosa. But the Jayhawks kept coming back to Mangino, who, of course, knew plenty about Kansas. During his days at K-State, and to a lesser extent at Oklahoma, he had butted heads with the Jayhawks on the field and on the recruiting trail. That Kansas was a downtrodden program without much of a football tradition actually appealed to him.

"I consider myself a builder," Mangino says. "I take pride in it. Just about every team I've been on, they were all programs that were down. I don't mind renaissance projects. In fact, I love them. But you've got to know who is going to support you. What athletic department has a history of supporting football? Who's really indifferent to it, but they need a head coach?"

In Bohl, the Jayhawks had a never-accept-no-for-an-answer salesman. Mangino kept telling Bohl he wasn't interested in the job. Bohl kept calling. This went on for a couple of weeks. At one point, Mangino issued a press release through the Oklahoma sports information office announcing he had taken his name out of the running for the position. Early the next morning, he got out of the shower to a ringing telephone. It was Bohl.

"He was relentless," Mangino says. And finally the coach relented. He was convinced that Bohl was a football AD. While at Toledo, the guy had hired Nick Saban and—small-world alert!—Gary Pinkel. Mangino was assured he would be given the resources and support he needed to succeed. After he hung up the phone at the end of an interview with the KU athletic advisory committee, the job was all but his. One of the committee members who participated in the conference call proclaimed, "He's our guy." It was Gale Sayers.

"The way it was presented to me was that basketball was doing great and would continue to do great, but the athletic department needed revenue and the only way to generate revenue was they needed football to win," Mangino says. "It was football, football, football. That was the selling point."

But don't let anybody kid you. At Kansas, it always has been and always will be about basketball, basketball, basketball. The Jayhawks have won three national championships and been to 14 Final Fours. They rank second in all-time victories, behind only Kentucky. James Naismith coached in Lawrence for a decade. Phog Allen Fieldhouse, named for the man who succeeded Naismith, is one of the most storied arenas in the college game. Fans can't wait for the start of basketball *practice*. Tom Keegan, sports columnist for the *Lawrence Journal-World*, says his department can expect phone calls or e-mails if the paper goes more than a couple of days in the off-season without any KU basketball fodder. In fact, when Roy Williams was the coach, during one particularly slow summer news day, the *Journal-World* ran a brief under the headline: "KU's Williams has head cold."

Mangino knew full well about the passion Kansas fans have for their basketball team. "I wasn't blind," he says. "Basketball is very important to the University of Kansas. And I'd say rightfully so. The guy invented the game. You can't get any more tradition than that, can you?"

Still, when he arrived in Lawrence in late 2001, he was floored by what he saw. He may have been called to nastier car crashes during his days on the Pennsylvania Turnpike, but the football program was in its own right an unsightly wreck. "It was in disarray," Mangino says. "There was a lot of apathy within the program, within the athletic department, within the university for the football team. Players hadn't developed any type of work ethic. They thought they were working hard. I talked to the seniors who were leaving. You know how kids are—they blame everybody else. After visiting with about 20 of them, they thought they were working hard."

Then there was the recruiting issue. Drawing from his experience in Manhattan, Mangino understood the culture as well as the challenges of attracting in-state talent. He also knew there were not enough prospects in Kansas to sustain two Big 12 programs. So he and his assistants were often recruiting, as he puts it, "on somebody else's turf," typically in Missouri or Oklahoma or Texas. When they walked into a high school, the host coach would often chuckle, then tell the Kansas staff he would see what he could do. Mangino had one thing going for him: He was a year removed from winning a national championship. Even if he didn't sign the players he wanted, he was at least getting in the door. Still, pitching prep coaches about the virtues of Kansas football was a tough sell.

"There were a lot of times you would go into a school and the coach would say, 'Well, I've got five guys who can play for you,' " Mangino recalls. "And they've got three other guys they won't let you talk to because they don't think your program's good enough. They want the five guys who were probably going to go to Stephen F. Austin or somewhere like that."

No offense to the Lumberjacks, but rebuilding with Division I-AA talent would have put Mangino on the unemployment line sooner rather than later. In his first season, the Jayhawks finished 2–10 (0–8 in the Big 12), so in 2003 he applied a tourniquet to a hemorrhaging program, signing a dozen junior college transfers. Kansas turned a corner, going 6–7, winning three Big 12 games and getting an invitation to the Tangerine Bowl, where Philip Rivers and North Carolina State inflicted a 56–26 defeat. Meticulous with his every move, Mangino was making headway, even if the progress was slower than he would have liked.

"We outlined the structure of our program," he says. "If you were playing at KU during my tenure, you could go to a calendar any day of the year, put your finger on it, and as a player you would know what you were going to do that day and what your responsibilities were. The kids liked that. There were no surprises. There were no tricks. They knew what was coming every day, so they mentally and physically prepared for it."

Surprisingly, the turning point came late in 2004, in the midst of a heartbreaking season in which the Jayhawks lost seven of their last nine games. Kansas opened with victories over Tulsa and Toledo, only to cough up fourth-quarter leads to Northwestern and Texas Tech. Next came a six-point loss to Nebraska, but after the Jayhawks rallied in the last three minutes to beat Kansas State, they went on a three-game skid. They were 3–6, and whatever faint bowl hopes they had were gone. Now, sixth-ranked Texas was coming to town. The Longhorns trailed Oklahoma in the Big 12 South, but they were in the hunt for a lucrative BCS at-large bid. Nary an eyebrow was raised when oddsmakers installed the Horns as 22-point favorites.

However, on a crisp, windswept November afternoon, the Jayhawks played the game of their lives. They couldn't stop the Texas tandem of Vince Young and Cedric Benson—the Longhorns piled up 292 yards through the air and another 289 on the ground—but Kansas forced three turnovers and moved the ball effectively through the air, passing for 308 yards. When Brian Luke and Lyone Anderson connected on a one-yard touchdown pass with 7:41 left, the Jayhawks led 23–13, stunning the Longhorns and a partisan crowd at Memorial Stadium, which was a good 12,000 short of capacity.

Texas answered with a 13-play, 87-yard touchdown drive, and three snaps later came the play that would keep the Longhorns' BCS hopes alive—and change the culture of Kansas football under Mangino. On third-and-seven from his own 26, Luke completed a 16-yard pass to Charles Gordon, who made a lunging grab in front of the Texas bench. The Jayhawks were basically a first down away from the upset. Or so they thought. Side judge Freeman Johns had thrown a flag, and officials stepped off a 13-yard penalty against Gordon for offensive pass interference. It was a phantom penalty, a call that conspiracy theorists alleged was made in the best interests of the Big 12—to keep alive the Longhorns' BCS chances. Others around the conference, particularly in the North division, had already grown weary of what they perceived to be preferential treatment toward the Horns both on the field and in executive sessions, to the point that they joked the league should be renamed the Big Texas Conference.

Kansas punted, the Longhorns drove 32 yards in seven plays and then Young threw a 21-yard strike to Tony Jeffery for the winning score with 11 seconds left. (It's worth noting that the Jayhawks would have prevailed had they not allowed Young to scramble for 22 yards on fourth-and-18.) When it was over, Mangino walked into a devastated locker room. For the fifth time in 2004, Kansas had lost a game by six points or less. The Jayhawks had rallied from 10 points down only to fall at Northwestern. They had lost on a 70-yard touchdown run in the dying minutes against Texas Tech. They had come within a whisker of beating Nebraska for the first time since 1968. But nothing stung like this defeat. The Texas game was stolen from them. It was robbery without a gun.

Mangino dialed up a handful of coaching clichés, telling his players they had to learn from the experience and move on, that he thought they had won the game but that the scoreboard said otherwise. Then he retreated to the solitude of coaches' room to collect his thoughts, and as he sipped on a Gatorade, he decided he couldn't let the opportunity pass. He had to show his players he believed in them. So he stormed into the interview room and went on a tirade that would be replayed on highlight shows from coast to coast.

"You know what this is all about, don't you?" Mangino told the media. "That's right, BCS. That's what made the difference today in the game. That's what made a difference today in a call in front of their bench. Dollar signs." Later, he added, "I'm not going to be pushed around—and [have] this university pushed around—because we're not the big spenders, we're not the big BCS team in the league."

Mangino apologized later in the day, but the Big 12 acted swiftly with a public reprimand and a $5,000 fine. The calculated gamble, it turns out, was worth every penny. The head coach showed his players he had their backs. The players had a newfound confidence. They believed they could play with anybody. Players and coaches grew closer than they had ever been.

"Let me tell you what that game was all about," says Mangino, still sounding agitated as he looked back eight years later. "The call was highly questionable, but let's take that away from the equation. The point was we had a chance to win a game against a great program, and we didn't do it. I felt like the call was incorrect, but the circumstances leading up to the call bothered me because their bench was working over that guy really good from an earlier call he had made.

"Everybody said, 'Mangino flipped out.' I didn't flip out. I should have won an Emmy."

Lo and behold, the next week, again with nothing to play for, the Jayhawks traveled to Columbia and upset Missouri, 31–14. The visitors were so dominant that the Tigers finished with minus six yards rushing, thanks largely to a half-dozen sacks of Brad Smith. Mangino had his second consecutive double-digit victory over Missouri and, more important, the trust of his players. "All season, our kids never gave up," Mangino said afterward. "That's why I love these guys."

Memories of the games against Mizzou are particularly vivid—and not just because of what transpired on the field. "I knew it was a big thing, but I'll be honest: I didn't know how big it was," Mangino says. "I was involved in the Red River Shootout [Texas-OU], but I've never been anywhere where the word *hate* is used so much. We might be opponents and even enemies, but I can't say I ever hated the team across the field. I never told the KU fans that because they might have run me out of town."

He describes his relationship with Pinkel as cordial and says the two were always complimentary of one another's program. The fans? Not so much.

"We'd come down the ramp [at Faurot Field] and their fans would say how much they hate you," Mangino says. "And when Missouri came to Lawrence, I wondered if our fans would say the same things. Yep, they did."

As both programs continued their slow climbs, the animosity only intensified. The 2005 KU season started impressively enough, with three victories in Lawrence by a combined score of 100–41. So what if the competition was Florida Atlantic, Appalachian State and Louisiana Tech. The Jayhawks were winning football games. But when Big 12 play started, they went into another tailspin, losing four straight games, none by less than nine points. Missouri was next on the schedule. The Tigers were 5–2 and riding high after a 41–24 victory over Nebraska. They were averaging almost 37 points a game. The prospects of ending the skid didn't seem promising.

Kansas, however, had a defense it could lean on. The Jayhawks were ranked second in the country against the run, and for the second straight year they bottled up Smith. Missouri ran for a season-low 33 yards, with Smith gaining 38 yards on 20 carries. Kansas walked away with a 13–3 victory.

The man behind the schemes was long-time college assistant Bill Young, a defensive wizard whose career was into its fifth decade. Before moving to Lawrence, the nomadic Young made stops at Oklahoma State (where he played as a defensive end and linebacker), Iowa State, Tulsa, Arizona State, Ohio State, Oklahoma and USC. In 2001, he was hired as the defensive line coach of the Detroit Lions, but before the season was even over, Young knew the NFL wasn't for him. Enter Mangino, who as he was filling out his staff in early 2002 looked high and low for a defensive coordinator. He brought in a couple of candidates for interviews, but nothing clicked. One day, a staff member asked Mangino if he'd be interested in hiring Young.

"I've never been anywhere where the word *hate* is used so much," Mangino says. "We might be opponents and even enemies, but I can't say I ever hated the team across the field."

"I said, 'He'd be willing to leave Detroit and come here?' " Mangino recalls. "And he said, 'Yeah, he would.' "

Mangino knew about Young's reputation. He loved to work with the defense, and whatever aspirations he had of being a head coach had long since passed. He didn't mince words, and he had a burning desire to get back into the college game. The offensive-minded Mangino was perfectly comfortable turning the defense over to a seasoned pro.

"I was thinking I'd get this young guy who was going to fly around the practice field and all that," Mangino says. "I decided to go with wisdom and knowledge and experience. It paid off."

It paid off to the point that in 2005 the Jayhawks finished eighth in the country against the run (even after being gashed for 336 rushing yards in a 66–14 loss to Texas and Young, who was a bit perturbed that Mangino didn't give the Longhorns credit for their comeback victory in '04). Building on the victory over Missouri, Kansas pounded Nebraska, 40–15. A record Memorial Stadium crowd of 51,750 watched the Jayhawks snap a 36-game losing streak to the Cornhuskers. In the finale, KU got bowl-eligible with a 24–21 overtime victory over Iowa State, tying the game in the same fashion it had lost so many times in 2004, on a touchdown with 65 ticks left. And the season was capped with a 42–13 triumph over Houston in the Fort Worth Bowl. Mangino had led the Jayhawks to their second bowl in three years—reason enough for a parade down

Massachusetts Avenue—but he saw the season as an opportunity wasted. And he pointed the finger directly at himself.

"We squandered a great defensive effort that season," he says. "And it's because we couldn't get settled at quarterback. Either somebody got injured or we weren't productive, and I did a poor job of managing that thing. If we had just had a half-decent offense in terms of stability at the quarterback position, we could have won some more games. I accept the responsibility for that. I didn't handle it well. It was bad, and I probably made it worse."

It was Mangino's subtle way of saying he sorely needed a quarterback. If basketball coach Bill Self needed a point guard to direct his offense, he had his pick of five-star recruits from around the country. Mangino? He was selling Kansas *football*. He had been on the job for four years and had a 24–29 record to show for his efforts. His architectural project was starting to take shape, but construction was at a snail's pace. As Year Five approached, he needed to find a playmaking quarterback. The sooner, the better.

Chapter 9

Sparky

The complicated tale of how a schoolboy quarterback who was
lighting up scoreboards across the Texas Hill Country landed in Lawrence,
Kan., is best told by the quarterback himself. So allow Todd Reesing to
explain how his highlight video turned up on the desk of Mark Mangino:
"My godfather's son married a girl whose dad was a former coach and
worked in the athletic office [at Kansas]."

As a junior at Lake Travis High in Austin in 2004, Reesing led the
Cavaliers to the first district championship in school history and was
named the Class 4A Player of the Year. He beat out, among others,
Highland Park's Matthew Stafford, a Georgia commitment and the first
pick in the 2008 NFL draft, and Stephenville's Jevon Snead, who backed
out of a commitment to Florida (after Tim Tebow announced his
intentions) before playing at Texas and Ole Miss. (Daniel was busy leading
Southlake Carroll to the Class 5A Division II state championship that fall.)
Despite the accolades, Reesing was struggling to fill out his itinerary for
the five official recruiting visits the NCAA allows. Worse yet, he was
drawing next to no interest from the 119 programs that were playing
Division I-A football. Kansas State and Bill Snyder had offered. So had
Duke. That was about it.

"Everybody told me I was too small, didn't have a strong enough arm,
wasn't fast enough," says the 5-foot-10 Reesing. "We had a few guys who
were getting looks, but they were a lot like me. They were undersized guys
who were getting looks from lower-level schools."

The notion of playing at a small school was unappealing to the
too-small quarterback. First and foremost, Reesing was going to college to
get an education. He wasn't expecting to make a career of football, so his
college choice wasn't going to be dictated by who recruited him the
hardest. Nor would he be lured by promises and guarantees from a
Division I-AA program.

"I never would have gone to play football at a lower-level school,"
Reesing says. "That was something I talked to my parents about. If you get

a chance to play at a good university, absolutely go and do it. But I wasn't going to be chasing dreams of playing football if I didn't get a scholarship to a big-time school.

"Education was very important to me. My brother and I graduated from high school with very high honors. We had an A-only policy in our household."

Reesing would have gladly stayed home. He was born in Austin and had grown up a Longhorns fan, and his dad is a Texas alum. Todd was in Darrell K. Royal Memorial Stadium in November 1998 when Ricky Williams broke the Division I-A rushing record, and although Reesing was only 11, he could see himself one day donning the burnt orange. Playing college football in Texas is the dream of most every kid in the Lone Star State who buckles a chinstrap on fall Friday nights. So if not Texas, certainly there would be a spot for him at Texas A&M or Texas Tech or Baylor or one of the five other Division I-A programs in the state.

But even as Reesing kept making plays at Lake Travis—6,497 passing yards and 70 touchdown passes over his last two seasons—everyone kept coming back to his vital statistics: Five-foot-10, 180 pounds. Recruiters were reluctant to take a flier on an undersized quarterback with an average arm.

"You get tired of hearing it," Reesing says. "Everybody telling you, 'You can't do this, you can't do that, because of your physical limitations.' Yet you see guys like Doug Flutie [of Boston College] and Drew Brees [Purdue] who have played at the college level and had huge success. I knew it could be done."

Just as they had passed on the local kid Brees, who would become one of college football's most prolific passers and an NFL and Super Bowl MVP, the Longhorns showed relatively little interest in Reesing. At least the Texas coaches showed some tact. A Texas A&M assistant phoned Reesing to tell him he was on the Aggies' B-list of potential quarterback recruits. According to Reesing, the coach said he wasn't "as fast or as strong-armed as those other guys, but we've got you on our list if things fall through."

B-list? It was the insult of insults for a player whose confidence rivaled Daniel's. Surely the A&M coaches had viewed the video—a jaw-dropping collection of highlights that showed Reesing making all of the throws and keeping plays alive with his legs. Snyder had seen it, and he was quick to offer a scholarship. Now, in the summer of 2005, the video had found Mangino's desk, courtesy of that round-about family connection. He, too, liked what he saw, so conveniently enough, after Reesing participated in a football camp at Kansas State, Mangino invited the QB and his parents to make the 80-mile drive over from Manhattan. Why not, Reesing thought. What did he have to lose?

"I was walking into a school I didn't know much about," he says. "I didn't know what they had done before or who their great players were." He did know this much: "I realized how much more I liked Lawrence than Manhattan."

Mangino could relate. Ask him about the Little Apple and he says, "You're out on the prairie. You can get in trouble, but not too much." He offered Reesing a scholarship on the spot, without asking to see a wind sprint or a single pass. Two weeks before a senior season in

"I had heard there was a lot of traffic through Lake Travis that spring," Mangino says. "I don't know what conclusion you can make other than Todd was too small, because when you watched his tape, he was fantastic."

which he threw for 3,340 yards and 41 touchdowns (against only five interceptions), Reesing committed to Kansas. He graduated early from Lake Travis and was in Lawrence for the start of the second semester in January 2006.

"We talked as a staff and said we need to recruit a playmaker, a guy who can help you with his arm and his feet," Mangino says. "And we needed a guy who had some intellect. We didn't have to spoon-feed him through every read and every check.

"He came on the unofficial visit, and he looked me in the eye. Now he wasn't a big guy. I knew what I was getting. But there was something about him. He gave me that look. He was confident, he was smart, he had that presence about him."

To this day, reflecting on a situation that was eerily similar to Pinkel's evaluation of Smith, Mangino wonders what he saw that so many other coaches were missing. He kept going back to the highlight video.

"I had heard there was a lot of traffic through Lake Travis that spring," Mangino says. "I don't know what conclusion you can make other than Todd was too small, because when you watched his tape, he was fantastic."

Reesing was also relatively green—like Daniel at Southlake Carroll, he had played quarterback at Lake Travis for only two years—so the decision to redshirt him in 2006 was an easy one. Redshirt freshman Kerry Meier and senior Adam Barmann would compete for the starting job. Reesing would spend the year getting acquainted with the offense and getting off to a good start in KU's honors program as he tackled a double major of economics and later finance.

"I traveled with the team," Reesing says. "I was the guy with the ball cap who was signaling in plays. I was still involved in practice, but I had very, very limited reps."

Nevertheless, as the 2006 season kicked off, Mangino entertained thoughts of burning Reesing's redshirt. When he made the rounds at practice, the coach occasionally would ask his freshman quarterback if he wanted to be thrown into the fire. Reesing always responded with the same one-word answer: "Sure." What competitor in his right mind wouldn't? There was another factor in play, and it had nothing to do with football. The coaching staff knew full well how important academics were to Reesing, and there were concerns he might graduate in three or 3½ years, then take advantage of a quirky NCAA rule that allows grad students to transfer to a school that offers a major not available at the student's original college and play without having to sit out a year. "This guy's so bright," Mangino says. "He could bounce out of here and go play somewhere else, for somebody who has a Masters in international business or something we don't have. That was running through my mind, even though I wanted to redshirt him. I thought it would be great to have him for four years."

However, the problems that plagued the Jayhawks at quarterback in 2005 resurfaced in 2006. Kansas lost at Toledo in double overtime, and an overtime loss at Nebraska was the first of four straight Big 12 losses. Meier couldn't stay healthy. At 3–5 and back home for a meeting with Colorado on the last Saturday of October, Mangino watched in disgust as his offense stumbled to 90 yards on 29 first-half snaps. "They had nothing going," Keegan recalls. "I mean *nothing*." Meier was injured, and Barmann had thrown a pair of ugly first-half interceptions. Playing a bend-but-don't-break scheme, Young's defense kept things from getting out of hand—limiting the Buffaloes to three short field goals. By this time, Reesing had resigned himself to the fact he wouldn't be playing in 2006. During the week, Mangino hadn't even mentioned the possibility of calling No. 5's number.

"All these guys on the team were saying, 'Don't worry. They're not going to burn your redshirt this late in the year,' " says Reesing. "I went into that game thinking there was no way on earth I was going to play."

The second quarter was winding down, and in the press box, Bill Self had made his way to the perch from which the assembled media was watching the debacle. Basketball practice had started—now there was something to get excited about!—and the KU coach, as is his custom at home football games, was chatting up beat writers and columnists. Self was in the middle of a story when Keegan noticed Reesing warming up behind the KU bench. "I bet they're going to rip the redshirt off of him," Keegan thought. Mangino had seen enough. The true freshman was trading in his ball cap for a helmet.

"Coach called me over right before halftime and said, 'Todd, we're going to start you in the second half,' " Reesing recalls. "He looked at me and said, 'Put it this way. You can't do any worse.' I guess that was his way of trying to get me to relax. My jaw dropped, my eyes got real wide, and I'm like, 'O.K. this is actually happening. Relax and have fun.' "

Because they won the coin toss and had deferred, the Jayhawks received the second-half kickoff. On the first snap of his college career, Reesing handed off to Jon Cornish, who ran for five yards. On second down, looking to get its new quarterback an easy completion, KU called a play-action rollout, but the ball was tipped and fell incomplete. Somewhere, a certain Texas A&M assistant had to be snickering. On third down ...

"We were trying to run simple slant routes on the inside and outside," Reesing says. "I tried to thread the needle. The guy was open, but the ball got tipped by a linebacker who was filling the passing lane and fell into the arms of a safety."

A stadium that moments earlier had been buzzing over the surprise entrance of a freshman savior suddenly went silent. As he jogged off the field, Reesing couldn't remember a worse feeling. What fun!

Mangino could only laugh. "His interception looked good," he remembers thinking.

On KU's next possession, Reesing and the offense stayed on the field for eight snaps before punting. Then, on his third series, he essentially took over the game. First came a 42-yard completion to running back Jake Sharp, and three plays later Reesing hooked up with Cornish for a 22-yard touchdown. The Jayhawks needed only four plays and 2:10 to cover the 76 yards. Now *this* was fun. Reesing was settling in, though he admits, "I didn't really know what to do, what to expect. I just went off of reaction."

On the fourth play of the fourth quarter, Reesing put Kansas ahead with a three-yard touchdown run, then capped a seven-play, 53-yard drive with a five-yard touchdown pass to tight end Derek Fine. In a mere 11:38, he had rallied the Jayhawks from a 9–0 hole to a 20–9 advantage.

Sounding somewhat regretful, Reesing says his night on the town was *not* the third coming of Joe Namath and Max McGee. Memorial Stadium was rocking, at least as rocking as it could be with the remnants of an announced crowd of 39,313. When he wasn't making throws, Reesing was keeping plays alive with his feet. He was cutting another highlight video. He was, in a word, electric.

Asked for his impressions from his first college game, Reesing says, "The speed of the game is faster than high school, and there's a lot more to think about. Play calls are more complex, you have checks, you have to read defenses. When it's all happening so fast and you're just trying to keep your breath without your heart rate going too high, I didn't think that much. I just reacted and played football. That's why I scrambled a lot. I actually graded out pretty poorly as a quarterback."

Not surprisingly, he wasn't without his shaky moments. Three plays before his touchdown run, he fumbled, but left tackle Anthony Collins fell on the ball. Then, on the snap after he scrambled for 63 yards to the Colorado three-yard line, Reesing fumbled again; Buffs free safety Ryan Walters picked up the loose ball and scampered 95 yards for a touchdown, and the Kansas faithful watched the final 3:17 of a 20–15 victory with sweaty palms.

"It was surreal," says Reesing. "Two days before, I was signaling plays in and hanging out at practice. Now I was the one who brought us back from a deficit and kept us where we had a chance to go to a bowl game. If we had lost that game, we would've been out of bowl contention."

The line was respectable enough: seven carries for 93 yards and a touchdown (the 63-yarder would be the longest of a career during which Reesing was credited with 335 rushes) to go with seven completions in 11 attempts for 106 yards, with two touchdowns and the buzz-killing interception. Most important, directing an attack that piled up 251 yards on 32 snaps, Reesing had almost tripled KU's first-half production.

Nobody could have predicted it, but a legend was born. And in the days after the comeback kid rallied the Jayhawks to their first Big 12 victory of 2006, the legend was burnished. Word spread that Reesing had been spotted on Massachusetts Avenue on the night before the 1 o'clock Saturday kickoff. True enough, Reesing says now, but could you really fault the kid? He was a 19-year-old freshman who was enjoying college life. He wasn't the only KU football player seen on the streets of downtown Lawrence that Friday night. Some of his teammates who were out on the town knew they would be playing the next day. And hadn't Reesing been told more than once that there was no way his redshirt would be pulled in the ninth game of the season? Plus, it was Halloween weekend, and Reesing was eager to trot out his Scooby-Doo costume.

So, yeah, he was decked out in orange from head to toe as he strolled up and down Mass Avenue, but that's where the story starts to get hazy. Reports ranged from his dancing on the bar at Brothers to his downing shots into the wee hours to his being found slumped over the wheel of his car at six o'clock on Saturday morning, motor running. Just to set the record straight, Reesing did go out with friends (and teammates), had a few laughs, caught some curious looks and called it an early night. Sounding somewhat regretful, he says his night on the town was *not* the third coming of Joe Namath and Max McGee.

"I've heard more versions of this story than you'd ever believe," Reesing says. "It would be funny if there were a better version, but I guess the one everybody has heard has grown over the years."

As it turns out, that last weekend in October would be the highlight of Reesing's freshman season. Meier returned for a 41–10 victory over Iowa State; Reesing pitched in with a touchdown through the air and another on the ground. He was surprised he never took a snap during a 39–20 win over Kansas State, and he got only mop-up duty in a 42–17 loss at Missouri. He also got an eye-opening introduction to the rivalry.

"Coming from Texas, you really don't know about the Kansas-Missouri game," Reesing says. "But once I heard all the history and the background on the rivalry and heard all the hatred …" He pauses. "Until we got to Columbia and I heard all the things that were said, you just don't understand the passion that these people have for the rivalry and how much it is more like a war. That's why the term *Border War* is appropriate."

There would be no bowl game at the end of a 6–6 season, but the significance of the last four games of 2006 wasn't lost on Mangino. "It worked out perfectly," he says, "because in 2007 Todd wasn't a rookie. If we had not played him in 2006, he would not have been prepared to play the way he did in 2007. If we had started him as a rookie in 2007, you wouldn't be talking to me about this book."

As his record-setting career was winding down, Reesing was often asked if he regretted burning the redshirt. The answer was always a resounding no.

"Going into Week 1 [of 2007], I didn't feel the nerves of a first-year player because I had been in some games, played twice on the road," he says. "I had been in some tough situations that helped me mature a lot quicker. I felt like I had a whole year under me, even though I only played in a couple of games."

Yet as the calendar turned to 2007, not even the cocksure Reesing would have been brazen enough to suggest the Jayhawks were about to embark on the greatest season in program history.

Chapter 10

Chase's Time

Chase Daniel needed exactly 29 minutes and three seconds to put his name alongside Brad Smith's in the annals of Missouri football. And another 20:04 to separate Smith from one of his 69 records. Making his first start as a Tiger on Sept. 2, 2006, Daniel threw for four first-half touchdowns against Murray State, tying the school record for TD passes in a game, and when he added a fifth scoring toss early in the fourth quarter, the record was his and his alone.

Before the clock wound down on Missouri's 47–7 victory, Daniel had completed 23 of 32 passes for 320 yards. He directed touchdown drives on the Tigers' first two possessions, connected on his first eight passes and spread the ball around to eight receivers. The only black marks on an otherwise stellar debut were a second-quarter fumble and the five sacks allowed against a Division I-AA opponent coming off a 2–9 season. Daniel acknowledged the negatives. "It was good to go out there and get the win, but that third quarter was pretty sloppy," he said afterward. "We need to take that up. [Those are] things that are going to get you beat later in the season."

Pinkel promises players and recruits that every position is up for grabs in spring ball and again at the start of fall practice. The quarterback position is no different. Brandon Coleman, a senior from Miami, was in the mix in '06. Patton, the 6-foot-5, 220-pound hometown star, was back for his sophomore season and eager to show off an arm that had made him one of the top recruits in the country. But the fact that Daniel would be the starting quarterback against the Racers was the worst-kept secret in Columbia.

"I think it was an open competition," Daniel says. "BC and Chase and I were great friends, and we competed our butts off. Again, I had three good scrimmages."

Then he adds, "There was no way in heck I was going to lose that job."

Patton believes the staff gave him every opportunity to win the position. "Even after Chase established himself, we'd go into spring and they'd say, 'Push him as much as you can. Who's to say you can't beat him out?'" Patton says. "I do think they meant it. It was impressive what [Daniel] could do. He made me a better player. And I think I pushed him to make him a better player."

Courted by Tennessee, Iowa, Kansas State and UCLA, among others, Patton remembers the day he received his official offer letter from Missouri. It arrived in a neatly addressed, padded envelope and was mounted on foam board, but he came home from school to find that Bruin, the family mutt, had ripped the package in half. Maybe that was an omen.

"It was impressive what [Daniel] could do," says Patton. "He made me a better player. And I think I pushed him to make him a better player."

"I was real close to going to Tennessee," Patton says. "Erik Ainge [a four-star from Hillsboro, Ore., who would sign with the Vols] and I took our official visit at the same time. We were feeling each other out."

In the end, Patton was enamored by the prospect of playing in a stadium 10 minutes from home, on the field where he had watched so many games as a kid. Patton wonders if his just-happy-to-be-there attitude might have a detriment.

"We were great friends," he says of Daniel. "I don't create conflict. I'm easy to get along with. Maybe that was my downfall. Maybe I didn't have enough of an edge when he came in. I worked my butt off, but I got sucked into the system and never got the competitive drive going. Looking back, I think I could have done more."

Matter describes Patton as a good kid who was good for the program. Nobody remembers so much as a complaint or the mention of a transfer. He had the respect and admiration of his teammates and coaches, including Daniel. Had Daniel pursued that 11th-hour inquiry from the Longhorns, the other Chase probably would have become a pretty salty signal-caller. "I think Patton, if given some time, would have developed nicely and been a pretty good Big 12 quarterback," says Matter. "It was just going to take time."

The Tigers, however, didn't have time — least of all Pinkel. He was beginning his sixth season in Columbia, and his record was a pedestrian 29–30. He found the right quarterback in Daniel, who knew only one thing: winning. The sense of urgency was evident in the roster decisions the coaches were making and the quality of recruit they were starting to attract. Daniel, Hood, Coffman and linebacker Brock Christopher played as true freshmen in 2005, and against Murray State, fans got their first glimpse of three newcomers who would emerge as key cogs in Missouri's 2007 title run.

Sean Weatherspoon was a loud, overlooked linebacker from Jasper, Texas, whose recruitment was waylaid after Hurricane Rita ravaged the southeast Texas coastline in late September 2005. That Spoon was only rated a two-star spoke more to the chaos and uncertainty that surrounded his life than it did to his football talents. Jasper became a safe haven for Rita refugees, and Weatherspoon got lost in the recruiting shuffle, moving from relative to relative while sometimes playing two games a week. Even after he committed to Houston, the Mizzou coaches stayed aggressive. They liked him as a linebacker, but Weatherspoon was so athletic as a receiver that Eberflus, his primary recruiter, jokes he was reluctant to share Spoon's highlight video with receivers coach Andy Hill.

"He looked O.K. at linebacker," Eberflus says. "Then I went to the school and put on his tape at receiver. He was off the chain, running over guys, running tunnel screens for touchdowns. You could really see his athleticism."

Weatherspoon put that athleticism on display at a scouting combine in Westbrook, Texas. He was one of about five dozen prospects at the workout, and Eberflus came away even more impressed. "He was in a tight-fit shirt. He looked ripped," the coach recalls. "He was pretty big at that point. He was about 215, 220 [pounds]. He was moving really, really well."

In other words, Weatherspoon was all but impossible to miss. Yet there may have been a perfectly good reason why other programs overlooked him. "Most of the guys who recruit for schools in East Texas also have another area, like Houston or Austin," says Eberflus. "They've got this huge area to cover. Where Gary was smart, he put a recruiter in East Texas only. I could comb the bushes for players and spend time with the coaches and build relationships with them. That's just a function of logistics — Pinkel and his organization in terms of recruiting."

Weatherspoon felt wanted—"We stayed on him," says Eberflus—and as Christmas approached in 2005, two events changed his thinking: First, two days before the holiday, Houston lost, 42–13, in the Fort Worth Bowl. The Cougars played as poorly as the score suggested, and Spoon began having second thoughts about his college choice. Coincidentally, the beating came courtesy of Mangino and the Jayhawks. Then, while killing time at an area mall, Spoon walked by a sporting goods store and happened upon a single black hoodie with "Missouri" stitched across the front. That, he says, was like a message from above, and on the day after Christmas, he committed to the Tigers.

Some 200 miles to the west of Jasper, linebackers coach Dave Steckel was doing some bush-combing of his own, and in Marlin, he stumbled upon an even more obscure recruit. So unknown was Danario Alexander that his first name was incorrectly spelled on the Rivals recruiting web site (and as of July 2013 still was). He was a two-star receiver with a rating even lower than Weatherspoon's, and he caught Steckel's eye only when he was evaluating another Marlin player. What wasn't to like about a 6-foot-3, 185-pound burner who swallowed up yards with an effortless stride? Three days after Weatherspoon pledged to Mizzou, Alexander did the same.

The Texas twosome, however, had nothing on Jeff Wolfert. As the calendar turned to 2006, Wolfert was already on the Missouri campus. He was even taking up residence in the football locker room, though he estimates that half of his teammates didn't know his name. A multi-sport athlete growing up in Overland Park, Kan., he took his talents as a soccer player to the football field as a senior at Blue Valley West High in 2003. Alas, in his first game as a Jaguar, on his first kickoff, Wolfert snapped his right hip. The fracture, doctors surmised, was the result of over-kicking in preparation for his maiden season on the football field.

It would be a year before he could even think about kicking again, but Wolfert had options. He was an accomplished and heavily recruited diver, so he took official visits to Missouri, Auburn, Minnesota, North Carolina and Purdue with the idea that he might one day walk on to the football team while continuing his career in the pool. "It came down to North Carolina and Missouri," he says. "Missouri was the better fit."

Wolfert had a successful freshman season, finishing in the top five on the platform and in the top 10 on the one- and three-meter boards at the NCAA Zone Diving Championships. However, he never lost his passion for kicking. In 2004, he was one of about a half-dozen kickers invited by Yost to an informal audition. Wolfert didn't get a call-back, but he kept grinding. At night, he would sneak into the indoor facility and work on his technique in the dark. "I was just trying to keep the dream alive because I wanted to try out again," he says.

He got another shot in the spring of 2005, and this time Yost came away impressed. "He said, 'You know what? We've got a spot for you,'" Wolfert recalls.

There was one problem. Pinkel wasn't crazy about the idea of raiding other programs on campus for their athletes. "First of all, I said I didn't want to upset the diving coach," he says. "We had to communicate this well so it was done right."

The coaching staff was also understandably reluctant to steal an accomplished athlete from one sport and roll the dice on a player who had not attempted so much as an extra point in high school. Yet Wolfert was willing to surrender his diving scholarship to walk on at a major-college football program without a guarantee he would ever put on a uniform. He gave the staff an ultimatum.

"I said, 'I'll take the decision out of your hands,'" Wolfert remembers. "'If you don't let me on the football team, I'm going to go elsewhere.'"

Bold as it might have sounded, it was pretty much an idle threat. Because the clock was already ticking on his eligibility and he didn't want to sit out a year, he knew a transfer would have meant pursuing his dream at a lower-division program. He would have been O.K. with that, but for a guy who oozed confidence, Wolfert had no intention of leaving Columbia. "I never had that transition where I was doubting my abilities to kick a football," he says. "I grew up a well-rounded athlete. I played lots of soccer, so I was really good with my feet. I played every sport imaginable growing up. Pressure and performing were never an issue. I always believed in my ability."

Though disappointed he never got an opportunity in 2005, Wolfert wasn't surprised. The job belonged to Adam Crossett, a strong-legged sophomore who also happened to be Yost's brother-in-law. "I knew that going in," says Wolfert. "It was just another one of the roadblocks." Crossett, however, was as inconsistent as his right leg was explosive (in the Independence Bowl, he shoved a 22-yard field-goal attempt, then nailed a 50-yarder on his next kick), and in the spring of '06 the kicking competition was opened up. "That's when it got serious," Wolfert says. And that's when the staff began to take him seriously.

"That's when my name was starting to become known," he says. "I was building relationships with some of the more pivotal people on the team. It was becoming evident that I was going to be an important player."

Of course, Wolfert knew as well as anyone he still had to prove himself. But the pressure wasn't overwhelming because he also knew how low the bar was set. What kind of expectations could Pinkel and Yost put on a walk-on who had never kicked in a college game? Any game.

Imagine how awkward the dinner conversations must have been in the Yost household in the days leading up to the opener, because in the middle of the week, Wolfert was moved to the top of the depth chart. "I benched my brother-in-law," Yost says half-jokingly. Wolfert's leg might not have been as strong as Crossett's, but he was certainly more consistent.

It was a typically hot summer afternoon, so stifling it would have been easy to understand why the players might lose focus. That excuse didn't fly with Williams. He slammed his helmet to the ground and lit into his teammates. Like that, a leader was reborn.

The athlete who turned in his Speedo for a pair of football cleats remembers his first two field-goal attempts like they were yesterday. "A 41-yarder, right hash, and a 38-yarder, left pole [upright]," he says without hesitation of the opportunities he got against the Racers.

The first attempt came early in the second quarter with Mizzou sitting on a 21–0 lead. The ball sailed wide left, though Wolfert, like any good kicker, contends it traveled directly over the upright and easily could have been called good. Whatever, the bar now was being raised several levels. As he jogged onto the field midway through the third quarter in a game the Tigers led 37–0, Wolfert understood the stakes. "I knew if I didn't make it, I could be done," he says. "It was a pretty easy field goal. I relaxed, made good contact and that was it. I got in a groove and kept moving along."

His new teammates followed right in step. Weatherspoon blocked a third-quarter punt out of the end zone for a safety, while Alexander caught a 13-yard, fourth-quarter pass from Coleman. And although he didn't make any headlines, backup safety Cornelius Brown, a junior college transfer by way of Adel, Ga., debuted with a tackle, three assists and a successful fair catch of a first-quarter punt.

When the Tigers followed with a dominating 34–7 victory over what was supposed to be a formidable Ole Miss team, Pinkel moved his record above .500 for the second time. This time there would be no turning back.

Not with Daniel, who passed for another 243 yards and, flashing the running skills he had displayed at Southlake Carroll, rushed for a team-high 89 yards. Equally impressive was the way the Tigers flew to the ball on defense. They limited the Rebels to 162 yards on 57 snaps.

The leader of the defense was—who else?—Williams. The prelude to his epiphany came in July 2006, at a team barbecue on the first anniversary of O'Neal's death. Ivey pulled Williams aside and asked him how he was feeling. The strength coach already had the answer, knowing full well that A.O.'s passing was still eating at Zo. He also believed it was important for Williams to acknowledge as much.

Then Ivey told Williams he was one of the most special players he had coached. "You are going to be a leader of this program," Zo remembers Ivey saying. "You can't look at [A.O.'s death] like it was your fault. You can't let this affect the way you play this game and [you have to] lead these guys because a lot of people look up to you right now. You just don't know it."

The revelation came soon enough. During August two-a-days, the Tigers were trudging through a particularly sloppy session, a period so brutal they were instructed to start it over. It was a typically hot summer afternoon, so stifling it would have been easy to understand why the players might lose focus. That excuse didn't fly with Williams. He slammed his helmet to the ground and lit into his teammates. Like that, a leader was reborn.

"I'd been playing football since I was four," says Zo. "I've always been a leader."

Finally, just as Ivey predicted, the light went off. Williams was now the ringleader of a defense that in the wake of victories over New Mexico, Ohio and Colorado was ranked 10th in the country. Skeptics questioned whom the Tigers had really beaten, and a road game against Texas Tech would provide plenty of answers. In fact, it proved that Pinkel didn't have to lean on his offense to win games. On consecutive second-quarter possessions, Jackson and Moore returned interceptions for touchdowns, and before Tech's explosive offense had crossed midfield, Missouri led 24–0. Celebrating his 20th birthday and playing in his home state for the first time, Daniel passed for only 171 yards. Yet the Tigers left Lubbock with a 38–21 victory, their first 6–0 start since 1973 and a No. 19 national ranking.

"It was a good feeling," says Daniel. "Everyone knows how hard it is to win at Texas Tech, especially at night."

The following week, when William Franklin scored on an apparent 65-yard touchdown reception at Texas A&M on the third play from scrimmage, Mizzou seemed headed for a magical season. It seemed too good to be true. And it was. The touchdown was overturned after a replay review—Franklin was stripped from behind a split second before crossing the goal line, and the ball rolled out of the end zone for a touchback. Missouri couldn't overcome two other first-half fumbles and was unsuccessful on a baffling fake field goal, and in a game that featured six lead changes, A&M scratched out a 25–19 victory.

And thus the tailspin began. Though they rallied for a 41–21 victory over Kansas State that snapped a 13-game losing streak to the Wildcats, the Tigers dropped a much-anticipated game at Faurot to Oklahoma, 26–10. They fell into an early hole in a 34–20 loss at Nebraska. It was no consolation that Daniel set the school single-season record for passing yards against the Cornhuskers or that Wolfert drilled a 54-yard field goal, and after a third consecutive defeat—a 21–16 loss at Iowa State to a team that had dropped six straight—Missouri was again portrayed as a program that had nothing left in the tank come November. Making the setback especially hard to accept was the fact the Tigers rallied from a 21–10 deficit and scored the go-ahead touchdown in the final half-minute, only to have it nullified by a phantom holding penalty. Sure enough, two days later the Big 12 office notified Pinkel that officials had blown the call.

"We had some tough games there," he says, pointing to the Iowa State game. "Good teams find ways to win games. I flat told our team that we did the right things to win. Bottom line, we did."

Except, they didn't—get credit for the victory anyway. On Senior Day, the Tigers took some satisfaction from a 42–17 pounding of Kansas that snapped a three-game losing streak to the Jayhawks and denied them a bowl bid. Even without a 75-yard touchdown pass that was wiped out by questionable offsetting personal-foul penalties, Daniel threw for a career-high 356 yards and four touchdowns and the Tigers racked up 493 yards of offense. It was the most points Mizzou had scored against KU in 10 years. Still, after a 6–0 start, the last thing these Tigers anticipated was an 8–4 finish. They accepted a bid to the Sun Bowl and a meeting with Oregon State. If nothing else, El Paso beat Shreveport as a bowl destination.

Winners of seven of their last eight games, the Beavers entered as the hotter team, but for the first 48 minutes, Missouri looked like its old self. Alexander hauled in a 74-yard touchdown pass, Temple repeatedly gashed the OSU defense and when Daniel and Coffman connected on an 18-yard touchdown pass with 12:08 left, the Tigers led 38–24. Then they found a new way to lose a game. The Beavers answered with a 76-yard touchdown drive, and after a 39-yard punt return, they took advantage of a short field to pull to 38–37 with 23 seconds left. Coach Mike Riley sent out his kicking team for the tie, but when Missouri called timeout, wanting to give the replay official more time to review the touchdown reception, Riley reconsidered. Running off left guard against the Tigers' kick-block formation, Yvenson Bernard burrowed into the pile and, best anyone could tell, into the end zone. Williams took the blame.

"To lose five times, that was tough," Daniel says. "That was not the standard for me. I felt disgusted. I said, 'This is not the way we do things around here.'"

"I knew they weren't going to kick it," he says. "They ran right over my butt. We had push right, which is a field-goal block. I'm the only person over the guard, and there's nobody else around me. The center, guard and tackle came down right on top of me. That is the day I *really* became a leader, because that was my fault more than anything. Who you going to blame? Just me. What are you going to do from here out? I never want to feel like this again."

Missouri squandered several opportunities in 2006, but none was more catastrophic than the meltdown in the Sun Bowl. Daniel passed for 330 yards, Temple ran for 194 more and the Tigers had seven plays of at least 29 yards. Add it up, and they finished with 591 yards of total offense. And a 39–38 defeat, the team's fourth in five games. Same ol' Mizzou. It was no way to send out the seniors, and the returning players would have to sleep on the loss for eight months.

"The '06 season was about learning how to win," says DeArmond. "They won a lot, but they didn't know how. I think '06 taught them some lessons that showed up in '07."

Adds Pinkel, "Sometimes you have to go through those things, especially for a program that has not been winning consistently."

Fair enough, but don't try selling that logic to Daniel. In two seasons as a starter at Southlake Carroll, he had lost once in 32 games. Now, for the fifth time in seven games, he had fallen short. He wouldn't tolerate losing. It made his stomach turn.

"Growing up in Texas and playing Texas high school football, I had different expectations," Daniel says. "To lose five times, that was tough. That was not the standard for me. I felt disgusted. I said, 'This is not the way we do things around here.'

"People in Missouri were like, 'Oh, we had a pretty good season.' The expectation level was not there. My job, and what I took pride in, was raising that expectation level, not only for the fans, but for the players as well."

A couple of hours after the latest kick in the gut, Mike Kelly stepped off an escalator at El Paso International Airport. It was New Year's Eve, but no one in the Missouri travel party was popping corks. As he scanned the concourse, Kelly saw a solitary figure sitting glumly on a bench.

Kelly walked over and thanked Daniel for a memorable season. Then he added, "There are many, many great times ahead for you."

Daniel looked Kelly squarely in the eye. Without hesitation, he replied, "And it begins when we get back [to Columbia]. We're going to learn from this as soon as we get back."

Chapter 11
2007: Chaos

Aqib Talib has never been shy in front of a microphone, so the assembled scribes and broadcasters didn't so much as blink when the Kansas cornerback made a bold prediction at the Big 12 media gathering in Dallas in July 2007. Asked what he would consider a successful season for the Jayhawks, the bombastic Talib, a pre-season All-America selection, replied, "Realistic, for us, is to have nine wins and play in the Big 12 championship game."

Realistic? Based on what exactly? Kansas was coming off a .500 season. The Jayhawks *hoped* they had found a quarterback, the school's all-time leading rusher had graduated, the three interior offensive line positions had to be filled and only 11 of 22 starters returned. That the media picked Kansas to finish fourth in the six-team North division— behind Missouri, Nebraska and Kansas State—may have been kind. Granted, the non-conference slate was softer than soft and neither Oklahoma nor Texas nor Texas Tech (the top three teams in the South) was on the schedule, but in its first 11 years in the Big 12, Kansas had never won more than three conference games in a season. Now, assuming a 4–0 September, Talib was forecasting five league victories, maybe more.

In the formidable Big 12? Certainly, the do-it-all corner had heard the February rant of Dan Hawkins. Reacting to a parent who suggested players were getting too little time off before the start of summer conditioning, the Colorado coach famously screeched, "Go play intramurals, brother! It's Division I football! It's the Big 12!"

Tom Keegan was at the Big 12 media extravaganza. After a career that included stops in New York and Los Angeles, Keegan arrived at the *Journal-World* in the summer of 2005. He had sat courtside at countless NBA snooze-fests and in press boxes for too many NFL and Major League Baseball games to remember, but his passion for college sports drew him to Lawrence. He was excited about the opportunity to cover Kansas basketball, of course, but at the same time he was intrigued by the football program.

"It was weird a school that didn't have any football tradition to speak of could have produced John Hadl, John Riggins and Gale Sayers," Keegan says. "That seemed so strange to me."

And although the ever-quotable Talib was a sports columnist's dream, Keegan wasn't buying 9–3, especially after having sat through a couple of uninspiring seasons of KU football. "I was still conditioned at that point to think, 'They're doing everything right, and they're doing as well as they can with the athletes who are willing to say yes to Kansas in recruiting,' " Keegan says. "But my brain was still conditioned to think that 3–5 is the best that Kansas can ever do in the Big 12. It's 1–7 for most years, but this looks like a 3–5 team."

"My brain was still conditioned to think that 3–5 is the best that Kansas can ever do in the Big 12," says Keegan. "It's 1–7 for most years, but this looks like a 3–5 team."

If only Keegan and his colleagues who were at that Dallas hotel had been witness to the off-season conditioning the Jayhawks subjected themselves to. Players challenged each other to get stronger—both physically and mentally. Upperclassmen such as Talib, running back Brandon McAnderson, tight end Derek Fine, defensive tackle James McClinton and linebacker Mike Rivera stepped up. Reesing, for one, remembers the first two months of 2007 as being program-changing. There was a sense of urgency in the weight room and on the practice field. Forget the recruiting rankings. The players believed they could be special. Still, they approached every sprint and ever rep on the bench press as if they were too small, too slow and too soft to battle with the behemoths of the Big 12.

"We had to outwork everybody, because we didn't have as good a natural athletes, we didn't have as big a linemen, we didn't have as fast a players," Reesing says. "So if we wanted to beat people, we were going to have to outwork them in the off-season and be more disciplined and part of a team. The thought process that made us a good team really started during that off-season program, and that carried over to spring ball."

Then, flashing back to all of those close calls in 2006 that turned a potential breakthrough year into yet another season without a bowl—in one six-week span, Kansas lost five games by a total of 23 points— Reesing says the Jayhawks adopted a mantra: "*Finish* the fourth quarter. *Finish* the workout. Whatever you're doing, just *finish*."

As spring practice began, the new but familiar face with the whistle around his neck was offensive coordinator Ed Warinner. The relationship between Mangino and Warinner is Exhibit A of how tight the coaching fraternity can be. Over the years, the two men bumped into each other on the recruiting trail and shared the occasional dinner or phone call. Mangino came away from Oklahoma's 2001 game at Air Force impressed by the play of the Falcons' offensive front, and when he was looking for an o-line coach in 2003, he hired his colleague. Two years later, Warinner moved on to Illinois, but during a casual conversation in January 2007, Mangino mentioned he was in the market for an offensive coordinator. Warinner said he might be interested, and a day later he had an offer.

Warinner and Mangino had the same vision: Their one-back, no-huddle spread would use the pass to set up the run; they would get creative with three- and four-receiver sets; they would stretch the field vertically; and they would incorporate the running back into the passing game.

Revamping the offense was a challenge in itself, but Mangino and Warinner were dealing with another issue as well—the psyche of the players who would be plugged into the new system. "Ed and I spent a lot of time working on the emotional aspect," Mangino says. "The kids were fragile—mentally fragile. As soon as someone made a bad play, there was a sigh. *Here we go again.*"

The coaches became psychologists. Dropped passes and bad reads and missed blocks would be greeted with back slaps and words of encouragement. Mangino's message to his players: "You've got to have a short memory."

There was also the question of who would run the spread. Through-out the spring, Meier and Reesing engaged in a heated battle, as Mangino and Warinner charted their every play. The coaches had lengthy discussions, and by early in August two-a-days, Reesing had won the job.

Still, Mangino knew he was rolling the dice. The youngest of four brothers to play college football, Meier was a prototypical quarterback. He was 6-foot-4 and 235 pounds, and the term most often used to describe him was *physical specimen*. And although Reesing had shown flashes during his abbreviated freshman campaign, Mangino and Warinner were staking their futures on an undersized quarterback who had thrown all of 24 passes as a collegian. No wonder sports information director Mike Strauss was somewhat startled when Mangino ambled over one day during drills to announce he'd named Reesing the starter and that both quarterbacks would be available at a post-practice media session. "I asked, 'How's Kerry doing?'" Strauss recalls. "Coach said, 'Don't worry about Kerry.'"

When Strauss approached the two players, they were leaning against a goalpost, stretched out and engaged in conversation about the world's bigger problems. Or not. Strauss knew how much Meier wanted to be the man, but there he was shooting the breeze with the guy who had taken his job from him. "They were such good friends," says Strauss. "Kerry cared, but he was fine with it. He handled things so well."

Says Mangino, "We were dealing with two very intelligent guys who could see the big picture."

As the 2007 college football season swung into full gear on Sept. 1, the Jayhawks weren't in the big picture. They were nowhere near the frame. Not only were they unranked, they also had failed to receive a single vote from the 65 writers and broadcasters who cast ballots in the preseason AP poll. Forty-seven teams had received at least one vote— 47!—but none of them was named Kansas. Hadn't at least one voter been listening to Talib? But what transpired on the first Saturday afternoon in September in Ann Arbor, Mich., should have given fans of Kansas and Boston College and South Florida and other middling programs around the country hope. Nobody knew it yet, but the sport was about to embark on a rollercoaster season filled with ridiculous twists and turns. *Chaos, disorder* and *confusion* were just three of the words used to describe the events of 2007.

Michigan was ranked fifth in the country, quarterback Chad Henne, running back Mike Hart and offensive tackle Jake Long had passed on the opportunity to declare for the NFL draft, and the Wolverines had designs on their first national championship in a decade. Appalachian State was in town. The Mountaineers were the two-time defending Division I-AA national champions and owners of a 14-game winning streak, but let's be honest. Nobody in the crowd of 109,218 expected a little ol' program from Boone, N.C., to put up a fight against mighty Michigan in the Big House. No I-AA team had ever beaten a Top 25 program. Like most every one of their cohorts who schedule these games, the Mountaineers were in it for the money—a guaranteed $400,000 payout to be a scrimmage opponent for an afternoon. So excited were Big Ten executives that the matchup was relegated to the conference's fledgling television network. And with only two major cable carriers on board, the inaugural telecast on the Big Ten Network was there for none of the college football world to see. Basically you had to be in the Big House to believe it. App State stunned Michigan, 34–32.

In Lawrence, Mangino's men were still a couple of hours away from the kickoff of their season opener against Central Michigan. Every attempt was being made to build up the Chippewas—they were the defending Mid-American Conference champs, after all—but if the Jayhawks couldn't handle Central Michigan, how exactly did Talib plan on getting to nine victories? And with games the following three weeks against Southeastern Louisiana, Toledo and Florida International (all of them at home), the table could not have been better set to start 4–0.

A Memorial Stadium crowd of 46,815, the largest to see a home opener in 13 years, witnessed a 52–7 beat-down. Reesing completed 20 of 29 passes for 269 yards and four first-half touchdowns. There were no turnovers. The defense was steady if not spectacular, limiting the Chippewas to 294 total yards. Yet if not for a sideline spectacle midway through the second quarter, nobody outside of Lawrence would have paid KU's convincing victory much attention.

Raimond Pendleton had just punctuated his 77-yard punt return for a touchdown with a swan dive into the end zone. Officials littered the field with flags for excessive celebration, but it wasn't hard to understand the reason for Pendleton's exuberance—the redshirt sophomore was playing for the first time in almost three years. Mangino could not have cared less. He greeted Pendleton as he came off the field with a 30-second, profanity-laced tirade, grabbing his facemask while asking his return man if he really thought he had scored the TD on his own. Mangino's rant went viral. It wasn't exactly the kind of pub the program was looking for, but it was a start.

Afterward, Mangino was more interested in singing the praises of Reesing. "He's starting his first game, and you'd think he'd been doing this for 10 years," the coach said. "The way he approached the game, the way he warmed up on the sideline. You know, courage is a good thing to have. He has it."

It may have only been one game, and the opponent may have only been Central Michigan, but there was plenty more to be optimistic about.

The Jayhawks passed for 308 yards and ran for 230 more, as both McAnderson and Jake Sharp went over the 100-yard mark. There were five completions of at least 20 yards, the longest coming on a 49-yard touchdown strike to Talib. It was all part of Mangino's plan to use *every* playmaker on the roster. The last TD came on a 21-yard pass from Meier to Pendleton. There was no flag for excessive celebration. "We have a different style of players now," Mangino said afterward. "We're matching that style with the offense. We've made a commitment to put pressure on a defense vertically."

So impressed was Keegan that he started his Sunday column with a simple five-word lead: *Heisman campaigns must start somewhere.* He was joking. (We think.) And so impressive were the Jayhawks that they collected a vote—one 25th-place vote—in the AP poll. You must start somewhere.

Three days later, the following appeared near the bottom of a *Journal-World* notes column: *KU associate athletic director Jim Marchiony said Tuesday that 69,000 tickets had been sold for the Kansas-Missouri game, which will be played Nov. 24 at Arrowhead Stadium in Kansas City, Mo.* Nobody other than Carl Peterson paid the 32-word nugget much attention.

Of course, the Jayhawks had a Division I-AA opponent on the schedule, and, of course, Mangino mentioned Michigan as Southeastern Louisiana came calling in Week 2. But I-AA squads just don't beat I-A teams: Of the 42 programs from BCS conferences that had such a matchup in 2007, only Iowa State (to Northern Iowa) and Minnesota (North Dakota State) joined Michigan as embarrassed losers. Kansas won its exhibition, 62–0, notching its first shutout in seven seasons and scoring at least 50 points in a second consecutive week for the first time in program history.

The Jayhawks followed with victories over Toledo, 45–13, and Florida International, 55–3. They were 4–0 and had outscored their opponents, 214–23, but what had they really proven? The most recent victim was in its third season of I-A football and lost for the 16th consecutive time. KU was the only Big 12 team that hadn't played a road game. So impressed were pollsters that the AP vote total was up to six.

However, as early as Week 2, Strauss sensed that the Jayhawks might have something. "You could tell how good they were," he says. "They played nobody, but just the way they executed and the way they defended, you got the feeling they could do that against anybody."

Mangino was a little slower to come around, but he too liked what he was seeing. Even as the games got out of hand, the Jayhawks didn't lose focus. And they were disciplined. They weren't turning the ball over—five fumbles and an interception in 301 snaps—and they were among the least-penalized teams in the country, with 17.

"Even when you're playing a non-conference schedule that's not a difficult one, you can see the execution of your team, you can see the way they operate, you can see their mind-set, how they play fundamentally," Mangino says. "By the time we got to game six or seven, I began to think that we could be a really special football team."

The offense was piling up the yards: 2,211, to be exact. McAnderson had rushed for 327 yards and six TDs. Sharp, Lightning to McAnderson's Thunder, had chipped in 307 yards and three scores. Reesing? Despite not taking a fourth-quarter snap, he had thrown for 1,199 yards with 11 touchdowns and the one interception. There was no doubt in Keegan's mind that Mangino and Warinner had found the guy to direct the offense. Reesing could extend a three-second play another seven or eight seconds, and those kinds of magic acts would translate to better competition. There's more.

"When you're Kansas, when you're in the second tier in recruiting, the place where you get hurt the most is in the lines," says Keegan. "If you're a lineman, you think you're going to be a first stringer. The first three strings go to Nebraska, so Kansas is left with …." The leftovers.

"You need a scrambler," adds Keegan. "Every time you watch [Reesing], you think of Fran Tarkenton. In all my years of watching football, I think of those two. There are better runners but not better scramblers. You saw the receivers change. They kept running their routes because they knew the play was never over."

Reesing's success came at a price. Meier was fast becoming a forgotten man. Yeah, the Jayhawks were winning and he was getting mop-up duty (along with several chances as the emergency punter), but he wanted to be on the field for significant snaps. In mid-September, Mangino dropped a hint about his backup quarterback when he told Bob Lutz of the *Wichita Eagle*, "Believe me, the Kerry Meier chapter in this book has not been finished." Not long after, Warinner called Meier into his office and asked if he wanted to continue to be primarily a clipboard holder. Against Florida International, Meier got his first action at wide receiver. On his first play, he caught a 15-yard pass; on the second, he motioned into the backfield, took an option pitch from Reesing and ran for six yards.

Meier became the busiest Jayhawk at practice, taking snaps and keeping his arm loose, attending quarterback meetings and running routes at wide receiver, all the while donning a red, no-contact vest. As Mangino saw it, by getting Reesing and Meier on the field at the same time, KU helped itself at two positions.

"I've said this before and I'll say it again. We've had great players at KU, and Kerry Meier is among them," Mangino says. "But Kerry might have played the most important role in the turnaround of our program."

"Kerry Meier might be the ultimate team player," Mangino says. "He was very unselfish. He cared about winning. I've said this before and I'll say it again. We've had great players at KU, and Kerry Meier is among them. But Kerry might have played the most important role in the turnaround of our program. Because of his unselfishness, a lot of kids looked up to him and respected him. He was a role model for a lot of players on our team."

Kansas had a bye on the last Saturday of September, but the dominoes around the country were starting to fall. No. 4 Florida lost in Gainesville to Auburn. Two other top 10 teams fell closer to home—in the Big 12. First, Colorado stunned No. 5 Oklahoma, 27–24, in Boulder. Later that night, Kansas State rocked No. 7 Texas, 41–21, in Austin, handing Mack Brown his worst home loss in 10 seasons with the Longhorns. The AP voters rewarded the one-loss Wildcats with a No. 24 national ranking. The Jayhawks? They were still residing in the "also receiving votes" neighborhood, down three points from the previous week, tied with Boise State and Virginia.

At least KU was finally in a position to do something about it. As luck would have it, the Sunflower State rivals squared off on the first Saturday in October. In what would become a recurring theme, Kansas was labeled as a team that was in over its head. In addition to hammering Texas, Kansas State had gone toe to toe with Auburn on the road before losing, 23–13. KU was leaving Lawrence for the first time. Though Mangino deserved credit for learning a thing or two from his old boss Bill Snyder about what favorable scheduling can do for a team's confidence, KU's four non-conference victories were a combined 3–13. Never mind that they hadn't won in the Little Apple in 18 years; the Jayhawks hadn't scored a touchdown there since 1999. Plus, Mangino's record in Big 12 road games was 2–18.

Sports Illustrated was intrigued enough by the matchup that it dispatched staff writer Mark Beech to Manhattan. After receiving apologies from the college football editor for being sent to the middle of nowhere, Beech was assigned a 700-word column. He would write about the winner. Based on its demolition of the Longhorns, K-State seemed the sexier story, but Beech covered his bases and contacted Strauss, who recalls, "He said he was here to write about Kansas State, but if we won he'd come see us. I said, 'Well, you never know.' "

Reesing threw an interception on the first play from scrimmage, and the Wildcats jumped to a 7–0 lead midway through the first quarter. However, five seconds before halftime, the Jayhawks knotted the score at 14 on a five-yard touchdown grab by Talib, who scored a TD in his sixth straight game dating to 2006. The second half was a seesaw affair. KU went up 21–14, and after K-State scored 10 consecutive points, Reesing showed what he could do if given an opportunity to play in the final 15 minutes. He needed only 65 seconds to get back the lead, on a 30-yard strike to freshman wideout Dexton Fields with 6:27 left. The Jayhawks won the fourth quarter, 9–7, and the game, 30–24. In the Oct. 15 issue of SI, Beech began his one-page column: *It's time to reevaluate Kansas.*

Ask him to identify KU's breakthrough game, and without hesitation, Reesing points to the meeting in Manhattan. "We hadn't won in that place in 18 years," he says. "The defense came up big with some stops. It was a total team win, and it showed our resiliency because we played all the way into the fourth. That became a staple of this team. When the fourth quarter came, we really beat people up, because with our conditioning and our mental toughness, that's when we were at our best. That game showed we could win the hard way. Those were the games we always lost in 2006."

Though he was intercepted three times, Reesing threw for 267 yards and three scores. Playing for the first time in the fourth quarter, he brought KU from behind. "Sawed-off quarterback Todd Reesing is a winner," Jason Whitlock wrote in *The Kansas City Star.* "He's Kansas' answer to Missouri's sawed-off Chase Daniel."

Keegan, who in the *Journal-World* had predicted a KU victory, nevertheless walked away pleasantly surprised. "By that time, I thought,

'This team might just go 4-4 in the Big 12,' " he says with a laugh. "Which would be pretty darn good."

Kansas finally entered the AP poll at No. 20, a spot behind Wisconsin, which dropped 15 places after losing at Illinois. That the Jayhawks were ranked for the first time in 11 years might have made for more headlines if not for the stunning upset that transpired after most of the college football world had called it a night. Stanford, a 41-point underdog, shocked No. 2 Southern Cal, 24–23, at the Coliseum on a touchdown with 49 seconds left. LSU became the unanimous No. 1.

The newly ranked Jayhawks returned home for a meeting with Baylor. Lightning proved more daunting than the Bears, as the game was delayed for 98 minutes before kickoff and another 45 minutes in the first quarter. The teams traded early field goals, but after Marcus Hereford returned a kickoff 88 yards for a touchdown, the rout was on. Kansas won, 58–10, piled up a record point total for a conference game and became bowl-eligible. On Oct 13. At halftime, Riggins was inducted into the Memorial Stadium Ring of Honor. A member of the Pro Football Hall of Fame, Riggins watched Sharp scoot for 110 yards and a touchdown. It marked the third time in six games that the sophomore had surpassed the 100-yard mark.

Sharp, the No. 1 recruit in Kansas in 2006 after running for a state-record 6,524 yards during his career and scoring 63 touchdowns as a senior at Salina Central High, was quietly working his way into the offense. Only 5-foot-10 and 190 pounds, he hid behind the Jayhawks' massive line, darting through holes and grabbing shovel passes from Reesing. However, even as the top-ranked recruit in the state, Sharp was only a three-star. His only other Division I-A offer came from Colorado State. Like so many other Jayhawks, he was playing with a chip on his shoulder.

"We liked being the underdog," says Reesing. "We wanted to keep proving people wrong. There was a certain satisfaction each week when people said you can't win and then you continue to win."

At least KU was starting to get a little respect in the polls. Perhaps the voters were starting to understand how damned difficult it was to win in college football. That week, No. 1 LSU (in overtime at Kentucky) and No. 2 Cal (at home to Oregon State) both lost. It marked the first time in 11 years that the two top teams had lost on the same weekend. The new No. 1 was Ohio State, which started the season ranked 11th. One of six undefeated teams left in the country, the Jayhawks jumped five spots to No. 15. They were tied with ... Missouri, which lost for the first time, at Oklahoma. And if you didn't have a ticket to the Nov. 24 game at Arrowhead, you were out of luck. Several days before the Baylor game, the contest was announced as a sellout.

"I think everybody in our locker room had an eye on that game at Arrowhead," says Reesing. "Everyone knew we were headed for the ultimate throw-down."

Both teams still had five games to navigate, and with a trip to Colorado looming, the talk started up again. The Jayhawks might have been 6–0, but here it was the middle of October and they had yet to leave the state. They'd also lost nine of their last 10 games in Boulder, and lest anybody forget, the Buffaloes were three weeks removed from the upset of Oklahoma at Folsom Field.

As was the case in Manhattan, KU fell behind in the third quarter, yet Reesing wasted no time seizing back the lead. The Jayhawks covered 58 yards in five plays, with Sharp running the last two yards for a 10–7 lead. There were some anxious moments when Colorado pulled to 19–14 with 3:42 left, but after getting the ball back 86 seconds later the Buffs went four-and-out. KU matched the school record for Big 12 victories in a season, and Mangino equaled his conference win total on the road for his first five seasons.

"They play a lot harder than any of the other teams we have played," said Colorado quarterback Cody Hawkins, whose team had faced Arizona State, Florida State and Oklahoma. "You're going to come out with a chip on your shoulder when everybody is doubting you."

Even Mangino seemed to be carrying around a rather large chunk of lumber. Talking about the mentality of his defense when it took the field for the final possession, he said he sensed "they had a little swagger to them." Then, asked about whether he thought his team should be taken seriously, he threw the question back at reporters: "I'm not going to say whether we're for real. You watch the games. You see whether we're for real." Finally, he harped on the psychology of college football. "Every Division I football team in America has a weight room," he said. "What separates the good teams from the not-so-good teams—the mental preparation and the mental edge."

Interestingly, the Jayhawks broke the tie in the AP poll with the Tigers, moving a spot ahead of their rival at No. 12. Around the time of the kickoff in Boulder, Missouri was putting the finishing touches on a 41–10 rout of No. 22 Texas Tech. KU was a spot behind South Florida, which plummeted nine places after losing at Rutgers. The list of unbeatens was shrinking by the week. Of the five teams without a blemish, only Ohio State and Hawaii started the season in the Top 25. In the second week of the BCS rankings, Boston College and Arizona State shot to second and fourth, respectively. Kansas, at ninth, was climbing but still pretty much an afterthought.

The Jayhawks, however, were 7–0 and a victory at Texas A&M from matching the program's best start in 98 years. None of the 26 Texans on the KU roster was more excited about the road trip than Reesing. He would be playing in his home state for the first time. His grandparents were lifelong Aggies fans, and there were other A&M fanatics in the family. Some of his high school friends were attending school in College Station. Kyle Field is one of the best atmospheres in college football, not to mention one of the loudest. And never mind that Reesing had grown up a Longhorns fan. Don't think for a moment he hadn't forgotten how the A&M coaching staff had turned its back on him during recruiting. The date had long been circled on his calendar.

"That whole week," Reesing recalls, "Coach Mangino came up to me in practice, just behind the huddle or just behind me in the shotgun and whispered in my ear, 'They said you were a B-list quarterback; they said you weren't good enough.' "

Against the Aggies, Reesing was good enough. Though he didn't throw a touchdown pass for the first time all season, he was an efficient 21 of 33 for 181 yards. Most important, for the third consecutive game, he didn't turn the ball over. KU won, 19–11.

"It was real cool," he says of playing at Kyle Field, "but it was a lot cooler when they were dead silent. That was just a hard-fought victory—another total team victory on the road, which again affirmed our belief that when it comes to the fourth quarter, we're ready to go."

It was more than that. "On paper, this was KU's most impressive victory of the season," J. Brady McCollough wrote in *The Star*. "Not because the Aggies are better than Kansas State or Colorado, but because teams just don't come into College Station and push them around."

The workhorse was McAnderson, who carried 21 times for a career-high 183 yards and two touchdowns. A fullback during his first three years at KU, McAnderson was another in the long line of lightly recruited Jayhawks. He got looks from Iowa, Kansas State and Missouri, but the knock was that he was too slow and, at 5-foot-10, too short. Mangino, however, took a liking to McAnderson while watching him take handoffs from Tommy Mangino at Lawrence High. Say this much for McAnderson: He had a nose for the end zone. He scored five touchdowns as a junior, and his two TDs against the Aggies pushed his 2007 total to nine. (He was also most likely the only 1,000-yard rusher in Division I-A who was on the punt-coverage team. McAnderson was credited with the tackle on the punt return before Colorado's final series.)

The Jayhawks weren't just winning. Now they were getting into their opponents' heads. "They played better than I thought they could play," said A&M defensive coordinator Gary Darnell. "I thought we'd hold up inside well enough to make them put the ball on the edge. I didn't think they could beat us throwing the football, and I *really* didn't think they could beat us running the ball."

That's exactly what they did. Sharp chipped in with 70 yards, and although Reesing was sacked four times, KU still piled up 227 rushing yards. As for A&M's vaunted ground game, a swarming defense led by Rivera and fellow linebackers James Holt and Joe Mortensen slammed the door. It was becoming a pattern. Kansas State had run for 53 yards, and Colorado had managed only 66. The Aggies boasted the nation's fifth-ranked rushing attack and were coming off a game in which they gashed Nebraska for 359 yards. Yet against the Jayhawks, A&M went nine yards in reverse in the third quarter and finished with 74 rushing yards.

Mangino didn't have to tell anybody. These guys really were for real.

"It was that way week to week," Reesing says. "We'd go out and get a win on the road and people would say, 'Oh, they're going to slip up this week. They're going to get beat. Their run's going to be over.' No one except for our team and our true fans thought we were worthy of playing with the best in college football."

The one negative to the victory in College Station was that Scott Webb missed three of five field-goal attempts. Nobody in the KU camp thought much of it, though. After all, in the first seven games, Webb had missed only one of 12 attempts, the Jayhawks were 8–0 and ranked eighth, and Nebraska was coming to town.

If there was a year to schedule the Big Red for homecoming, 2007 was it. The Cornhuskers had dropped four straight, athletic director Steve Patterson had been ousted (and replaced by Tom Osborne) and it was no secret that coach Bill Callahan was a dead man walking. The vaunted Black Shirts defense had given up 49 points to Southern Cal, 40 to Ball State (Ball State!), 41 to Missouri, 45 to Oklahoma State and 36 to Texas A&M. Lincoln was starting to look at lot like Lawrence of yesteryear; the self-proclaimed best fans in college football weren't bothering to stick around for the Cornhusker Marching Band's halftime show.

This is how dramatically the tables turned in 2007. Kansas opened as a 14-point favorite over Nebraska, and by kickoff the number had ballooned to 20.

In 2005, KU snapped a 36-year losing streak to Nebraska, but the 40–15 victory didn't exactly even the score. Consider that during those 36 years of frustration, the Cornhuskers scored at least 40 points on 26 occasions, while the Jayhawks were shut out eight times and scored a touchdown or less eight other times. During a four-year stretch beginning in 1971, KU lost 55–0, 56–0 and 56–0. Those were just three of the 17 times that Nebraska put up at least 50 points. In those meetings, the average score was 58–8. The capper came in 1986, a 70–0 laugher; the next year the final was 54–2.

Yet this is how dramatically the tables turned in 2007: Kansas opened as a 14-point favorite over Nebraska, and by kickoff the number had ballooned to 20. For once, Memorial Stadium wasn't a sea of Cornhusker red, and a record crowd of 51,910 could smell blood. The typically slow-starting Jayhawks went three-and-out on their first series. Then they scored. And scored. And scored. In fact, they scored on 11 of their next 12 possessions, Nebraska's only "stop" coming when Reesing took a knee after KU got possession five seconds before halftime. Reesing passed for a school-record six touchdowns, McAnderson tied a school record with four rushing touchdowns and Nebraska gave up the most points in its proud 118-year history. So efficient was the offense that in their 90 snaps, the Jayhawks had one penalty and no turnovers. KU won, 76–39.

"It was just pure joy," says Reesing. "I made a comment that it was like practice. It was like playing a junior varsity team. We were clicking on all cylinders to the point that whatever play we called worked. For the fans who suffered so many beat-downs, it was good to give them a good, thorough beating of Nebraska."

Insisting he did everything he could to keep the score down, Mangino says "it just came unraveled" for the Cornhuskers. Reesing isn't so sure. The Jayhawks led 69–31 after three quarters, and the starters were on the field for the final touchdown, which came with 11:12 left.

"We didn't want to take the foot off the gas," says Reesing, who was 30 of 41 for 354 yards. "We were trying to score as many points as possible. They did that to us for years and years and years."

A Colorado native, Strauss knew the reputation the Cornhuskers had developed around Big Eight and Big 12 country. "We got calls from everybody around the league thanking us for beating Nebraska like that," he says, "because they did that to everyone for so many years."

Mangino preferred to focus on all the things his team was doing right. The talk of the soft schedule was getting old. So what if the Jayhawks hadn't beaten anyone that was even getting votes in the AP poll. They were 9–0, and after No. 2 Boston College lost at home to Florida State and No. 6 Arizona State fell at home to Oregon, KU was one of three undefeated programs in college football. Mangino talked about his team having a target on its back, how it was "getting everybody's best shot." He went so far as to compare the '07 Jayhawks to his 2000 national-title team at Oklahoma. "They're focused," he said after the drubbing. "They're smart. They play hard every week."

They were also climbing in the AP poll. The Jayhawks jumped three spots to No. 5, and more important, they cracked the top five in the BCS, at No. 4. Even the ever-skeptical Keegan was coming around. For the first time, he started looking down the road to the Missouri game—and wondering whether anyone in the KU administration was having regrets about the decision to surrender what was scheduled to be a home game for the neutral-site setting at Arrowhead.

First things first. There was one more road hurdle to clear—against Oklahoma State in Stillwater. The Cowboys were only 5–4, but night games on the road are dicey. They're especially dicey when they're played before a national television audience and the already oversized target on the visiting team's back has grown to epic proportions. Less than two hours earlier, No. 1 Ohio State, a 15-point favorite, had fallen at home to Illinois (marking the seventh time in eight weeks a top three team had lost). There was now but a single undefeated team from all the BCS conferences—the Kansas Jayhawks. No pressure there.

All night on ABC, Brent Musburger and Kirk Herbstreit marveled at the Jayhawks' unlikely story. They also said it was time to take the kids from Lawrence seriously. When you are disciplined and are the least-penalized team in Division I-A and you don't turn the ball over and you are playing with a chip on your shoulder, good things happen. Even when a 33–14 lead over the Cowboys dwindled to five points, KU didn't panic. Reesing answered with an 11-play, 87-yard drive that he capped with a four-yard touchdown pass to wideout Marcus Henry. Webb tacked on a short field goal, and Kansas had a 43–28 victory.

It was another week featuring another star for the Jayhawks. Henry, a senior, made a triumphant return to his home state with eight receptions for 199 yards and three touchdowns. He thought he was headed from Eisenhower High in Lawton to junior college in 2004, but then he had a breakout performance in a summer all-star game. Duly impressed, the KU coaches offered Henry a scholarship. Now he had blossomed into the Jayhawks' leading receiver.

The countless feel-good stories—Reesing, Meier, McAnderson, Talib and Henry, just to name five—were a journalist's dream. Writers descended on Lawrence, and for once they weren't there to chronicle KU basketball. Mangino always started his weekday press conferences at noon. Not 12:01. High noon. "He and I would be in the hallway, and he would stand there and do this," says Strauss, touching his wrist with his index finger as if it were a watch. "And then he'd say, 'Now!' It was to the second."

Mangino would walk into the room, and Strauss would follow closely behind, shutting *and* bolting the door behind them. There was, after all, a schedule to keep. Mangino couldn't be distracted by a tardy beat writer who might saunter into the room with cell phone to ear while the coach was in mid-sentence. Besides, he was forever preaching discipline to his players, and what kind of message would bending the rules for a late-arriving outsider send? Strauss still laughs about the time in 2007 when Steve Wieberg of *USA Today* came to town. He arrived for a press conference a couple of minutes late to find the door locked.

"He wasn't there [at noon]," recalls Strauss. "We said, 'You're not coming in.' I'm like, 'Geez, we're telling the *USA Today* college football writer no.' I've known Steve for 20 years. His kid worked in our office that year. I'm like, 'Sorry, Steve.' "

Around town, the excitement was building. Keegan remembers a day when his late-model convertible predictably broke down. Conveniently, there was a taxi at the gas station where he was stranded—"one of maybe three cabs in Lawrence," he says—and the cabbie agreed to give him a lift. Racing to campus to make the noon Mangino lock-in, Keegan was astounded when the driver struck up a conversation about KU *football*. "He said, 'This is the first time I can remember that there are more people talking about KU football than there are people talking about KU basketball,' " Keegan says. "Everybody was in a good mood when that football team was going great. You know how it is. People figure it's going to last forever."

After the victory over Oklahoma State, Kansas climbed to third in the BCS rankings and fourth in the AP poll. The Jayhawks even got a first-place vote, from Doug Lesmerises of *The Plain-Dealer* in Cleveland. But the wackiness of the college football season was evident in the way pollsters around the country perceived KU. One voter had the only undefeated team from a BCS conference ranked ninth. Missouri, winner of four straight, was lurking at No. 5 and No. 6 in the BCS and the AP poll, respectively.

The Tigers had already kicked off against Kansas State when KU took the field for Senior Day, against Iowa State. The Jayhawks may have been 27-point favorites, but with the game against Missouri looming, Mangino didn't want any distractions. So he instructed the stadium staff not to update the crowd on the proceedings in Manhattan. No worries. Reesing completed 17 of 18 passes for 221 yards and four touchdowns—in the first half. For the fifth time in 2007, he didn't take a fourth-quarter snap. On a spectacular, 60-degree fall afternoon, Kansas won in a walk, 45–7, and for the first time as a college head coach, Mangino was a winner. His career record climbed to 36–35.

"The community was so buzzed and everybody was so excited about football," says Reesing. "And to be a part of that, especially for the older guys who knew what it was like to play in a stadium that wasn't half-full. At the same time, it was so surreal. Five months before that, I was just trying to win a starting job."

Meier may have ceded the quarterback position to Reesing, but he had arguably his finest hour of 2007 against the Cyclones. He caught three passes for 41 yards and a touchdown. He completed all nine of his pass attempts for 101 yards and another touchdown. And he graced the cover of the following week's *Sports Illustrated*, hauling in a pass with a packed, picturesque Memorial Stadium serving as the backdrop. The cover billing said it all: "Dream Season."

"I'm glad he stuck around because he turned into one hell of a receiver," Reesing says of Meier. "It was a blessing in disguise. I couldn't have been happier, because I knew Kerry just wanted to play, just wanted to help the team. Being able to find a spot for him on the field was great, because he was such an athlete. There was no way you couldn't put him on the field."

Even before the home finale against Iowa State, No. 2 Oregon had lost a Thursday night game at Arizona. Later on Saturday, No. 3 Oklahoma fell at Texas Tech. The math was simple. When the rankings came out on Sunday, Kansas would be No. 2 in the AP poll and the BCS, behind one-loss LSU. In less than three months, the Jayhawks had gone from *not receiving votes* to No. 2. They were 11–0, and this much was clear: KU was two victories from playing for the national championship. The doubters would just have to deal with it.

"We believe that your ship doesn't come in," Mangino said after the victory over the Cyclones. "You have to swim out to it. I don't believe in that destiny stuff. You have to earn your way in life."

In a jubilant Jayhawks locker room, McClinton, an all-Big 12 defensive tackle, proclaimed: "We're ready for No. 12."

Everybody knew who that was.

Chapter 12

Strictly Business

In essence, the 2007 Missouri football season began on a dreary winter day in a meeting room at the Tom Taylor Building. That's when a group of seniors requested one of those clear-the-air confabs with their head coach. Granted, the Tigers had been to consecutive bowls, but 8–5 seasons weren't what Williams and Rucker and Ray envisioned when they engaged in those dorm-room discussions in 2003. (Don't even get Daniel started.) These guys were in it to win a championship, and they had but one round left in the chamber. So Pinkel laid everything on the table, told the players they would have to be more committed than ever, take their preparation and film study to another level. He said the fire in November had to match the intensity in September, probably even exceed it. He then got back to the basics, reminding the players that the secrets to success were eliminating turnovers and careless penalties as well as winning the kicking game.

"That's when it clicked," Williams says. "I'm like, 'Why can't we do that? This should not be that hard.'"

Zo's final season in Columbia was already off to a rousing start. Like many juniors and redshirt sophomores, he had tested the NFL waters, but his draft evaluation rated him no better than a sixth-round selection. He held his breath as other draft-eligible teammates awaited word, but none of them, most notably Rucker and Franklin, got a high enough grade to warrant jumping for the money. Plus, Ivey had declined an offer to join the Kansas City Chiefs.

Under Ivey's watchful eye, the Tigers trained hard. During breaks, they talked about what it would take to deliver Mizzou its first conference championship since 1969. The dorm-room discussions spilled into the locker room and around a crowded table at Shakespeare's, the legendary pizza haunt at the corner of Ninth and Elm.

"We would go running in the summer before fall practice," Ray recalls. "Someone would say that Oklahoma and other schools were doing the same thing. We would say, 'What makes us different?' It was an open-ended question. Why should we be a team that competes for a championship?

"Zo said, 'Everybody's going to lift weights, everybody's going to run wind sprints. But what bond do you have with the group of guys you're going to work with?' You develop this [bond] over time. It happens behind closed doors. It happens in workouts in the summer. It starts with all of the things you *don't* see on Saturday."

Pinkel saw it. He was beginning his seventh year in Columbia, and he sensed that all of the pieces of his grand plan were finally in place. The lessons learned from 2004 had helped mold the '05 and '06 teams. The '07 group was truly taking ownership of the program.

"You develop this [bond] over time," says Ray. "It happens behind closed doors. It happens in workouts in the summer. It starts with all of the things you *don't* see on Saturday."

"That was their team," Pinkel says. "It wasn't Gary Pinkel's team. The work ethic and the leadership were at the highest level since we'd been here."

So was the talent. The Tigers were particularly loaded on offense. Daniel knew the Missouri Spread inside and out. Coming off his record-setting performance in the Sun Bowl, Temple was healthy and primed for a huge senior season. Three starters returned on the offensive line. With Rucker, Franklin, Ray, Coffman, Alexander, Tommy Saunders and Jeremy Maclin, Mizzou was dangerous and especially deep at receiver.

"We had a lot of playmakers," says Christensen. "We had the guys on the perimeter, a couple of All-America tight ends, good backs, a great quarterback, explosive receivers, a big, athletic line. We felt like we had all the ingredients to do with that offense what we wanted to do."

The Tigers were pretty salty on defense as well. As early as spring ball—when ones battle against ones—Eberflus believed his defense had a few playmakers of its own. "We did a lot of competitive stuff in the spring," he says. "That's the way Coach wanted it. I loved that part of it. I could tell early on that our guys were pretty fiery, pretty competitive. We were getting after [the offense] pretty good. The only thing about Chase Daniel is if you get after him, you can guarantee that at the next practice he's coming after you."

Even the circumspect Pinkel believed the '07 Tigers might have had something. "I never go into a season and say, 'Well, we're good enough to win eight games. Or we're good enough to win 10 games,' " he says. "My thinking is that we'll win every game every year. But I also thought we were a really good football team. Playing in the national championship game? I don't think I would have gone that far."

Team captains are elected during practice in August, and the first two picks—Williams and Rucker—were no-brainers. Ray was the third choice, but for the final spot, the players made a somewhat surprising selection. At least to Pinkel it was. Cornelius Brown, who made one start at safety in '06, was entering his second and final season at Mizzou, and by now everyone in the program was calling him by his nickname: Pig. When Ivey first saw Brown wandering around the weight room, he didn't even know his name. "He was like 235 pounds," Ivey says. "I thought he was a walk-on. We came in here as a staff and said, 'Who's the guy with the hair and the dreads?' Somebody said, 'Cornelius Brown.' I said, 'He doesn't look good, but he's got some pretty good feet.' "

When he delivered his annual summer workout report to Pinkel in the days leading up to August two-a-days, Ivey told his boss that Brown was the player who had impressed him the most. He talked about his worth ethic and noted that Pig, so named by his mother for his sloppy eating habits as a child, had dropped 40 pounds. "I've talked to a few players," Ivey recalls telling Pinkel, "and they all say he's dynamic in the locker room. They say he's good [on the field], but in the locker room he's the Man."

Pinkel was still understandably reluctant to bestow a coveted captaincy on a guy who been in the program for all of one season, but he also knew he had turned over ownership of the team to the players. If they saw Brown as a worthy captain, who was he to question it? "We honor what our players want to do," Pinkel says. "They chose a great kid, high energy. The guy could make some plays too."

By now, everyone in the locker room knew Wolfert's name. After a sophomore season during which he made a school-record 18 field goals (on 20 attempts) and was perfect on all 45 extra-point tries, the diver-turned-Lou-Groza-Award-semifinalist was even rubbing elbows with Daniel. He remembers a comment the QB made at the onset of camp. "He looked at me and said, 'Dude, we are going to be *good*,' " says Wolfert. "That's when I was starting to believe. When you look at the guys we had, look at the experience we had, there were a lot of things lining up that gave us the opportunity to have a phenomenal season."

Two-a-days are "all ball," as Ray puts it, and as camp dragged on, he was just trying to get his body right. Players not only have to learn how to pace themselves in the summer heat, but they also have to be cognizant of how they spend time away from practice. One night, Ray was nodding off in his dorm room when a vision came to him. In his dream, Temple was scoring a touchdown. Ray was trailing closely behind, and when the two went to celebrate, rather than bear-hug or high-five or chest-bump his teammate, Ray shook Temple's hand. Ray took his idea to the receiving corps and suggested they give the handshake a try. And that is how a touchdown celebration was dreamed up.

"It's all business, like a business transaction," says Ray, a marketing major with a minor in English. "I tried to get everybody to do it during camp. I didn't think it would get much press."

The Tigers pretty much had it all: playmakers on both sides of the ball, experience, strong-willed leaders, a tremendous work ethic and even a unique TD celebration. The only thing lacking was respect. It was one thing that NFL personnel executives didn't think too highly of their talents. The '07 season could be used as a platform to prove the pros wrong and elevate draft stock. But what was up with the 65 voters in The Associated Press poll? When the rankings were released in mid-August, Missouri headed the "also receiving votes" category, nosed out of the Top 25 by Boise State and Texas A&M.

"I remember going into the season telling anybody who would listen," says Moller. "Again we were under the radar. We had lost the bowl game to Oregon State, and for some reason people discount you. They read way too much into the result of a bowl game, both for the season it was played in and looking ahead to the next year."

So as if they needed any more motivation, the Tigers were playing with large chips on their shoulders heading into the opener against Illinois in St. Louis. It seemed like an ideal first act. The Illini were coming off a 2–10 season, and the Tigers were a solid favorite. Missouri was sitting on a 7–6, second-quarter lead when Brown picked up a fumble in his own end zone and ran 100 yards for a touchdown. Pig recovered another fumble, and the Tigers tacked on 10 points in the final 20 seconds of the first half for a 23–6 lead.

Enter Maclin. Unquestionably the biggest recruit Pinkel had ever landed (and a St. Louis kid, to boot), the four-star wideout had been penciled into the Tigers' plans as a true freshman in 2006, but during voluntary seven-on-seven drills in July, he landed awkwardly and tore the ACL, the lateral collateral ligament and the posterolateral capsule in his right knee. So catastrophic was the injury that team doctors wondered whether Maclin's college career would be over before it ever started. Even then, Kelly remembers an encounter with the surprisingly upbeat freshman during August two-a-days.

"He was sitting under a tent by himself watching practice," Kelly says. "I went over and introduced myself. I told him I knew it was tough going through this, but that he would be better in the long run and that everything was going to work out great. He said, 'I know it is. I know I'm in the right place.'"

Maclin had come too far to walk away from the game he loved. He was raised by a single parent, and Cleo Maclin King was overwhelmed by the burden of caring for Jeremy and his two older brothers. A youth football coach came to the rescue. Jeff Parres routinely gave Jeremy a ride home after practice. The car would often pull up in front of a darkened house, and one night Parres was alarmed to see Jeremy climb through a window to get inside. Parres kept a watchful eye, and Maclin became a frequent guest at his home, hanging out with Jeff and Cindy's two sons. Finally, during his sophomore season at Kirkwood High and with his mother's blessing, Maclin moved in permanently. Jeff and Cindy Parres, a white couple living in an upper-middle-class neighborhood, treated Jeremy, a black youth with a dark past, as if he were their own son. They also may have saved a young man's life.

"We came in here as a staff and said, 'Who's the guy with the hair and the dreads?'" Ivey recalls. "Somebody said, 'Cornelius Brown.' I said, 'He doesn't look good, but he's got some pretty good feet.'"

"They love him so much; they love my child," Maclin King told Gregorian for a *New York Times* feature in September 2007. "I am so blessed. I really, really am."

Her son was also blessed—blessed with electrifying speed and the ability to change a game in a flash. Thanks to the miracles of modern medicine and the drive of a determined young man, Maclin returned from the injury a step or two faster. Fast-forward to a practice during spring drills in '07.

"He caught the ball in the middle," Kelly says, "then weaved his way around three defenders with seemingly very little effort and got to the

133

sideline on the east side of the field. Then, boom, he was gone. I remember thinking, 'Missouri hasn't had players like this.' This was a new dynamic."

Now fast-forward to the third quarter of the Illinois game. Back in his hometown for his college debut, Maclin was dynamite. His first reception came on an 18-yard sideline route, and on the next play he hauled in a 25-yard TD pass from Daniel. On his next touch, Maclin returned a punt 66 yards for a touchdown. Three consecutive touches, 109 all-purpose yards. Like that, Mizzou led 37–13.

"Anybody who had any misgivings about the idea of how a St. Louis kid might do at Missouri at that point simply had no argument," says Gregorian. "I know it was just one game and one moment, but that was amazing."

Then, as they had done too many times before, the Tigers let an opponent back off the mat. A pair of fumbles led to a couple of quick scores, and the lead dwindled to 37–34. The clock was approaching the 5:00 mark when Daniel took a snap on third-and-seven from his own 26. After eluding a rusher from his blind side, Daniel scrambled up the middle. However, as he dove forward at the end of a 17-yard gain, he was helicoptered on a helmet-to-helmet hit by strong safety Justin Harrison. Daniel lay flat on his back. Finally sitting upright but still dazed, he didn't get on his feet for more than a minute, and as he staggered off the field, his body language suggested he was done for the day.

On the sideline, Patton hurriedly grabbed a football and began loosening up. His opportunity had arrived. "I thought for sure I was in for the rest of the game," he says. "They took [Daniel's] helmet away."

The first play was *Rhino Left*, a Temple run that gained three yards. The next call was a play-action pass. Patton was ecstatic; at long last, he was going to get to showcase his cannon of an arm. He readied for the shotgun snap, made the signal with right hand for the ball to be delivered and … felt a tap on his right shoulder. It was Daniel.

Yellow flags flew, and Mizzou was penalized for an illegal substitution. *Rhino Left* would be the first and the last meaningful snap of Patton's college career. He walked behind the bench, took his helmet off with his left hand and slapped the headgear with his right. "I had that feeling," he says of an opportunity suddenly snatched away. "I could feel it clicking in."

In the ESPN2 booth, Dave Pasch and Andre Ware shared a laugh, saying they couldn't remember a team being flagged for "having too many quarterbacks on the field." Even Patton had to chuckle. "It was really funny," he says, "but it was also, 'There goes another shot.' "

Patton knew as well as anybody that this was his namesake's offense. Daniel wasn't going to let a ding to the head—later ruled a mild concussion—keep him out of a game that hung in the balance.

"That was the only time I've been knocked out of a game," says Daniel. "It was a great hit. I was a little woozy. I don't like to be out. I know Chase would have done a great job, but when you've got a grasp on something and you care about something so much, you want to be in there."

Two plays later, on third-and-11, he rifled a 33-yard pass down the middle to Alexander, but when Wolfert's 49-yard field-goal attempt slid wide left, the Illini still had life, down six.

Brown saved the day. In the final minute, on first down from the Missouri 22, he made a leaping goal-line interception of a pass from backup Eddie McGee. Brown was a playmaker, all right. He had two fumble recoveries (and the TD), a blocked extra point, five tackles and the interception. Missouri escaped with a 40–34 victory.

Pinkel, who as the clock wound down put both hands on his head in a gesture that suggested utter relief, called his team's performance—four fumbles, a blocked punt, 10 penalties, the Daniel-Patton Keystone Kops scene—"a comedy of errors." (The handshake needed a little work as well, as most of the TDs were still celebrated with bear hugs.) No mistake, however, had more potential for disaster than the coach's own decision to go for two after Brown's momentum-turning return. Pinkel cited the two-point chart he carried for the dubious call, but on *Tiger Talk* two days later, he acknowledged he had misread the sheet. Never mind that it was too early in the game to even consider going for two. The Tigers were up seven points, not six. Loud and clear, the chart screamed: Kick it! Pinkel knew how lucky he was he hadn't cost his team a game. "An error was made," he told Kelly. "That's inexcusable."

In Week 2, Mizzou traveled to Oxford for a meeting with Ole Miss. The Rebels were the home of Archie and Eli Manning (and the Grove is arguably the top tail-gating venue in college football), but they were also just an average SEC program. Nevertheless, a road game against a team from college football's premier conference would serve as a good measuring stick for the Tigers, and over a span of 20:15 in the second and third quarters, they scored 38 points. Daniel threw for a school-record four touchdowns in the second quarter, and with the third period barely five minutes old, Mizzou led 38–13. "Shock and awe," *Tribune* columnist Joe Walljasper called it.

"We were focused," Pinkel says. "That told me a lot about our team."

Again, however, the Tigers struggled while playing with a sizeable lead. In the second half, McGee had directed Illinois to 313 yards and 28 points. In a 38–25 defeat, Ole Miss piled up 539 yards. Especially troubling were the 226 rushing yards racked up by BenJarvis Green-Ellis. There were flashbacks to 2004 and the '06 Sun Bowl. So at the weekly Monday captains meeting, Pinkel mentioned the inability to finish games. Much to the surprise of his three teammates, Williams brought up a sore subject. The Tigers, Zo reminded his coach, were practicing too hard.

The topic was first discussed during August two-a-days. Williams remembers how he and his teammates would joke with the staff that they were being overworked. One day Pinkel asked the players what they could do to be a better team, and this time Zo got serious, suggesting that practice was so intense it was as if the Tigers were playing three games a week. Considering the defenders spent a good part of the sessions chasing their explosive counterparts all over the field, Williams' observation didn't seem so outlandish. "We would get our butts kicked by the offense," Zo admits.

Pinkel's reaction? "He was like, 'Excuse me?' " Williams says.

Zo reasoned that if practice were a bit less intense, the defensive starters would have their legs under them in the third and fourth quarters of close games. "He lost his mind," Williams says. "*He lost his mind*. He said, 'Are you trying to tell me how to coach my team?' "

Pinkel may have opened himself up to his players, and he was trying his damnedest to get to know them, but the line had to be drawn somewhere. No player, not even someone as respected as Williams, was going to tell a coach who had been in the business more than three decades how to run practice. Williams says Pinkel called him into his office and told him if he ever broached the subject again, he'd be stripped of his captaincy. Yet, when in the wake of the Ole Miss game, Pinkel posed the question about the second-half conundrum, Williams was quick with a solution. "He lost it again," says Zo.

Rucker, one part stunned that Williams wouldn't let the issue die but equally amused, remembers the exchange like it was yesterday. "Coach blew up on him," he says with a laugh. "And you know how it runs downhill. Coach blew up on the defensive coordinator [Eberflus], and he blew up on the position coach [Craig Kuligowski] and Zo got it from all three of them."

The soap opera didn't make headlines because the offense was stealing them. Christensen was the mastermind. Five players had already taken direct shotgun snaps—and two of them were even quarterbacks. Before the home opener against Western Michigan, so as not to befuddle the officiating crew, Pinkel handed over a folder filled with diagrams of the Tigers' array of exotic formations. They were all legal, of course. One was called the Monster. It featured line splits estimated between five and eight yards.

> **"In the 25 years I've seen Missouri football, it's hard to think of a guy who could take your breath away as [Maclin] could," Gregorian says. "It was like, 'This is a new era.'"**

Mizzou again started fast, jumping to a 31–3 halftime lead. All told, the Tigers amassed 619 yards of total offense, and in mop-up duty, Patton capped a 94-yard drive with an 18-yard touchdown run. Maclin, now starting because Alexander had dislocated his left wrist late in the victory over Illinois, accounted for 275 all-purpose yards. Through three games, he was the only player in college football with 100 yards in rushing, receiving, kickoff returns and punt returns. While quick to acknowledge Smith, Gregorian marvels at the multitude of ways that Maclin could impact a game. "In the 25 years I've seen Missouri football, it's hard to think of a guy who could take your breath away as he could," he says. "It was like, 'This is a new era.'"

There were a couple of downers in the 52–24 victory: Daniel's Big 12 record streak without throwing an interception was snapped at 254 passes, leaving him 17 shy of the national record, set by Fresno State's Trent Dilfer in 1993. And with two touchdowns early in the fourth quarter, the Broncos crawled to within 38–24. But the Tigers were 3–0, and on Sunday they snuck into the rankings at No. 25, just behind Nebraska.

Only a victory over Illinois State stood between Missouri and a much-anticipated meeting with the Cornhuskers—and for the first time since 1905 and '06, a second consecutive 4–0 start. Though they weren't on the same level as Appalachian State, the Redbirds were a top 20 Division I-AA program. Still, they were no match for a faster, deeper and more experienced team. Before the first snap, Illinois State called timeout because it was a player short on defense. Out of the break, Missouri lined up in the same formation, and Daniel hit Franklin on a slant for a 57-yard touchdown. The last Mizzou score in a 38–17 victory came courtesy of a 64-yard punt return from Maclin, who tied the school record for punt-return touchdowns in a career in his fourth game as a collegian.

Writing for *The Pantagraph* in Bloomington, Ill., Randy Reinhardt noted the Tigers were impossible to defend because they used 14 players at a time on offense. He was joking, of course, but it must have seemed that way after watching Missouri rack up 581 yards of offense.

"Playing a team like that defensively is like running a marathon," said Redbirds coach Denver Johnson. "You're just absolutely wasted after it's over. We may have to take a day off this week in order to get our guys back physically."

The Tigers were averaging 544 yards and 42 points a game. Most impressively, the average time of their 24 scoring drives was 2:08. Daniel and Co. knew only one way to play: Fast! But as efficient as the offense was, the benefit of having a quick-strike attack was coming at a price. Despite averaging 82 snaps, the offense was on the field for only 26 minutes a game through the first four weeks. That meant Williams and his mates were buckling their headgear for 34 minutes a game and often back off the bench before they could so much as ponder a defensive adjustment. Fatigue was becoming a factor too, and the Tigers had not even begun Big 12 play.

It is one thing when an NFL-caliber tailback such as BenJarvis Green-Ellis runs at will on your defense. But when the immortal Geno Blow, a backup from a Division I-AA program in Normal, Ill., rips off 116 yards, something has to change. On the Tuesday after the victory over Illinois State, the coaching staff announced the starters would get fewer reps per practice period.

"Coach Pinkel was like, 'Don't even say anything,' " Williams recalls.

Pinkel doesn't remember the practice debate being as melodramatic as Williams and Rucker portrayed it. In fact, he gets almost defensive when asked for his side of the story. But he adds, "Coming from Zo, it was a guy who had a great work ethic. It wasn't a guy who was trying to get out of something. It was just an observation he had."

Conveniently enough, the bye fell the week before the showdown against Nebraska, giving Missouri's defenders two weeks to rest their weary legs. Good thing. The game matching Top 25 rivals was billed as the most anticipated in a generation, "the beginning of a defining eight-game stretch for Pinkel," as Walljasper wrote. Later, he added, "If Missouri is going to become something more than the Texas Tech of the North, this should be the year."

Mizzou may have enjoyed a two-game home winning streak over the Cornhuskers, but this was different. Those games were contested in relative obscurity, without much on the line. Now the Tigers saw themselves as the favorite in the Big 12 North, if not the entire conference. ESPN was in town for the prime-time telecast, and the college football world would be watching. School officials urged fans to wear gold, and the first official Gold Rush in program history drew an overflow crowd of 70,049. Overhead shots showed Faurot Field as it had never been captured before—a sea of gold lighting up the night sky. It had been almost a decade in the making, a scene Alden envisioned when he took over the athletic department in 1998.

"As you look at it for the state of Missouri and the university, to see that and know that you are on the national stage and people now are recognizing Mizzou at a higher level than they probably have for 30 years —30 years!—that gave us such satisfaction," he says.

During an impassioned speech on the eve of what he acknowledged was at the time the biggest game of his career, Williams destroyed a blackboard at the team hotel and put a hole in conference room wall. A night later, the Tigers followed their captain's lead.

On its first two drives, Mizzou effortlessly drove 80 and 79 yards for touchdowns. On their first two drives of the second half, the Tigers scored TDs on drives covering 64 and 69 yards, needing but six plays for each. Even the handshakes were crisp. In a game that ended minutes before he turned 21, Daniel had a night to remember. He finished 33 of 47 for a career-high 401 yards, ran 11 times for 72 yards and had a pair of touchdowns passing and running. His last scoring strike came on a third-quarter dart to Alexander, who as a result of the wrist injury was considered for a redshirt. But did the Tigers really want to sit a playmaker who could help them win a championship? Alexander's 48-yard TD reception came on a route across the middle; he reached over his head on the dead run to snatch the ball out of the cool night air, then raced untouched to the left-front corner of the north end zone. Just what Daniel needed—another weapon.

"From an offensive perspective, we were on fire that night," says Daniel. "It felt like you could have put an NFL team out there, and they wouldn't have stopped us."

Missouri shredded the famed Blackshirt defense for 606 yards, prompting Mitch Sherman of the *Omaha World-Herald* to write: "There's no effective way to defend Missouri and QB Chase Daniel without a dominant pass rush."

Impressed by the gunslinger's laser-like accuracy, DeArmond wrote, "Daniel could have forced a football through your mother's wedding ring."

The much-maligned defense? A unit that entered the game ranked 93rd in the country put the clamps on the Cornhuskers. Marlon Lucky, the Big 12's leading rusher, was limited to 67 yards on 17 carries, and Nebraska, which was averaging more than 35 points a game, failed to score a touchdown against Missouri for the first time in 60 years.

"Daniel could have forced a football through your mother's wedding ring," DeArmond wrote.

"It was our night," says Rucker, who naturally took great delight in the thumping. "We knew we had something special, and we had been here before. We were going to start fast, and once we got ahead, we weren't going to let up."

As the party kicked into high gear all around Faurot, the only lingering question was how badly the Tigers would embarrass the Cornhuskers. One of the knocks that Missouri fans have against Pinkel is that he's too quick to take his foot off the gas. (Late in a 51–13 victory over Miami of Ohio in 2010, he ordered four sneaks into the middle of the line from the RedHawks' 11-yard line. He was none too pleased when the first play gained five yards; the next three netted four.) Up 34–6 in the fourth quarter and methodically driving for another score, the Tigers stalled after a personal foul penalty, so on fourth down from the Nebraska 10, Wolfert was summoned. In the huddle, Rucker's pupils got as big as saucers.

"When it got to that point," he says, "I didn't think we'd run it."

It was a fake field goal the Tigers had put in during the bye week. Rucker would line up on the right wing, feign a block, then slide to his left, parallel to the line of scrimmage. Saunders, the holder, would catch the snap and, with the flick of the right wrist, pitch the ball to Rucker. Sounds simple enough. Not so fast, says Rucker.

"If you go too early, you can mess it up," he says. "But you get real antsy. I was like, 'Do your steps, catch the ball (*catch the ball!*) and then worry about everything else.' It was like clockwork."

Just like the Blackshirts, the Nebraska field-goal defense put up next to no resistance. As Rucker cut upfield hell-bent on scoring what would be the most satisfying of his 18 career touchdowns, he was disappointed to see an expanse of green in front of him. Wasn't there somebody he could run over? Anybody? Turns out there was. He immediately recognized the player in the white jersey wearing No. 51.

"There was one guy standing between the end zone and me," Rucker says. "It was Bo Ruud."

When he attended the Nebraska camp during high school, Rucker remembers Ruud as being the player who graded out at the top of all the performance drills. The coaches were lavish in their praise. Everything was all about the linebacker from right there in Lincoln. Bo Ruud *was* Nebraska football.

As the lyrics go, Rucker could've gone left. Or he could've gone right. Taking either route, he could have walked into the end zone. But what fun would that have been? So he ran directly at Ruud and tumbled into the end zone. "I put my head down and sprinted right at him," Rucker says. "And ran him over. It was like I was giving it to Nebraska, I was giving it to Bo, I was giving it to everybody."

In the front row on the east side of Faurot stood two enterprising students. One was holding a yellow cardboard cutout that said "wound" while the other shook another sign that was shaped like a salt shaker and sported the letter "S." It most certainly was a curious time to call a fake field goal. And to T, of all people? But Pinkel insists he was not trying to run up the score. He is adamant about it.

"No! No! No!" he says. "I don't do that. We design those during the week because we see something we think will work or give us an advantage. I'm not naïve enough to think the game is over even when it seems it's over. There's something good about showing those things because it might pay off down the road. I can see where the Nebraska people thought it was running up the score. Anybody who has been around me knows that I try not to embarrass opponents."

In this one case, Christensen would beg to differ. He may not have been around for the beat-downs Nebraska inflicted upon previous regimes, but he also knows there was no love lost between the programs. "Believe me, there were messages being sent," he says.

Pinkel's reaction seemed to say as much. "It's one of the few times I've seen him smile on the sideline," says Matter. "The smile was very mischievous. The cameras caught him."

Matter's colleague summed up the situation best. Writing about the 41–6 drubbing in the Sunday *Tribune*, Walljasper suggested the fake field goal was "the sort of extended middle-finger play call normally saved for a team's most bitter rival. At last check, that rival is still Kansas, but Nebraska runs second these days."

Oklahoma was undoubtedly third in line, and the following week the Tigers stepped onto an even bigger stage. The rout of Nebraska had gotten everyone's attention. It was time to take 11th-ranked Mizzou seriously. In a feature sizing up the 11 remaining undefeated teams, the *Times-Picayune* put the odds of the Tigers getting to New Orleans for the BCS championship game at 21–1. "If this were the Arena Bowl, possibly," the paper wrote. (Citing its favorable conference schedule, Kansas was listed at 18–1.)

In *USA Today*, Steve Wieberg wrote, "Nationwide, the spread is now a staple. But few, if any, are as tricked-out as the one run by the Tigers, who will snap the ball to tight ends and receivers, split out their tackles and, in a typical game, run a half a dozen or more trick plays."

It was what Daniel came to Columbia for. He was playing with a swagger, and his teammates were feeding off him. He was in his element. "I had a lot of say in what plays were called during the week and what I felt comfortable with," he says. "Coach C [Christensen] did a great job of tailoring the offense to what fit me best. We threw the ball around—a lot. We had a lot of these gadget plays. And they always worked. It's fun when you're putting up 400 yards of offense and 30 points."

The prospect of a Norman conquest, however, was daunting. The Tigers hadn't won there since 1966, and with all due respect to Texas and Nebraska, the Sooners were the kings of the Big 12. They were the defending conference champs and had won four of the previous six crowns. Plus, no one defended the Missouri Spread better than OU. In 2006, the Sooners held the Tigers to 10 points and 360 yards, and they intercepted Daniel three times in a 26–10 victory. The line was set at 12 points.

Regardless, from the first snap, the Tigers had the full attention of the Sooners—and their fans. "I remember Gary telling me that after Missouri's first possession, the fans knew his team was good based on the way the crowd reacted," recalls Kelly. "He said the noise level and the intensity changed when we took the ball for the first time."

Mizzou jumped to a 7–0 lead when Maclin scored on a five-yard double reverse around left end. Finally, the Tigers had a burner who could run with, if not blow by, the Sooners. Maclin had been a popular subject of game-week coverage because he had originally committed to OU, only to reconsider and pledge with Mizzou two months later. It was easy to see why Bob Stoops wanted Maclin on his side.

"That in itself was a big deal," Gregorian says of Maclin's signing with the Tigers. "He was a St. Louis guy who not only chooses Missouri, but he chooses them over Oklahoma and in fact turns his back on Oklahoma to do it. That became a big building block. Of course, it's not a big building block unless Jeremy becomes who he did."

Oklahoma rallied for a 17–10 halftime lead, which it extended to 23–10, but Mizzou wouldn't go away. Maclin scored on another double reverse (this one from 10 yards), Jimmy Jackson added a four-yard TD run and the Tigers took a one-point lead into the fourth quarter.

On the Missouri sideline, Williams and his teammates had a difficult time comprehending it all. "Everybody was looking around and thinking, 'Man, we're about to beat OU,' " he says.

If not for two unfortunate breaks during an eight-play stretch early in the fourth quarter, that might well have happened. The first came on a play from the Mizzou 33. Sam Bradford threw deep down the middle into double coverage, but the pass sailed into the waiting arms of Brown, who broke on the ball as he crossed into the end zone. It was as easy a turnover opportunity as the Tigers would have in 2007, the kind of play the defense had been making routinely all year. But the ball slipped through Brown's hands, and five plays later the Sooners punched it in for a touchdown and a 29–24 lead.

Missouri was still brimming with confidence. The offense had scored on its previous two possessions, and with 12:26 left, there was no reason to hit the panic button. On the second snap, however, came the play that essentially sealed the defeat. To this day, plays for the Tigers' no-huddle attack are relayed from the sideline to the field through an intricate array of hand signals. It looks rather silly at times as a handful of assistants go through their gyrations. On second down from the Mizzou 20, 11 Tigers looked to the east sideline for the play. Ten of them got one call. Daniel got another. So when he dashed from right to left in front of his quarterback, Maclin wasn't expecting the ball to be shoved into his mid-section. The ball hit the ground, and linebacker Curtis Lofton scooped up the gift and rumbled 12 yards, dragging Daniel and Maclin into the end zone.

Afterward, OU defensive coordinator Brent Venables credited his unit, and specifically Lofton, saying Maclin dropped the ball because he glimpsed a defender crashing from the outside. Actually, due to a communication problem, a graduate assistant had signaled the wrong play to Daniel.

"To have a lead in the fourth quarter against a top five team on the road, it gives you a lot of confidence," says Daniel. "It was a couple of mistakes here and there."

Pinkel took responsibility after the 41–31 gut-wrencher. "Gosh darn, you take so much pride in being well-coached and doing all the little things," he says. "One thing I had to do was tell my players they had nothing to do with that. It was a coaching error. I went in the locker room and told our players, 'We can beat anybody in the country.' "

Pinkel, says Williams, took the loss harder than any other he can remember: harder than the debacle at Troy, the '06 loss at Iowa State, the Sun Bowl collapse. And while admiring his coach's willingness to take responsibility, Zo would have none of it. "Everyone looked around and said, 'Coach, shut up. We all lost this game together. We're going to walk out of here with our heads up, talk to the media and go back to work and get this thing going again.' "

Then Williams returned to his locker. He took a seat next to Brown, and he remembers Pig's mentioning how they had let one slip away. "I said, 'I know,' " Williams says. "'Don't you think it's weird that we almost beat OU in Norman?' He said, 'I think we're good.' I said, 'Yeah, me too.' "

No one had time to feel sorry for himself. No. 22 Texas Tech was coming to town, and the Red Raiders led the nation in total offense and passing offense (with a staggering 500.4 yards a game), and they were averaging 50 points. With 31 touchdown passes against only three interceptions, Graham Harrell was slinging it even more than Daniel. It would be the Tigers' third straight game against a ranked opponent. If there was ever an opportunity to mail one in, this was it.

Knowing he had to get his players' undivided attention, Pinkel dropped a bombshell at the captains' meeting. In so doing, he ignored a coaching tenet, did something unheard of in today's one-game-at-a-time cliché-fest. He looked six weeks down the road. "Coach said, 'Anybody been paying attention to KU?'" Williams recalls.

Pinkel told his captains this would be the first and last time he would mention the K word. He said he didn't want to hear anybody talking about it. Then he mentioned he had studied the Jayhawks' schedule and could say with certainty that KU wasn't going to lose any of its next five games. So if the Tigers wanted the Nov. 24 meeting to mean anything, there could be no more of the two-interception, two-fumble, three-sack slop-fests like the one turned in at Oklahoma. He said the message had to be subtly conveyed in the locker room—the 2007 Tigers were a special team, but to have the opportunity to be truly special, they had to win the next five.

"I rarely talk about games, but they were a mature group of kids," says Pinkel. "I flat told them that we knew Kansas was good. I wanted to present the rest-of-the-season story. If you want the big prize at the end, there cannot be any mistakes. We've got to come out focused week in and week out. It wasn't a full discussion. It was easy to get the point across. They were well aware of what was going on."

That they were. "It was no secret anymore," says Rucker.

To at least one long-time observer, the challenge was proof that Pinkel was getting it. "It speaks to the confidence that Gary had in those guys," DeArmond says, "and it speaks to the understanding that Gary has of the Missouri fans. The KU game, by that time, was as important to Pinkel as it was to average Joe-rabid-I-hate-the-Jayhawks fan. *Here's my piece of raw meat. You've got to win out, and here's my piece of raw meat.*"

If only Kelly had known. How he would have loved to ask Pinkel about looking six weeks down the road on *Tiger Talk*. "I think he probably would have used the line that he's used many times before: 'That's not one of your better questions,'" Kelly says with a laugh.

No question, Pinkel got his message across. "Ruck's big thing was that Coach obviously trusted us a lot to bring us in here and say that to us," says Williams, "and he trusted us to go into that locker room and not let people get complacent or feel sorry for themselves for losing. Pick it up and start winning."

Brown took the lead. "I've got Crabtree," he told his teammates.

Michael Crabtree was only a redshirt freshman, but he was already being lauded as the top receiver in college football. Rightfully so. Most wideouts would die to have a season anything like the 6-foot-3, 214-pound Crabtree's first seven games as a collegian: 78 receptions for 1,244 yards and 17 TDs.

On his fourth snap, Harrell threw across the middle to his favorite target. Brown arrived at the same time as the ball, which ricocheted high in the air and back toward the line of scrimmage. Defensive end Stryker Sulak snatched the ball and burst 38 yards for a touchdown.

It was a sign of things to come. Reliving his '06 nightmare against Mizzou, Harrell would throw four interceptions (one more than he had tossed in 347 attempts coming in), and although he passed for 397 yards, 68 of those came on a second-quarter touchdown pass. He was sacked three times, the Red Raiders finished with minus-nine yards rushing and they never took a snap in the red zone. Held under the century mark for the first time all season, Crabtree finished with 10 catches for a pedestrian 72 yards. Brown filled up another stat line: 14 tackles, including 4½ for a loss, an interception and two pass breakups in the 41-10 victory.

> **"It didn't matter who the opponent was," says Ray. "Zo passed around a plate one week and said, 'Everybody's going to eat.' That became our mantra. *Who's the next team up?"*

"I always talked to our defense about having such a dominating performance you literally can see that the other team doesn't want to play you any more," Eberflus says. "You could see it on the field that day: *This isn't really fun for us. I don't think we want to play anymore."*

Eberflus always set goals for the defense, and the bar was raised especially high when the Tigers faced a scoring machine such as the Red Raiders: hit the quarterback as much as legally possible; attack receivers; create more opportunities for the offense by forcing turnovers (preferably five); and maybe even put a defensive score on the board. It may have fallen one turnover short, but the defense matched the Red Raiders touchdown for touchdown and turned them away on four of seven fourth-down attempts.

"Zo got those guys ready to go," says Rucker. "That was his side of the ball. I had full faith that was what he was going to do. It's all about accountability."

Adds Ray, "It didn't matter who the opponent was. Zo passed around a plate one week and said, 'Everybody's going to eat.' That became our mantra. *Who's the next team up?"*

The game attracted the second-largest crowd in Arrowhead history, and although Kansas was the home team, Mizzou fans reminded their bitter rivals that the game was being played on the Missouri side of the contentious border.

PHOTOS BY Mizzou Athletic Communications (*stadium*) and Bill Frakes (*fans, 2*)

WE'RE NOT IN KANSAS ANYMORE... THIS IS TIGER COUNTRY

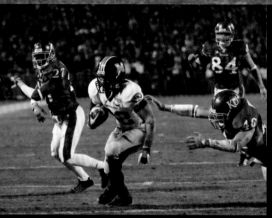

Kyle Tucker prevented a Maclin touchdown (above), but Temple (left) set up Rucker (82) for the game's first score. Meier (10) got KU rolling with a 39-yard reception on the first play of the second quarter.

"Great call," Daniel says of the empty-set, fourth-down touchdown pass to Rucker from the one-yard line. "Just a little bubble screen. Go block."

Moore's interception (above) was the game's biggest play, and Pinkel (near right) called Temple's 17-yard run from the goal line a "hit-you-in-the-mouth momentum play." Webb missed two first-half field goals, much to the dismay of Mangino (far right).

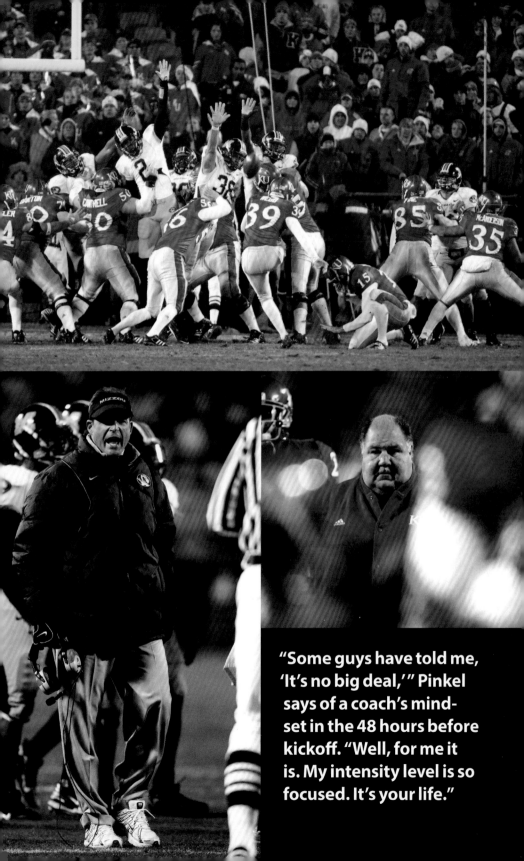

"Some guys have told me, 'It's no big deal,'" Pinkel says of a coach's mind-set in the 48 hours before kickoff. "Well, for me it is. My intensity level is so focused. It's your life."

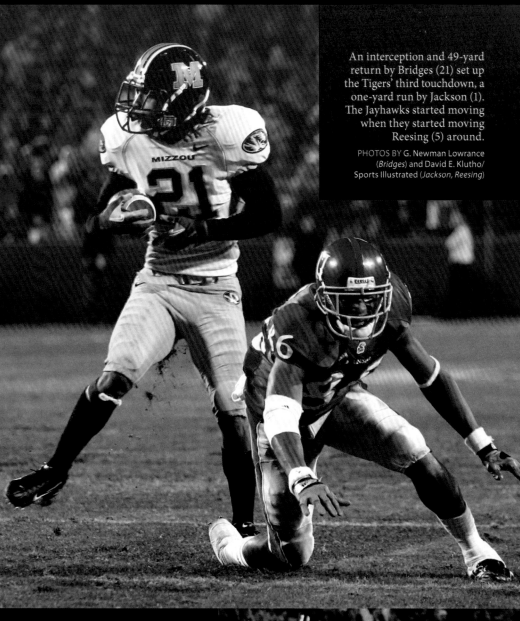

An interception and 49-yard return by Bridges (21) set up the Tigers' third touchdown, a one-yard run by Jackson (1). The Jayhawks started moving when they started moving Reesing (5) around.

"You get the feeling that Kansas is shell-shocked," Herbstreit said after Mizzou took a 21–0 lead. "It's almost like they don't know what hit them."

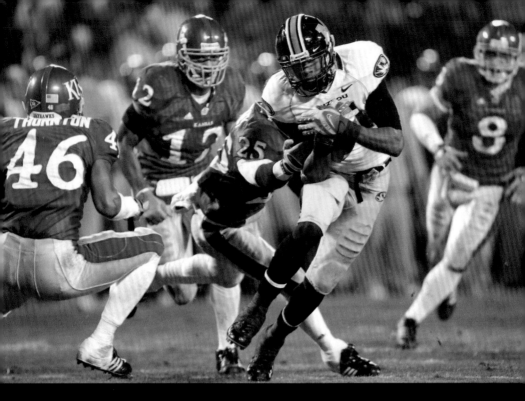

Alexander, with eight catches for 117 yards and a touchdown, had a breakout game, while it was just another day at the office for Daniel, who directed the Missouri Spread flawlessly and in the third quarter matched his jersey number by competing all 10 of his attempts.

Wolfert (99) delivered a pair of
43-yard field goals, the second after
KU had pulled within 10 points on
a TD reception by Fields (88). The
Missouri defense put the finishing
touches on a 36–28 victory, and Reesing
was left to pick sod out of his facemask.

PHOTOS BY David E. Klutho/Sports Illustrated
(*Wolfert, Fields, Reesing*) and Jamie Squire/
Getty Images (*sack*)

In a game that featured 64
points, 51 first downs and
910 yards of offense, the
clincher came courtesy of
Williams, Sulak and the
Missouri defense.

When it was over, Pinkel and Mangino shared a handshake at midfield, Williams walked off with the Lamar Hunt Trophy and Rucker went straight for the War Drum.

PHOTOS BY G. Newman Lowrance (*coaches*), David E. Klutho/Sports Illustrated (*Williams*) and Larry Smith/Icon SMI (*Rucker*)

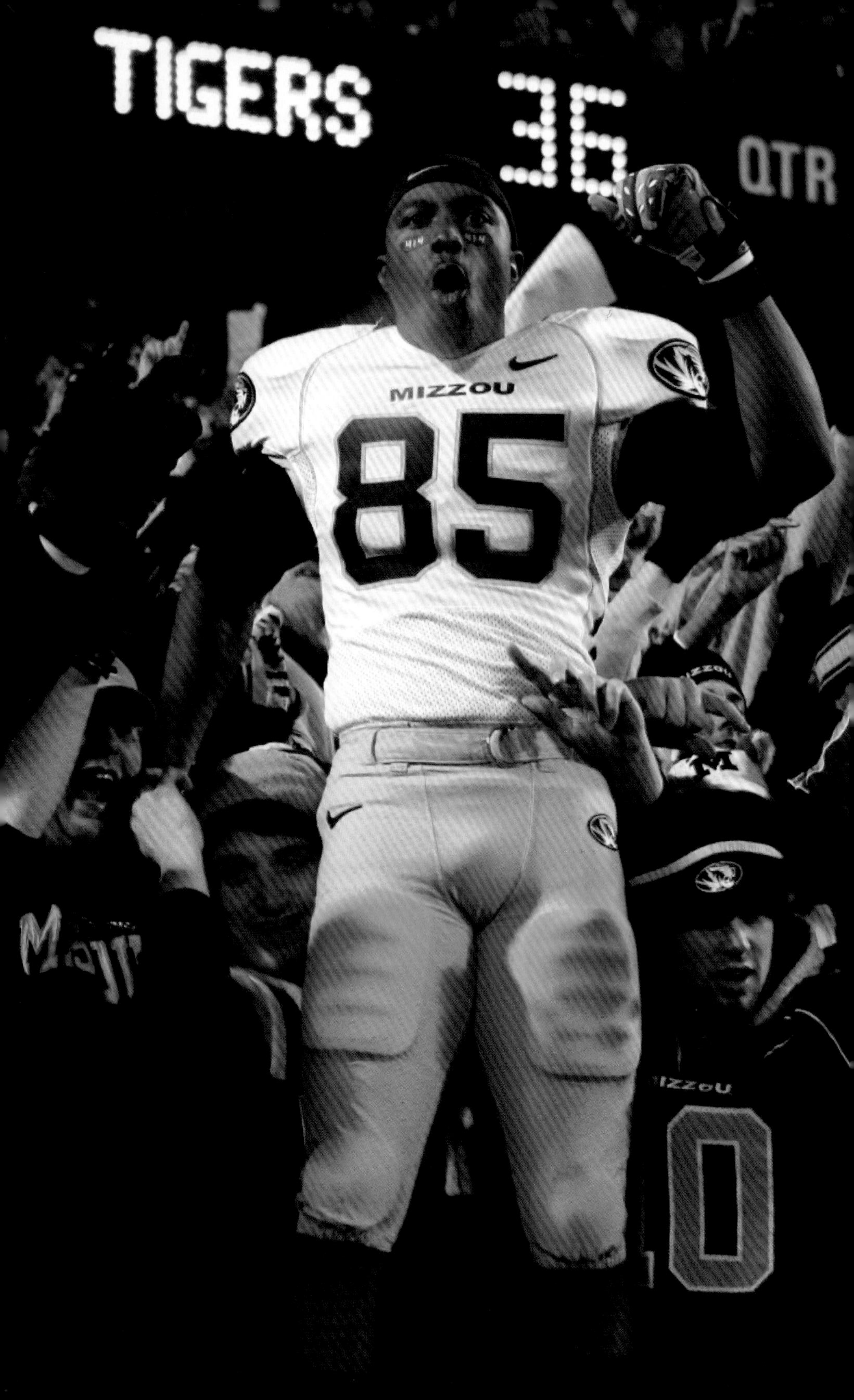
TIGERS
36
QTR
MIZZOU
85
MIZZOU

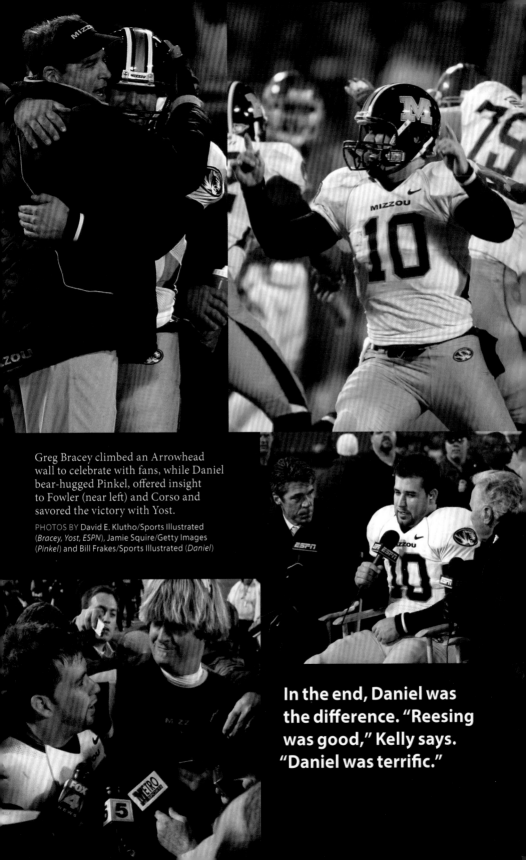

Greg Bracey climbed an Arrowhead wall to celebrate with fans, while Daniel bear-hugged Pinkel, offered insight to Fowler (near left) and Corso and savored the victory with Yost.

PHOTOS BY David E. Klutho/Sports Illustrated (*Bracey, Yost, ESPN*), Jamie Squire/Getty Images (*Pinkel*) and Bill Frakes/Sports Illustrated (*Daniel*)

In the end, Daniel was the difference. "Reesing was good," Kelly says. "Daniel was terrific."

HOW THE BROWNS LEARNED TO WIN BY DAMON HACK

Sports Illustrated

www.SI.com

THE HEISMAN RACE
BY PHIL TAYLOR

FLORIDA'S TIM TEBOW LEADS THE PACK

THE REST
Darren McFadden
Arkansas
Chase Daniel
Missouri
Pat White
West Virginia
Colt Brennan
Hawaii

MIZZOU
10

Mizzou, That's Who
The Tigers Are No. 1 for the First Time Since 1960
Can They Beat Oklahoma?
BY STEWART MANDEL

DECEMBER 3, 2007

Daniel, who completed 40 of 49 passes for 361 yards and three touchdowns, led the Tigers to their first No. 1 ranking in 47 years, vaulted into the middle of the Heisman discussion and appeared on the Dec. 3, 2007 cover of *Sports Illustrated.*

PHOTO BY Damian Strohmeyer for Sports Illustrated

Sports Illustrated dispatched senior writer Austin Murphy to Columbia to report on the anticipated shootout, but only Missouri held up its end of the bargain. It wasn't just that the Tigers moved the ball at will against the Red Raiders, it was the way they did it. Daniel's right arm got a well-deserved rest (a season-low 20 passes), and Mizzou rushed a season-high 50 times. For the second straight week, Temple was sidelined by an ankle sprain, so the Tigers went to a running back by committee. Jackson, Earl Goldsmith, Derrick Washington and Marcus Woods combined for 35 carries and 192 yards, with Jackson scoring on three short rushes.

It was a runner's paradise. The Red Raiders dropped their safeties deep and to the outside. They never adjusted, even after it became clear the Tigers were perfectly content running the ball. And when Mizzou went to an unbalanced line — the Swan formation, in which a tackle shifts to the other side of the line — the Tech defense didn't budge. "We ran unbalanced the whole game, but they wouldn't adjust to it," says Yost. "They refused: *We're not lining up like that. That's bullshit what you guys are doing.*"

Daniel and the video-game passing attack were happy to cede the spotlight. "Those kids never talked to me about throws, catches, touches," says Christensen. "Never."

Adds Wolfert: "Chase was never one to question a game plan. *Just tell me what the plan is, we'll discuss it and if that's what we're going with, I know how to make it work. And it will work.*"

Besides, it was about time that Missouri's hogs got their due. They were an unsung group, all five of the starters hailing from small Missouri towns. Center Adam Spieker, from Webb City, was making his 41st consecutive start. What are the odds of landing two players who would man one side of the line at a major college program from a hamlet whose population was just north of 3,000? Well, left tackle Tyler Luellen and left guard Ryan Madison both played at South Harrison High in little old Bethany. Right tackle Colin Brown, a one-time walk-on, grew up in Braymer, population 952. And right guard Kurtis Gregory was a converted defensive tackle out of Santa Fe High in Blackburn.

"Madison was the clown of the bunch," says Christensen. "He and Colin lived together. Tyler was the old boy of the group, had a bunch of surgeries and could barely get around. They had to speak for Spieker. He would only whisper to one of them. He wouldn't talk. Kurtis was extremely athletic and flexible. He had a lot of natural strength from working on his family's farm, baling hay and digging fence posts.

"Like all those kids, they worked so hard every single day. They never left the practice field and thought, 'Oh, man. I didn't give a great effort today.' They worked well together. They spent a lot of time together as a unit, watching video, talking through things."

In the end, Eberflus says the man in charge of the program deserves the lion's share of the credit for the bounce-back after the devastating loss in Norman. "Gary spun that thing with the players in such a positive light, about how well they played, how good we are as a team," he says. "They acted like they won the game. It was a great job in terms of psychologically working with the team."

After three high-pressure matchups, a letdown was to be expected, and it came the following week against Iowa State. The Cyclones were 1–8, and the Tigers were a 28½-point favorite. But Iowa State being Iowa State, the visitors hung around to the end. No. 13 Missouri staggered to a 42–28 victory. Considering four ranked opponents ahead of them had already lost on this Saturday, any victory was a good one. It was costly, however. In the game's dying minutes, Brown blew out his right Achilles' tendon. The Tigers would have to play the rest of the way without one of their unquestioned leaders.

They would turn the calendar as they moved forward. And during his first six years in Columbia, no stretch had been more unkind to Pinkel than the month of November.

Chapter 13

Finish!

How valuable was Brown? When the Tigers boarded the charter for Boulder on the first Friday in November, they saved a seat for the man called Pig. Pinkel's policy was that injured players didn't travel. But Brown was a captain and an inspirational leader, and he might be able to help coach up the secondary.

"He had been such an impact player for us," Pinkel says. "I felt I owed it to him. It was important for him to be on that trip with us."

Missouri needed every edge it could find against Colorado. Folsom Field was more like Folsom Prison for the Tigers, who hadn't won in Boulder since 1997. It was mentioned in every press conference and in every story leading up to the game. Pinkel, for one, grew tired of it. "There were so many things we had to overcome," he says, sounding almost indignant. "You hadn't beaten them in 25 years, you hadn't won there in 13 years. It was unbelievable. People talk about the altitude, said you have to go out there a day early. I got so upset. I talked to our players. I told them that altitude is a myth, an absolute myth."

Point taken. But the calendar had turned to November, and critics were eager to note Missouri's struggles under Pinkel in the last two months of the year—a .333 winning percentage to be exact. That's why November was a point of emphasis for the '07 Tigers. The message: "You've got to learn how to pedal downhill," Patton recalls. "If the season is going well or if a game is going well, you've got to learn how to finish. That was a big lesson."

Pinkel drilled into his players the importance of completing the job they had started. "At some point, he started making a big point about finishing in November," says Ivey. "It became a time to get your second wind. It became a time when the season didn't seem so long. [Pinkel] said, 'Those who finish in November will be remembered.' "

And this is how the '07 Tigers began November: On his first pass of the night against the Buffs, Daniel threw into a crowd near the line of scrimmage and was intercepted by defensive tackle George Hypolite.

Colorado needed three plays to score. The Missouri faithful would have been excused for breaking into a *here-we-go-again* refrain. The game wasn't 90 seconds old, and already the Tigers had dug a 7–0 hole.

Then, just as they brashly said they'd do, the Buffs went man—and Daniel went deep. The plan was to reintroduce Franklin to the offense—he had caught one pass in the previous two games—and on his second throw, Daniel delivered a laser down the right sideline. The catch-and-run went for 72 yards.

"They were talking noise in the media the entire week," Daniel says of the Buffs. "We were like, 'Do you not see us on film? Do you not see what we do to defenses?'"

"They were talking noise in the media the entire week," Daniel says of the Buffs. "We were like, 'Do you not see us on film? Do you not see what we do to defenses?' They were oblivious. In the film room, we were like, 'We might throw for 450 yards on these guys, because all they do is play man coverage.' "

Maybe Colorado had only bothered to punch up the Texas Tech video. In the second quarter alone, Daniel threw a 46-yard touchdown pass to Maclin, a 45-yard strike to Jared Perry and a 37-yarder to Franklin. Alexander got in the act with a 31-yard reception. And showing the athleticism that made him a defensive coordinator's nightmare, the 6-foot-6 Coffman caught five passes for 60 yards and three touchdowns. He eluded three Buffs on his first TD, hurdled a defender en route to his second score, then executed a nifty toe tap at the back of the end zone to complete the trifecta. All told, five receivers had at least one catch for 25 yards.

"I was put in some great situations to be able to get those touchdowns," says Coffman. "We had so many playmakers, so many people we could get the ball to. That's something that helps you in terms of blocking downfield. You always felt like somebody could spring it at any time."

Then, characteristic of a team that was loaded with as many selfless individuals as it had playmakers, Coffman says he got as excited about contributing to a big play as he did in making it. "It was just fun blocking for those guys, being on the highlight tape — *Yeah, yeah, I made that block. I did that*," he says. "We had a lot of people with so much talent that it was fun blocking when you didn't have the ball."

The selflessness had started to evolve a year earlier, and by the middle of the '07 season the team-first mantra was in full throat. "Will Franklin wanted to be the best receiver on the team, but he looked around and said, 'We're better if I'm not the No. 1,' " DeArmond says. "Rucker was totally comfortable splitting time with Coffman. And Coffman, too. I think they learned so much from '06, not at any one point, but collectively. *This is what you have to do to win. Sometimes I have to block. Sometimes I have to be a decoy.*"

Imagine the quandary faced by defensive coordinators. According to Daniel, opponents might do one thing on film, then show something completely different in the game. "Well, Colorado didn't," he says. "They showed man on film. We felt like we could beat them deep because we had better athletes. The game plan was to take shots. We did. And we took a lot of them."

If you were open, Daniel had a knack for finding you. After going four of 14 in the first quarter, he was 22 of 30 the rest of the way. He finished with a career-high 429 yards passing and tied his school record for TD passes with five, all in the first three quarters. "What you saw right there was not normal," Pinkel said afterward. "It's just not normal."

Daniel is quick to deflect the credit. "Coach C would be the first to tell you that he had the hardest job of all, trying to get the ball in all of our playmakers' hands," he says. "The quarterback is a distributor. You surround yourself with great playmakers, and they're going to make plays for you. Get the ball in their hands one way or another, and they will make plays. They make you look good."

And talk about finishing. Missouri scored the last 48 points in a 55–10 rout. With a guaranteed four games left on the schedule, Maclin had already set the school single-season record for all-purpose yards. The defense was not without its moments. It caused five fumbles, recovering two, and picked off a pass, and during one mid-game stretch it forced seven consecutive three-and-outs. The Buffs finished with 196 total yards.

"More than ever, it looks like Missouri and Kansas are on a collision course for the mother of all Border Wars on Nov. 24 at Arrowhead Stadium," Walljasper wrote in the *Tribune*.

In the *Post-Dispatch*, Bryan Burwell went a step further: "Each week, another ghost falls and another echo dissipates into thin air. Nebraska, done. Iowa State, history. The Folsom Field jinx? That's dead and gone, too. The season of vindication continues, and who knows where it will end."

All good things must come to an end, and for the 20 seniors on the 2007 Missouri roster, the last game at Faurot Field fell on Nov. 10, against Texas A&M. Senior Day is never easy for the head coach, and for Pinkel, this one was especially difficult.

"Those kids—all the adversity," he says. "They saw it all, all the things we were doing, changing attitudes. It was tough, but you are also very proud. You're thankful for them and all they did. It was a great senior class. It was very emotional."

The gratitude was especially deep for Williams and Rucker, who had bought what Pinkel and his staff were selling in 2003. Their roles in the rise of the program could not be overstated. "It was a big deal to them that guys were ready to play," Pinkel says. "There was no assumption. They were working the players. It was awesome to see."

It also made for great radio. "Zo and Rucker together," says Kelly. "Priceless. Just priceless." Allow the voice of the Tigers to take it from there:

"One of the things we do with *Tiger Talk* is we always have two players on. At the end we always say, 'Martin Rucker, tell us something about Lorenzo Williams that we don't know.' Those two were always on together, and the level of work they would do to come up with something on the other was remarkable.

"Their senior year, Lorenzo says, 'Since this is our last time on the show together, I've been saving this. I didn't know if you knew, but T's very self-conscious about the way he looks. On media day every Monday, he gets a facial, a manicure and a pedicure, complete with cucumbers on his eyes and things like that.' T starts laughing. He says, 'Well, I don't know if you all know this about Zo, but when he was younger, his mom made him take dance classes, and there are pictures of him in a tutu.' The place erupted."

Late-morning kickoff be damned, Faurot Field on Senior Day was rocking as well. During pre-game ceremonies, the seniors were saluted one by one. The players were greeted by thunderous roars and met near midfield by family members. As is tradition, the four captains were the last to be introduced.

"It was the reason we went there," says Rucker, "to give all these fans something to cheer about, to restore Mizzou to national prominence, to be on TV, to have our games mean something. Everything was unfolding right in front of us. Everybody was just so happy. This was what college football was supposed to be about. Everybody in the stands was going nuts. It was why I went there."

Rucker didn't leave the locker room without passing on a little advice to his sidekick. "I told Zo not to cry," Ruck says. "He might have dropped a few, too. We came out of the locker room and Coach Pinkel was *bawling*. He was letting them go."

Temple was one of the last Tigers to be introduced. It had been a roller-coaster career for the highly touted running back, four years filled with more lows than highs. "I wanted to quit my freshman year," he says. "I wanted to transfer. They weren't playing me. I was the typical freshman."

Plus, he had come to Columbia with the understanding he would be taking handoffs out of a run-friendly set. That all changed in 2005, when the Tigers unveiled the Missouri Spread. "It was a transition," he says. "As a running back, it wasn't one of those things that registered. I used to get critiqued for running east and west. But that's the way the plays were designed."

Temple had already missed two games and most of a third in 2007, and his rushing total was nothing to get excited about: 418 yards on 89 carries. Senior Day wasn't playing out as planned either. Temple jogged out of the tunnel and onto the field to be greeted by exactly no one. His family was back home in Kansas City, preparing to bury Tony's grandmother. Stricken by cancer, Dolly Ringle died on the Thursday before the A&M game. Temple had spent the week shuttling between Columbia and Kansas City.

Tigers who don't practice typically don't play, but Pinkel made an exception. "Any time there is an issue with family, we adjust," he says. "We make that a priority. Other than that, it's true. If you don't practice, you don't play."

Temple came to play, all right. On Missouri's first possession, he ripped off a 44-yard touchdown run, his longest dash of the season. Running like he never had, he finished with 141 yards on 22 carries. "I didn't even know the game plan," he says. "It was all instinct and heart. All I could think about was my grandmother."

Much like Iowa State, the Aggies wouldn't go away. But Daniel, who finished 27 of 35 for 352 yards and three touchdowns, wasn't about to let the seniors lose on Senior Day, and in the fourth quarter he engineered a pair of textbook, 80-yard touchdown drives.

"The underclassmen took a lot of pride in sending those seniors off right, especially at Faurot Field," Daniel says. "We had a great, great, great group of seniors that year. They turned the program around. They set the tone."

Fittingly, Williams capped the 40–26 victory with an end-zone sack of Stephen McGee. It would be Zo's last play at Faurot. Temple wasn't around to see it. With the NCAA's blessing, Missouri had arranged to fly him back to Kansas City so he could pay his last respects to his grandmother. He arrived as the motorcade was pulling into the cemetery.

"I stood up and said, 'Everything we've worked for, all that we've done is great, but what does it all mean if we let K-State come back and beat us?'" says Williams. "Everybody was like, 'We're going to go down as the same ol' Mizzou.'"

Back in Columbia, Pinkel was singing the praises of his senior class. "These guys," he said, "have brought Missouri football back."

The Tigers had their first nine-win season since 1969, they had scored a school-record 418 points (and counting) and Pinkel was assured of his first winning record in Big 12 play. Plus, they were one victory from making the Nov. 24 meeting with Kansas mean something. Everything. Yet almost immediately, all anybody wanted to know was, could Missouri prevail in Manhattan? The Tigers hadn't won at Kansas State since 1989.

"Yeah, I heard all of that stuff, too," Pinkel says. "You can't win there either."

Of course, they could. This was not the same ol' Mizzou. That became evident midway through the first quarter when Maclin fielded a kickoff at the one-yard line, spun out of a pile at the 25 and zoomed down the left sideline for a touchdown. The Tigers had gone an unfathomable 287 games and 979 kickoffs without a TD return since Ricky Doby turned the trick in a 1982 game against Oklahoma State. Another demon had been exorcised.

Because he was under the employ of the school that owned the dubious streak, Moller had the unenviable weekly task of apprising fellow sports information directors of the Tigers' futility in the kickoff-return department. "I had to hold back the tears," he says of watching Maclin's magical runback. "I was sick of having to keep track of that note."

It was nice to get off the schneid, but Mizzou was in a dogfight. The halftime lead was only 21–18, and as they gathered in the locker room, one player after another made impassioned pleas. Brown was the first to speak up, but the next Tiger to talk came as a total surprise. It was Coffman.

"Chase was a quiet guy," says Pinkel. "Before games, he'd be falling asleep. I'd shake hands with every player before a game, and with him I'd put my hand on him for a few seconds and walk away. That's the way he got ready."

Adds Williams: "This is Chase Coffman's routine: Pre-game, come in, fall asleep for an hour. Goes back out, comes back in, falls asleep again. I don't know what's wrong with the dude, but he's always asleep. Then he goes out and just kills."

Coffman says the catnaps were the way he best knew how to prepare for a game. So he would throw a towel over his head and sit as stiff as a statue in front of his locker. "There are so many people listening to music and getting crazy," he says. "I feel I just needed to calm down a little."

By halftime in Manhattan, however, Coffman was as riled up as his teammates. He knew the Tigers were 30 minutes from their goal, and he wasn't about to walk off the field where his father, Paul, had starred in the 1970s with any regrets.

"He stood up and said, 'Are we really going to let these guys beat us after all the things we've done?' " recalls Williams. "Everybody was like, 'Why are you talking?' He was trying to be serious, and everybody started laughing."

Coffman's talk was the tension-breaker the Tigers sorely needed. Williams took it from there: "I stood up and said, 'Everything we've worked for, all that we've done is great, but what does it all mean if we let K-State come back and beat us?' Everybody was like, 'We're going to go down as the same ol' Mizzou.' "

No chance. Missouri scored four second-half touchdowns and coasted to a 49–32 victory. Daniel threw for 284 and four touchdowns. Challenged by his quarterback at halftime, Temple ripped off 66 yards and scored twice on a dozen second-half carries. The only player in college football in 2007 to score on a run, a reception, a punt return and a kickoff return, Maclin finished with a school-record 360 all-purpose yards and three touchdowns.

Kansas State coach Ron Prince was duly impressed. He had praised the Jayhawks after their six-point victory in Manhattan, calling them the best team he had seen in '07. Six Saturdays later, he was changing his tune. "This is clearly the best team that we've played this year," Prince said. "We played a team that has a legitimate chance, from a talent standpoint, from an organizational standpoint, to win the national championship."

This was *not* the same ol' Mizzou.

In the locker room, a beaming Daniel mentioned that he and his teammates were at last allowed to utter the K-word. Outside, in sections 17, 18 and 19 of Bill Snyder Family Stadium, a celebration broke out among the thousands of Missouri fans who had made the trek west. They were soon joined by Wildcats fans and members of the K-State band.

"Beat KU," they chanted in unison. "Beat KU."

Chapter 14
Game Day!

To call the Kansas City Chiefs an average NFL franchise when Carl Peterson was hired as president and general manager in December 1988 would have been kind. The Chiefs were coming off consecutive four-victory campaigns, and in the previous 15 seasons they'd finished above .500 exactly twice. Peterson had a monumental task on his hands. So imagine his surprise when during his first week on the job, iconic owner Lamar Hunt approached him to discuss his vision for a *college* football game.

"I walked into this beautiful Arrowhead Stadium,'" Peterson recalls, "and Lamar asked me, 'Carl, do you think we could ever host the oldest college football rivalry west of the Mississippi River?' I didn't want to embarrass myself, but, man, I was going through the Rolodex in my brain trying to figure out which rivalry this was. I knew it couldn't be my UCLA-USC. (Peterson is a UCLA grad.) Then I said, 'You mean MU-KU?' He said, 'Absolutely.' "

A native of the Lone Star State, Hunt had moved his beloved Dallas Texans of the AFL to Kansas City in 1963 (and renamed them the Chiefs) after coming to the realization that Big D wasn't big enough to support two professional football franchises. He brought his passion for the college game with him. He and his father, H.L., had served on the board of the Cotton Bowl Classic. Lamar was familiar with the story of how Dallas city officials persuaded administrators from Texas and Oklahoma to move their annual grudge match to a neutral site. That was in 1929. He couldn't see any reason why Missouri and Kansas shouldn't be playing in Kansas City.

It made perfect sense, actually. Lawrence was a mere 50 miles from Arrowhead. Columbia was 118 miles away, a straight shot across I-70. The Kansas City metropolitan area was a melting pot for students and alumni from the two schools. Peterson already had envisioned making Arrowhead the top tail-gating destination in the NFL. Why couldn't that translate to the college game?

"I knew how much people in the Midwest loved to tailgate," Peterson says. "I always thought that with a parking lot that held 26,000 cars, you could have the biggest tailgate party in the NFL. That was our marketing and sales emphasis with the Chiefs."

Persuading two college programs to give up a home game every other year was a tough sell. Local merchants count on the pile of revenue that a home game generates, and universities are reluctant to turn their back on those businesses. Peterson's predecessor, Jack Steadman, told him as much.

Hunt, however, didn't want to hear it, and Peterson was charged with brokering a deal. For the better part of 15 years, he would make annual trips to Columbia and Lawrence, meeting with the athletic directors and football coaches and often with the university presidents and chancellors. While on the scouting trail during the season, Peterson also sought out each school's athletic director. Alden was first approached by Peterson and Hunt not long after he took the job at Mizzou in 1998. He remembers Peterson's press-box visits.

"Carl would come for a game every year," Alden recalls. "Every time, he'd say, 'Don't forget, Mike. We want to play that game. Whenever you're ready.'"

"Carl would come for a game every year," Alden recalls. "Every time, he'd say, 'Don't forget, Mike. We want to play that game. Whenever you're ready. Whenever you're ready.' "

Alden's biggest issue was that his economic model was built around a schedule that featured a minimum of six home games a year. In 2002, the Tigers signed a deal for an annual game against Illinois in St. Louis. No one in Columbia was keen about the prospect of a second neutral-site game, even if it was played within the state borders.

Again, Hunt didn't care. By this time, the Chiefs had hosted a couple of Big 12 championship games, and they had started to attract other Division I-A programs—Kansas State and Iowa State, among them. "Finally, Lamar said, 'How can we get this done?' " Peterson recalls. "I said, 'Lamar, we're going to have to do what we did when we bid on Big 12 championship games. We're going to have to give them a guarantee.' "

Peterson went to work. His research showed that when a Big 12 team hosted another conference foe, its payout was about $900,000. Because the visiting team netted nothing, he proposed to Hunt that the Chiefs guarantee Missouri and KU $1 million each. In a two-year deal, each program would be guaranteed $2 million. Throw in a sold-out

Arrowhead along with the possibility of a title sponsor and TV revenues, and the pot had the potential to swell. How could either university turn its back on that?

"It got their attention," Peterson says.

The athletic director at KU was Lew Perkins, whom Peterson had known since the 1980s, when he was the president and GM of the Philadelphia Stars of the USFL and Perkins was at the University of Pennsylvania. "Lew is a businessman," says Peterson. "He immediately seized upon it and thought it was a great opportunity."

Many administrators might have been reluctant to strike such a deal, fearful of the backlash from local businesses, the lifeblood of many college towns. Not Perkins. According to Peterson, he convened a meeting with about 30 influential merchants. During the discussion, Perkins, who did not respond to several requests to be interviewed for this book, posed a question. He asked the movers and shakers if they'd be willing to pass the hat and make a $1 million donation to the athletic department in those years when the Jayhawks played the Tigers in Columbia. Nobody raised a hand. The decision was made.

Alden wasn't necessarily opposed to the idea, but he was a tougher sell. "He had to walk through a little political minefield to convince the administration and his head coach to play two neutral-site games a year," Peterson says. "Gary Pinkel was wonderful about it."

There was also the issue of placating Columbia merchants, who contended that KU had to be one of the six opponents to visit Faurot Field. When Alden asked why, the businesspeople claimed that more revenue was generated when the Jayhawks came calling. Alden knew otherwise.

"We did all the data analysis that showed whether you played Arkansas State in Columbia or you played KU in Columbia, there's not much of an appreciable difference," he says. "Once we laid the data out— we did that two or three years before the announcement was made—even though there was a lot of pushback, at least they had been prepped for it. We answered all of [the merchants'] concerns. We also appealed to the state of Missouri because we had eight football games in the state, and the tax revenue on that was pretty good."

And, as luck would have it, due to contractual obligations, 2007 was the first year that Missouri could take on a second neutral-site game and still maintain the six dates at Faurot it needed for Alden's economic model to work. That just happened to be the year the Tigers and Jayhawks were scheduled to play in Lawrence. The two-year deal was announced in January 2007.

"The stars aligned perfectly," Peterson says of the event that would be the most-anticipated game in college football that year.

Don Fambrough never seemed to be big on astronomy. He was a straight shooter who knew what the merchants in Lawrence meant to the university, how they had been there for the athletic department during lean times. He had a love affair with his community that spanned more than a half-century; remember, this was a guy who couldn't be run out of town even after being fired from the same job twice. No surprise, he was against the Arrowhead game from the start. He wasn't particularly fond of Perkins either.

"I don't like it, and I don't think the Missouri people like it either," Fambrough said in 2010, less than a year before he died. "All that [Perkins] was interested in was how much money he could put in *his* pocket—not the university's, not the athletic department's, but in *his* pocket."

Lamar Hunt did not live to see his vision became reality—he died in December 2006 at the age of 74, a month before the contract was signed—but Peterson saw the deal through. That's not to say there weren't sleepless nights. He knew exactly what the magic number was for the Chiefs to recoup their $2 million investment. "I'll be candid," he says. "Until we got 63,000 seats sold, this boy was real anxious."

No worries. The game sold out by early October, and by late on the afternoon on Nov. 17, the anxiety had given way to excitement. Kansas was 11–0 and ranked second in the country. Missouri held up its end of the bargain; in the wake of the loss to Oklahoma, the Tigers answered Pinkel's challenge, and they did so convincingly, winning five games by an average of 24 points. Mizzou was 10–1 and ranked fourth. The victor at Arrowhead would claim the Big 12 North and play the following Saturday for the conference championship, most likely against the Sooners. There was more. Each team was two victories from playing for the national championship.

No one can pinpoint the number of media who descended upon Columbia and Lawrence on the Monday before kickoff, but suffice to say the turnout was unlike anything either program had seen. "I remember getting some looks from the guys when they opened the door," says Moller. "It was like, 'Whoa, this is serious.' "

Williams estimates he sat through 18 interviews and didn't leave the Tom Taylor Building until nine o'clock that night. He walked out with

Rucker, Daniel and Temple. Moller knew he was walking a fine line. "It's not in my nature to turn down any of that," he says. "Deep down, that's what you want. That's what you dream for. But I did have concerns. I did wonder if I was asking our guys to do too much."

So chaotic was the scene that Pinkel postponed his seniors meeting. Yet while understandably wary of potential distractions, he didn't seem overly concerned. He reminded his players about the importance of sticking to their routine, of keeping their focus. "I trusted these guys," he says. "I had seniors who were running around like coaches. They were leading the band as much as I was. That whole senior class used the term *over-prepare*."

> **"All that [Perkins] was interested in was how much money he could put in his pocket—not the university's, not the athletic department's, but in *his* pocket," said Fambrough.**

They were undoubtedly feeding off the energy and drive of their head coach. Even on Monday night, when they got together for the weekly radio show, Kelly saw a man who was already dialed in. "At times, during breaks on *Tiger Talk*, he'd say, 'This is a big opportunity. This is a great opportunity. Do you know how *big* this is?' " Kelly recalls.

Because the players were off-limits to the press on Tuesdays, DeArmond typically headed home to Kansas City after filling up his notebook during the Monday media sessions. Considering the magnitude of the game, he decided to hang around for another day to gauge the atmosphere at practice. "There wasn't any joking around," he says.

Rucker agrees that the mind-set of the Handshake Gang was business as usual. This was the way the Tigers approached everything. Many of the players had waited four or five years for an opportunity like this. They had talked about it. Heck, they had expected it. "It was a big game," Rucker acknowledges. "You can't downplay that."

Adds Patton, "The whole discussion in team meetings was to keep us grounded. It was an amazing sense of calm and focus during the week. I remember being surprised at how we handled it, with that much on the line."

Daniel was Daniel. "Business as usual," he says of the mood at practice. "Our motto that whole year was that it's a big game because it's the next game. We didn't change anything. We said, 'If we play our ball game, we're going to win.'"

There was also a quiet confidence among the Missouri coaches. The week after Thanksgiving marked the start of a recruiting period. A victory meant the coaches would be staying home and cramming for the Big 12 title game. If the Tigers lost, everybody would be hitting the road.

"No one planned any travel to go recruiting that Sunday," says Yost. "We were that confident. No one even talked about it."

In Lawrence, there also was a remarkable sense of calm. It was no secret that Mizzou would be by far the best team KU had faced all year. The Tigers weren't just beating Big 12 foes; they were beating them soundly. Comparing results against the teams' five common victims, Missouri won by no fewer than 14 points. The Jayhawks won three of those games by six, five and eight points. And as impressive as KU's 37-point annihilation of Nebraska had been, was it any more dominating than Missouri's 35-point whipping?

"No one planned any travel to go recruiting that Sunday," says Yost. "We were that confident. No one even talked about it."

"We knew we were playing a really good football team, and that it was going to come down to the fourth quarter," Reesing says. "We knew how much this game meant to the university, our fans, our alumni. We knew how much was at stake."

Mangino liked what he was witnessing on the practice field and in the meeting rooms. The Jayhawks were still playing the underdog card and carrying that chip on their shoulders. "The buildup on campus was intense," he says, "but our players came to the compound every day grounded, willing to work, taking care of business. Just keep sawing wood."

Tuesday was the last day of classes before the Thanksgiving break (Missouri's students were dismissed the previous Friday), so the Jayhawks weren't faced with the distraction of back-slapping classmates reminding them they were about to play in the biggest football game of their lives.

"It was a positive anxiety," Reesing says. "I wanted the week to end so we could get to the game. I had so much raw energy. Those days couldn't go by fast enough. It was a long week, the longest week I ever had before playing a football game."

It was a long *two* weeks for Strauss. Though the game was being played at a neutral site, the Jayhawks were the designated home team. So to Strauss and his staff fell the unenviable task of handling media credentials—press-box seating, photographer arm bands and the ever-coveted parking passes. So intense was the crush that two weeks before kickoff, Strauss assigned two staff members to do nothing but handle media requests in the quiet confines of an upstairs office. This being the first game at Arrowhead, the department was in foreign territory. A game involving a pair of 6–5 teams would have provided enough challenges. Now everybody who had anything to do with college football (and a few who didn't) wanted in.

"It was overwhelming," Strauss says. "I always laugh because I had been at Utah State for 10 years. Our press box seated something like 36. Those two weeks I may have been cussed out more than any other time in my life. People couldn't understand that I couldn't just give them a pass."

One query came from the folks at ESPN. Carl Edwards wanted to watch from the sideline, and the network was eager to accommodate one of NASCAR's biggest stars. Strauss knew Edwards hailed from Columbia, but that had nothing to do with his rejection. He was flat out of passes, but if network execs believed it was that important for Edwards to be on the sideline, they could give him one of the credentials they had already been allotted. "They're like, 'You're telling Carl Edwards no?' " Strauss recalls. "I said, 'Yeah.' "

Peterson, meanwhile, was dealing with an issue he and Hunt could not have foreseen, not even in their wildest dreams. NFL scouts had their work to do—between the two teams, four players would become first-round draft picks and another 13 were also selected—but most of their cushy press-box seats were assigned to reporters and broadcasters. Many of the NFL types would be relegated to frigid, outdoor seating in the upper reaches of Arrowhead. "We had an excess number of requests from scouts and player personnel people who wanted to see it," Peterson says. "You hate to do that to fellow scouts because you don't want to be treated poorly when you go to their place."

Yes, the game had gotten *that* big. Kansas City was bracing for arguably its biggest sporting event ever—certainly the biggest since the Royals and the Cardinals squared off in Game 7 of the 1985 World Series. DeArmond says editors at *The Star* held daily meetings to ensure that every on- and off-field angle was covered. Typically, when two area teams are involved, the beat writer for the home team writes the game story, but so as to make it clear they weren't taking sides, executives gave the assignment to Big 12 correspondent Blair Kerkhoff. DeArmond and McCollough would work the locker rooms of their respective teams and write sidebars.

It was a mid-week McCollough story that made headlines and sent shock waves back to Columbia. In a feature about KU's giving up the home game, McCollough quoted Perkins as saying he projected the Jayhawks would enjoy a 70–30 crowd split. A panicked Alden got on the phone to his crew in the Mizzou ticket office and asked where Perkins was getting such a number. Alden had already assured Pinkel that Arrowhead would be split close to the middle. A crowd that was 70 percent KU meant there would be some 56,000 Jayhawks fans in the building. Everyone knew Kansas had included the game in its season-ticket package, but that only accounted for 31,000 seats. Plus, Mizzou was guaranteed 18,000 tickets, and those had been snatched up immediately.

"I'm thinking, 'We're going to go in there and they're going to have 70 percent of an 80,000-seat stadium,' " Alden recalls. "Our ticket people kept saying, 'We don't think that's accurate.' "

Alden only needed to place a call to *The Star*. Upon reading Perkins' prognostication, DeArmond was incredulous. At a Wednesday staff meeting, he asked McCollough where the 70–30 figure had come from. Perkins, of course. "I guarantee you that Lew pulled that number right out of his ass," says Keegan.

Like many in the Missouri camp, DeArmond believes Perkins was trying to allay the fears of a suddenly stoked fan base. The KU contingent undoubtedly was none too pleased its athletic director had sold what would have been the biggest home football game in program history for the almighty dollar.

"Lew knew exactly what he was doing," DeArmond says. "This is what Kansas does extremely well. They spin better than anybody I've ever seen. They're masters at it. And they're so much better at it than Missouri is. We printed that quote, and Grandma, who can't see the field, is going to that game."

Mangino was doing everything he could to treat the biggest game in program history as if it were being played at Memorial Stadium. Unlike most teams, the Jayhawks didn't retreat to a local hotel on the night before a home game. The players typically ate dinner together, had meetings and watched a movie before being sent on their way. The schedule for the Missouri game wasn't going to change, even if the home field was 50 miles away and across the state line. So on Friday, the Jayhawks made the one-hour trek to Arrowhead for their walkthrough, reboarded their buses and headed back to Lawrence.

"We wanted to treat it as a home game the best we could," says Mangino, "so we let the kids sleep in their own beds. Whether it was good, bad or indifferent, I don't know."

Upon further reflection, he points out that these are college athletes we're talking about. And with a chuckle, he adds, "Those kids will drive over to Kansas City to buy a pair of jeans and come back."

Reesing had no quibbles with the commuting schedule. He wisely notes that sequestered teams waste a lot of time and nervous energy at the hotel in the hours leading up to kickoff, particularly when the game is at night. "You feel confined while you're in your hotel room, and you're ready to get out of there once you wake up," he says. "When you're in your own locker room or facility, it makes the day go by quicker."

The Tigers left Columbia early on Friday afternoon and headed directly to Arrowhead for their walkthrough. They were somewhere on I-70 when the Arkansas-LSU game kicked off in Baton Rouge. The Bayou Bengals were No. 1 in the country and already had clinched a spot in the SEC championship game. Like Missouri and Kansas, LSU was two victories from playing for the national title. The Razorbacks were a respectable 7–4 and had won four of their last five games, but that didn't stop oddsmakers from making the Tigers a ho-hum, 13-point favorite.

Yet LSU walked into a fight it never expected. Darren McFadden rushed for 206 yards and three touchdowns and passed for 34 yards and another score out of the Wild Hog formation, and the Tigers needed a touchdown with 57 seconds left to knot the score at 28. In the third overtime, not long after the Missouri traveling party arrived at the Overland Park (Kan.) Marriott, 16 miles southwest of Arrowhead, Arkansas converted its two-point attempt, LSU didn't, and the Razorbacks had pulled off a 50–48 stunner. No. 1 had been vanquished.

As if the stakes weren't high enough, Missouri and Kansas would now be playing for the top ranking in college football. Word spread through the hotel. "Whether you wanted it to or not," says Pinkel. "We just had to make sure we took care of our business."

That included the customary Friday night flurry of meetings. Williams was on his way to a defensive session when he was stopped by a hotel security guard. "I've got something for you," the guard told Zo, "but I don't think you're going to like it." He was holding a box he had been instructed to give to Missouri's quartet of captains. Inside was an ice cream cake decorated with a fictitious bird and the words: "Go Jayhawks. Beat the Tigers." The guard said a minivan pulled up in front of the hotel, a gentleman got out, handed the box to him with the delivery instructions, got back in the vehicle and zoomed off. It might have been a KU fan, but it just as easily could have been a Mizzou fan looking to fire up his team.

If the stunt was intended as a motivational ploy, it worked. Williams lugged the box to the meeting and placed it under his chair. Someone asked what was in the box, Williams relayed what had happened, and the next thing you know, Weatherspoon was flying in from a couple of rows back and planting an elbow in the cake. "Everybody started going nuts," Williams says.

Christensen and Yost were holding court at a meeting with the offensive players. Included in the material distributed to the players was a one-page informational sheet. Printed on gold paper with black ink, it highlighted the keys to victory, among other things. It wasn't without its motivational messages. The first was right at the top.

"Those two weeks I may have been cussed out more than any other time in my life," Strauss says. "People couldn't understand that I couldn't just give them a pass."

Four weeks ago we set out on a mission to win in November. Tomorrow night in Arrowhead—You will decide how we finish it! Go into tomorrow night's game as the most confident, focused, disciplined, ass-kickin' physical team on the field. The Missouri offense will attack Kansas each and every play. Our big playmakers will show Kansas and a national [television] audience what we are all about.

At Arrowhead, the ESPN College GameDay set was in place for the following morning's two-hour pre-game show. Rolled out in 1993, GameDay has become the greatest traveling circus in college football— a live telecast featuring Chris Fowler, Kirk Herbstreit, Lee Corso and Desmond Howard. The crew typically sets up shop at the week's biggest game, and even before LSU lost, was there anyplace else to be on the morning of Nov. 24 than outside Arrowhead Stadium?

As it often does on Friday night, ESPN cut from SportsCenter to the GameDay set. There was plenty to tease: the LSU loss and its ramifications on the national title chase, No. 3 West Virginia's meeting with Connecticut and, of course, Mizzou-KU. Strauss was sitting in his Kansas City hotel room when his cell phone rang sometime around 10 o'clock. It was one of the Jayhawks' equipment managers. He was tuned in to ESPN and was shocked to see a KU helmet with an outdated logo on the set. He then suggested (rather loudly) that Strauss hustle the proper headgear over to Arrowhead. Strauss decided it was a trip he could put off until Saturday morning. During a week filled with throbbing headaches, the helmet snafu was a minor one. Perhaps it was also an omen.

"You always knew it would be a cold day before Kansas and Missouri would collide with college football's top ranking on the line." And that is how Fowler kicked off GameDay. The 120-minute program would draw two million viewers, a record for the show, and despite the unseasonably frigid temperatures, fans from both schools came out in force. For the first time in the history of the show, the adversaries were separated by metal partitions—Missouri fans to the right of the set, KU fans to the left. They came bearing signs that Fowler kindly called "creative." Behind the scenes, ESPN staffers frantically conducted Google searches to decipher the meaning of cryptic artwork and confiscated those deemed too offensive. One ESPN publicist called it the most challenging show the taste police had ever monitored. The wackiness of the 2007 season and the significance of the showdown at Arrowhead were encapsulated in the first 10 minutes of GameDay.

Flashing a graphic with the headline "Year of the Upset," Fowler noted it was the first time since 1990 the top-ranked team had lost four times in a season. It was also the first time since 1990 that No. 1 had lost on its home field twice in November (first Ohio State, then LSU). And finally, an unranked team had beaten a top five program a dozen times, including seven times on the ranked team's turf.

Corso pointed to the numbing cold that had enveloped Kansas City and suggested the team that best handled the adverse conditions could be the winner. Then he added, "With this kind of game, defense could take over. Advantage: Kansas."

Fowler gave the uninitiated a history lesson on the bitter rivalry, mentioning the 1863 burning of Lawrence, noting that Jayhawkers stormed across the border and terrorized Missourians and chuckling about the inability of the schools to agree on the series record. (Mizzou had it 53–53–9; KU, 54–52–9.) "For many fans, the hatred is very real and it's very raw and the players are just acting out the latest chapter in all that," Fowler said. After a pause, he added, "And you thought this was just about the Big 12 North."

ESPN had every angle covered. There was a graphic noting the rich and famous who attended each school. Don Johnson, Bob Dole and

Danni Boatwright (winner of *Survivor: Guatemala*) represented Kansas. Sam Walton, Sheryl Crow and Brad Pitt were presented on the Missouri side. "A slight edge to Missouri, I think, in star power," Fowler said (and that was a couple of years before Jon Hamm burst onto the scene as Don Draper). During a chilling piece on A.O., reporter Steve Cyphers eloquently said: "This team's unity is Aaron O'Neal's legacy."

Herbstreit, drawing on his experiences playing quarterback at Ohio State against a bitter border rival, reminded the audience that "as much as this is about the BCS and the winning team [will be] No. 1, remember this is a rivalry." Players and coaches from both teams told him that as magical as the year had been, the loser would consider its season a failure. "I want to see which team comes out and is able to put all of that hype and all of those distractions to the side and go out and execute the way they have for 11 weeks," Herbstreit said. "Because these are unchartered waters for both of these teams. Whoever handles it better wins."

One of the top analysts in the business, Herbstreit was on his game. Over the course of the show, he offered a handful of observations that would prove to be prophetic. Among them:

• On Reesing: "Missouri's got to do something to get him out of his comfort zone today—mix up looks, change it up, get him out of rhythm. Right now, Todd Reesing is as confident as any quarterback in college football."

• On Mizzou's offense: "It's my opinion looking at all these teams this year, the most explosive offensive in the country is the Missouri Tigers. It's because of Chase Daniel and his decision-making. And it's because of the tight ends, the big-play wide receivers … I'm telling you, right now this Missouri offense is clicking on all cylinders."

• On the key to victory: "Missouri is going to score touchdowns. To me the key to the game is Kansas. Todd Reesing is playing flawlessly. They're not having many penalties, they're not hurting themselves, they're not self-destructing. That has to continue tonight for Kansas to win this game. I see a shootout. I can't make the pick [because he was calling the game]. I'll let Lee make the pick. A lot of points [scored], in my opinion."

The GameDay show always culminates with Corso's slipping on the mascot head of the team he believes will win. "Headgear time," he calls it. Corso taunted the Mizzou fans, then looked to the KU side before slipping on an oversized Tigers' head. "No chance," he said twice as he waved his hands at the Jayhawks' fans. "Go Tigers."

Back at the Marriott, the Mizzou players were soaking it all in. For the first time, the magnitude of the game truly hit them. Williams walked into Moore's room. The defensive players always played spades on game day, but there they all were, staring in disbelief at the TV set. The comment on ESPN that the winner at Arrowhead would ascend to No. 1 in the BCS was lost on exactly no one.

"Dog, we're not playing spades today," Williams recalls one teammate saying. "I said, 'No, we need to play spades. If we keep looking at this, we're going to drive ourselves crazy. Let's do our normal thing. Get the spades game going. Let's not talk about it. Shut it up and move on.' "

Pinkel didn't sound overly concerned. He believes the opportunity to watch GameDay fueled his players. And hadn't they earned the right to enjoy their time in the spotlight?

"You always knew it would be a cold day before Kansas and Missouri would collide with college football's top ranking on the line," Fowler told the GameDay audience.

Plus, the ESPN show served as a nice diversion on what would be the longest day for every Tiger.

"We had played a bunch of night games, so we were used to those long Saturdays," Pinkel says. "We learned how to utilize the day better so you're not sitting around watching football on TV for eight straight hours."

And how was the man who was preparing for the biggest game of his career coping?

"I don't do a lot of relaxing," Pinkel says. "It's hard to describe what it's like for a head coach in the 48 hours before a game. Some guys have told me, 'It's not a big deal.' Well, for me it is. My intensity level is so focused. It's your life."

Life is at least made easier when your offense is in the hands of a quarterback like Daniel. Dating to his days at Southlake Carroll, he had played in too many big games to count. Though he was known to do fidgety things in the hours leading up to game time, his understudy and roommate on the road was amazed by Daniel's calm. "I was always impressed with how he prepared himself," Patton says. "He was amazingly focused that week. He prepared so well that he was confident and excited to play."

Adds Ivey: "Chase may be the person most responsible for how our guys watch film today. He was a student. It was like he already had the notes for the class. He knew how it was going to go, from the time he could walk and talk, how to be a champion."

It was for those very reasons that Corso and Herbstreit gave the edge at quarterback to the Tigers. Reesing hadn't thrown an interception in six games, and in three November games he had tossed 13 touchdown passes, but Herbie called Daniel "a linebacker playing quarterback." He had thrown 12 TD passes against only one interception in November, and he had almost two more years of experience than Reesing.

That didn't faze Keegan. After picking against the Jayhawks most of the season, he was finally coming over from the dark side. He forecast a KU victory because he thought Reesing "was the best player in the game. Chase Daniel was really, really good, but I didn't think he was as creative. I just thought Reesing would figure out a way." Howard also picked the Jayhawks. The *St. Louis Post-Dispatch* polled 11 writers and editors who had followed one team or the other all season. The voting fell pretty much along party lines. DeArmond picked his alma mater, 41–31. It was too close to call. Las Vegas oddsmakers installed KU as a two-point favorite, but more than 154,000 viewers who responded to a GameDay poll gave Mizzou a razor-thin edge: 50.3% to 49.7%.

For perspective, it's never a bad idea to turn to the backup quarterback. As he bides his time in the background on the practice field and on the sideline, he has plenty of time for observation and analysis. In fact, it has been said the No. 2 QB is the smartest player on the roster, because he would most certainly perform better than the starter if ever given the chance. Patton, a pre-med major, was no dummy, and though he had a rooting interest, he says analysts should have simply looked back to the 2006 meeting for clues on how the '07 game would play out.

"There was really no change in the rosters," he says. "They had the same people. We had the same people. So there was no reason for us not to be confident."

That's because Missouri won, 42–17. Yeah, the game was in Columbia, but the Tigers racked up 493 yards of offense, with Daniel completing 26 of 38 passes for 354 yards and four touchdowns. He accomplished all that without Franklin, who was sidelined with a shoulder injury. Franklin was healthy again, and now Mizzou was adding another weapon to the attack—the guy known as J-Mac.

"They tried to blitz us," Yost says of the '06 meeting. "I remember going in at halftime, Mangino said [to ABC], 'We've just got to get to the quarterback.' You don't get to Chase Daniel. If you blitz, he gets the ball off. You're better off not blitzing and trying to get there with your rush because we're going to hold the football when they're not blitzing. If they're blitzing, the ball's out. I didn't think they were going to blitz us to give us big plays.

"By then [in 2006 and '07] we saw all this zone. Chase was so amazing against zone coverage because of timing, understanding concepts, getting the ball out. If he ever struggled in a game, it was in man coverage. That's when you physically have to win some throws."

Turns out there was another way to slow Daniel and the Missouri Spread: traffic. Police escort and all, the Tigers' buses crawled to Arrowhead. The 16-mile trip took the better part of an hour. (Traveling in his own car and eventually separated from the motorcade, Moller walked into the press box 20 minutes before kickoff.) Arrowhead officials had prepared for the sellout crowd. What nobody could have anticipated were the countless fans who showed up without tickets, who just wanted to say they were on the property.

Those who enter Arrowhead from the east are treated to a panoramic view. The stadium sits below, and in the distance is the Kansas City skyline. As the Missouri motorcade inched along Blue Ridge Cutoff and made the right turn into the parking lot, passengers inside the library-quiet buses went dead silent. A haze hung over the lots, smoke pillowing from tailgate parties in the frigid, late-afternoon sky. Flags whipped in the wind. A glow emanated from the stadium. Even the hyper-focused Pinkel did a double-take.

"The greatest feeling was driving up in our buses," he says, his voice rising. "It was unbelievable. *Un-be-lievable.* Fans were running up and hitting the buses. There were roars and cheers. You went by the Kansas people and it was just the opposite. The environment was as good as it will ever get."

Adds Wolfert: "It was surreal. We came in from the top of the hill. Cars, tents, flags blowing in the wind. It was really dark, but there was this glow coming from the stadium. You've got people yelling at your bus, you've got people cheering for your bus, you've got people flipping you off.

"The bus rides are quiet, but they're quiet for the right reasons. Coming into the venue, you'd think that everybody would get pumped, but there are so many opportunities to get excited, and if you let that happen, you're going to be exhausted before the game even starts."

Daniel? "This is what football's about," he recalls thinking.

Because he never took a snap, Patton remembers the drive into the stadium as much as he does details from the game. "The scene—there was nothing like it," he says. "You could feel the hostility in the air."

It was some party. It was also Patton's 22nd birthday. He couldn't have imagined a better present than being the starting quarterback in the biggest game in Missouri football history. Asked what he would have been thinking when he signed his letter of intent in 2004 about the prospect of facing the Jayhawks on such a big stage, Patton says without hesitation, "I'll be playing in that game."

The Tigers' late arrival might have rattled the Pinkel of old, but this was a changed man. He knew the last thing his players needed to see was a flustered coach. "We are very much about attention to detail," he says. "When something like that is going on, I need to be very poised."

The Kansas contingent didn't fare any better with the bottleneck. Keegan caravanned over from Lawrence with other *Journal-World* staffers, and what should have been an uneventful one-hour drive turned into a three-hour ordeal. "I worked in L.A. for eight or nine years, so I dealt with traffic," says Keegan. "Never have I dealt with anything like this."

Oh, to be able to slip a blood-pressure cuff onto Mangino's arm as the Kansas buses idled. You want to talk about schedules and attention to detail? This was the guy who locked the *USA Today* college football writer out of a press conference because he was a couple of minutes late. Nevertheless, Mangino honored a commitment to do an interview with ABC when he stepped off the bus. "We were late, so that pissed him off," says Strauss. "But he did it. He hated those game-day interviews."

Mangino insists the delay didn't impact him, but others aren't so sure. "When things didn't go exactly right," says Strauss, "that would affect him."

Adds Keegan: "Not only did you have the buses being late, but then there's the anger that had to be building. It's like going to the first tee thinking about work. You're doomed."

Reesing stepped off the bus, looked directly into an ABC camera and shouted, "Showtime, baby!" Yet he was very much aware of the Jayhawks' predicament. "We pulled up and we started to realize, 'Hey, we're really behind,'" he says. "That cuts into your normal routine. We had to speed everything up. It definitely adds extra anxiety to the game."

At some point, Mangino must have been second-guessing the decision to stay in Lawrence on Friday night. (The following year, the

Jayhawks bunked in Overland Park. They got to the stadium on time— and won a 40–37 thriller.) And, of course, he wouldn't have been dealing with this migraine if the game were being played in Lawrence. Certainly, that thought crossed his mind. He laughs.

"Being successful in football as well as in life is being able to adjust," Mangino says. "Those things happen. Stay calm. Let your coaches figure out how we're going to do it."

Peterson was roaming the jammed parking lots with Clark Hunt, Lamar's son and the Chiefs' chairman and CEO. To reduce the possibility of scuffles, the Chiefs drew a border of their own. KU fans were encouraged to enter from the west side of Arrowhead, the Mizzou faithful from the east.

"One of my biggest regrets is that [Hunt] didn't live long enough to see KU–MU at Arrowhead," Peterson says.

"There was a lot of concern that these two schools have such a long rivalry it wouldn't be good for them to be in the parking lots at the same time," says Peterson. "I must tell you: Clark and I walked the lots that afternoon and evening. People were absolutely terrific. We didn't have one incident."

Looking back almost five years later, Peterson couldn't help but think about Lamar Hunt. "One of my biggest regrets is that he didn't live long enough to see KU–MU at Arrowhead," Peterson says.

My, how Hunt would have been impressed. It was quite the spectacle. Even 90 minutes before kickoff, Arrowhead was starting to fill up. That's about the time Ivey gathers the Tigers' skill-position players, linebackers and defensive backs for early stretching exercises. When away from Faurot, Ivey tries to pick a corner of the stadium where the players can feed off the energy of their fans. He was stunned not only by the number of spectators who were already in their seats, but also by the noise they were generating. The atmosphere was unlike anything he had ever experienced as a player or a coach. He checked his pulse and looked in the eyes of the Tigers. He didn't like the feedback he was getting.

"My heart rate was elevated, and their eyes were dilated," Ivey says. "I thought, 'O.K., this is different. This is *different*. What can I do right now?' I gathered everyone and said, 'Let's just take some deep breaths. We took three deep breaths—inhale, exhale. A lot of players had closed their eyes. They opened them up and you could just see—O.K., we're relaxed. We're ready now. Let's go."

Ask any Tiger for secrets to the program's success, and Ivey's name always comes up. He is so respected that players who have moved on to the NFL routinely return to Columbia for off-season training. "He worked his butt off to get us in the best shape and give our offense the opportunity to do what it needed—to be able to run no-huddle the whole game and just wear people down," says Patton.

Strength and conditioning, however, is only a small part of Ivey's job description. He is also involved in sports nutrition, and after the 2007 season, he began pursuing a PhD in sports psychology. That's when he came to understand what the Tigers were experiencing when they took the field that night.

"It was the arousal level," Ivey says. "We were too high. If your arousal level is too high, your performance drops. If your arousal level is too low, your performance is not the best. You want to be right in the middle. That's where you have maximized performance."

Once back in the cramped visitors' locker room, Ivey wasn't sure what to make of the players' mental state. "There were a lot of nervous guys," he says. "The butterflies were there. They were doing the best they knew how to get themselves ready. It was different. They didn't know if they should say something or be quiet."

Pinkel knew he had a team loaded with strong-willed leaders, but as he scanned the room, he was concerned. "We're pretty quiet anyway," he says, "but it was one of those things where you're looking around and thinking, 'Are they *too* wound up? Are they *too* focused?' "

Coffman was dozing, of course. Daniel didn't notice anything out of the ordinary, but that wasn't unusual. "I don't pay attention to that stuff," he says. "I really don't. I'm not going to worry about something if it doesn't have a direct impact on the game."

As was his custom, Daniel had on his headphones. Hip-hop was the genre of choice.

"I'm sure guys were nervous," he says. "Heck, I was nervous. I'm nervous before every game. If you aren't nervous, something's wrong."

The Kansas locker room was equally subdued, save for the guy the Jayhawks called Sparky.

"Most guys go pretty stone-cold in the face," Reesing says. "I was kind of the opposite. I was the one who was always loose in the locker room. I was jumping and dancing around, big smile on my face. For me, I'd done all the work, gone to all the practices, watched all the film. This is what I'm here for. I was going to be focused, but I didn't see any reason to put added pressure on myself. I was trying to enjoy it and soak it all in."

On the field, Alden was breathing a huge sigh of relief. Arrowhead was packed—the standing-room-only crowd of 80,537 would be the second largest in stadium history—but Perkins had been off on his 70–30 forecast. Way off. Here's why: According to the contract, Chiefs season-ticket holders, particularly on club level, got the first shot at tickets. And the lion's share of premium seat holders, Alden would learn later, were Mizzou fans. As for the tickets that were available to the general public, Tigers supporters snatched up more of those as well. Sorry, Grandma.

Pressed for an answer, Alden believes Arrowhead was a pro-Mizzou crowd, but he is quick to add, "Out of respect to KU, we're pretty confident in saying it was at least 50-50."

Moments before kickoff, Fowler and Corso were sitting in director's chairs on the KU sideline. ABC had thrown the telecast back to its Manhattan studio, but a camera remained trained on the set. Fowler's mike was on, and as he surveyed the stadium he made a request to Bill Bonnell, the producer of *ESPN Saturday Night Football*.

"Hey, Billy," Fowler said, "if you want to get a shot, we were told to expect a Kansas-heavy crowd. It doesn't feel like that at all in here. There's a lot of black and gold. If you have something to show, I might make reference to that."

Fowler turned to check out the north side of the stadium.

"I don't think it's going to be a pro-Kansas crowd in here," he said as he continued to look around. "We were told by a lot of people it would be 70-30. I'm telling you right now, it ain't 70-30. That's for sure. Unless the Kansas people are all stuck in traffic."

Alden was taking in the scene with associate athletic director Mark Alnutt. Arrowhead is arguably the loudest venue in the NFL, and already the place was rocking. Peterson happened to stroll by.

"Carl, can you believe this?" said Alden, gazing around in amazement.

"Never a doubt, Mike," Peterson replied. "Never a doubt."

Chapter 15

First Quarter
"Is that our best play?"

"Folks, let this sink in. If either Kansas or Missouri wins their next two games, they will play for the national championship."

And that is how Brent Musburger welcomed the ABC television audience to Arrowhead Stadium on the evening of Saturday, Nov. 24, 2007. More than 11 million viewers would tune into what would be the most-watched college football game of the 2007 regular season.

Back in the Manhattan studio, analysts Craig James and Doug Flutie were weighing in. Never one of the Tigers' biggest fans (or maybe just bitter about the way he had been burned in the '05 Independence Bowl), James said he was excited to see what Bill Young and the Jayhawks had in store for Missouri's dynamic attack.

"The discipline they have on defense is going to come into play for them against Chase Daniel," James said. "Missouri's offense is good. Make no mistake about it, they're really good. But when I visited with Mark Mangino, he really thinks his team on defense plays unselfish, disciplined, fast to the football."

Flutie chimed in, adding, "I agree with that. I think that's where they have the edge."

James and Flutie should've looked beyond the X's and O's, for there was a little-known piece of information that would have told them everything they needed to know about the matchup. Daniel was dancing. And when Vickie Daniel saw her son "bobbing and weaving," as he puts it, she knew good things were in store for the Tigers.

"I remember looking back on it, during pre-game warm-ups I was so loose," Chase says. "My mom always said, 'We knew when you were dancing to the music that you were going to have a good game.' "

Daniel was oblivious to it all. What he does remember is the remarkable sense of calm he felt all week and especially on game day, a feeling not unlike the one he experienced when he had the baptism by fire against Iowa State in 2005.

"I felt the most calm, cool and collected I had before any game I've played in," he says. "I can't tell you why. Maybe I slept well or had a good pre-game meal. I just felt really good, really confident."

He was also excited about the game plan. Really excited. Every Saturday morning, Yost would gather the quarterbacks in Daniel and Patton's hotel room and read through the 75-play script. Plays would be discussed, digested and visualized. Then, just before the team boarded the buses for the ride to the stadium, Daniel would pull out his marker and go to work. He would code the script from top to bottom, typically putting a circle next to the drop-back passes and a square next to the play-action calls and a star next to the bubble screens.

Asked what a review of his meticulous coding told him about the game plan, Daniel replies without hesitation: "I remember we were going to chuck it."

"We probably had five types of pass plays," he says. "I would get a feel for what to expect, what Coach C was thinking when he put that game plan together."

Asked what a review of his meticulous coding told him about the game plan for KU, Daniel replies without hesitation: "I remember we were going to chuck it. We felt like they had a really good line and front seven. We thought they were hurting a little on the back end, and we thought we could expose them."

Kickoff was a couple of minutes away, but even in the balmy 33-degree conditions, Arrowhead was abuzz. Fans were standing. Some wouldn't sit all night. And while there was section upon section of Mizzou fans or KU fans in one area of the stadium or another, the ABC cameras showed pockets where a fan decked out in black and gold was standing right next to another dressed in blue and red. They might have been old high school friends or neighbors or colleagues or cousins. Maybe even husband and wife.

Patton compared the atmosphere to the scene he witnessed during his recruiting visit to Tennessee. There may have been 20,000 fewer fans on hand than there were on the Saturday in 2003 he spent at Neyland Stadium, but they were making considerably more noise.

Lamar Hunt was right. Arrowhead was tailor-made to host a college football rivalry.

"It was deafening the entire game," Pinkel says. "It was non-stop. It was as loud as any place I've been."

No surprise, but both teams wanted the ball first. Mangino was looking "to get tempo and rhythm going." Missouri never deferred, and as the captains walked to midfield amid the din, Williams thought it was the perfect time to discuss the coin toss. Rucker always called it—and he always called tails because, he says, "tails never fails." Well, tails had failed T in St. Louis and Oxford and Norman and Manhattan. His average was hovering at .200, on the Mendoza Line, only because he finally got one right in Boulder. So couldn't Zo be excused for suggesting it might not be a bad idea to appoint a new spokesman? If nothing else, considering he was one-for-five on the season, shouldn't T at least consider *heads?* "We argued about it on the way out there," Williams says with a laugh. "Who was going to call it and what to call."

T called tails. Missouri got the ball.

More specifically, Maclin got the ball, and had he been a bit more patient, J-Mac might well have taken a kickoff to the house for the second consecutive week. Fielding the ball at his one-yard-line, he set off on an angle down the left side of the field. He was still in space as he crossed the 30, but there he ran up the back of Earl Goldsmith, one of his blockers. Maclin put out his right hand in an attempt to maneuver around Goldsmith, but he almost came to a stop before going down at the 37.

Daniel came out chuckin' it. Maclin dropped a sideline pass under tight coverage from Holt. A swing pass to J-Mac went for two yards. Facing a blitz on third down, Daniel threw high and slightly behind Saunders, who had found a seam along the right hash.

"We've got to calm Chase down a little," says Yost.

If a get-your-mind-right talk was in order, it would have to be delivered from across the field and several stories up, by way of telephone. It's because of those very situations that many quarterback coaches prefer to be on the sideline. Not Yost.

"I've always been upstairs," he says. "I have a better feel for seeing things. It's like electric football up there. I hate scrimmages, being on the sideline. I don't know what the defense is doing."

He is sitting in a pitch-black film room inside the Tom Taylor Building, rewatching and rewinding the Arrowhead game almost four years later.

"We sit in here all the time with the lights off watching video," Yost says. "Well, guess what? I'm not looking at [the quarterbacks] when I'm talking to them. I've got to be able to communicate by understanding their voice and their voice patterns and when they don't answer a question right or the way I expect them to."

So, were nerves to blame for the missed connection with Saunders? "Just a high throw," Daniel says.

Still, when the Tigers went three-and-out on their second series, James was looking like a genius. Even after Temple ran for six yards on first down, Missouri had to punt it back. In their first 11 games, the Tigers had gone three-and-out on consecutive possessions only three times. The Jayhawks forced a pair of three-and-outs right out of the gate: six plays, six yards.

"At first Kansas did a great job of understanding the rhythm of our snap count," says Yost. "They were able to show blitzes, Chase would get the line set one way, then they would blitz off the other side late. They were putting themselves in some precarious positions, but on certain plays it worked."

For all the good things the Jayhawks did in those first two series, however, they weren't even the best defense on the field. Eberflus' 57th-ranked unit had been much maligned, but the statistics the analysts used to identify a purported weakness were skewed by the defense's performance in the first four weeks of the season. Missouri turned a corner in the Nebraska game and never looked back. As for the statistics that were presented to make the case for KU, it's worth noting that the average ranking of the 10 Division I-A offenses the Tigers faced was 43rd, or 10 spots better than the average of those the Jayhawks encountered.

But how to defense a balanced attack that was averaging 289.6 yards a game through the air and another 210.6 on the ground?

"Kansas did the little things very well," says Eberflus. "They didn't run a lot of plays. They ran the same plays over and over, but they executed and they paid attention to detail. That's what made those guys so hard to defend."

Yet from the opening snap—a slow-developing option right to McAnderson that Weatherspoon and defensive end Tommy Chavis snuffed for a one-yard gain—the Mizzou defense set the tone. Cornerbacks were in press coverage, jamming receivers before they could get into their routes. Safeties cheated toward the line. The Tigers were flying all over the field. Eberflus knew he had to try and take something away from KU, and he decided it would be the run.

"They had the balance, and the quarterback had the ability to create once the play broke down," he says. "I thought he was real special that way. You also had to be careful when you played man coverage that nobody's got his back turned to the quarterback, and he takes off and runs. We had to do some things with the rush schemes to cover that up. If we were going to play man, we had to have somebody in the hole so we could have a guy on the quarterback if he did take off."

Missouri got consecutive three-and-outs to start as well, and again Maclin almost took one to the house. This time he fielded a punt at his 25 and broke down the right sideline. By the time he crossed the 50, he had only one man to beat. It was punter Kyle Tucker, and Alexander, looking over his right shoulder like a sprinter in a relay waiting to receive the baton, was already sizing up the last line of defense. Had he cut back inside near the 35, Maclin could have walked into the end zone. However, believing he could beat Tucker with his speed, he chose the straight line. Alexander didn't have the best angle, and Tucker impressively fought off the block and knocked J-Mac out of bounds at the KU 32. Alexander slapped both hands against his helmet, well aware of an opportunity lost.

"Our kids showed up and played extremely physical that night," says Christensen, sounding one part proud and one part appreciative.

Still, the 43-yard return gave Missouri a jolt. On the first play, Daniel found Saunders for 12 yards, but the Tigers gave those yards right back when Franklin was flagged for a questionable personal foul. Replays showed that Talib took the first swing during a pillow fight nowhere near the ball and Franklin merely shoved him back. (Had anybody reminded the officiating crew this was a rivalry game?) So on fourth-and-12, Pinkel sent out Wolfert for a 39-yard field-goal attempt. It was the logical thing to do. In two seasons of Big 12 play, Wolfert hadn't missed in 21 tries, and Mizzou had a chance to seize the lead.

But the Tigers had a gadget play in the game plan, and Pinkel decided to use it. While the idea began buzzing in the headsets of the coaching staff as soon as Missouri took possession, the decision was not a knee-jerk reaction. Far from it. So as to take emotion out of the equation, all trick plays are discussed during a Thursday staff meeting.

"We make all of these decisions in a calm, intelligent environment when you've got all this information," says Pinkel. "We have a Thursday check list, so you don't go out [on Saturday] and do stupid things."

Every trick play is assigned a yardage potential, and therein lay the biggest issue with this sleight of hand—a pass from Saunders, the holder, to Franklin, who was trying his best to blend in near the Missouri bench. The staff estimated that the play would gain seven or eight yards. The Tigers, remember, needed 12. The other problem, says Yost, was that the ball wasn't spotted on the side of the field where they would have preferred it.

"We probably should have used a timeout because how we got to it was so odd," he says. "We got the penalty, we weren't on the hash we were expecting to be on. We wanted to be on the right hash."

While understandably disappointed, Wolfert wasn't surprised the call was made. "I wanted to kick the field goal," he says. "I felt really confident. I knew we had a sure three points. Why not take the points?" But he also knows how these things go, so he is quick to add, "We had been practicing it all week, and to be honest, when we practice a fake field goal, the coaches are eager to use it as soon as they can."

Adds Yost, "The longer we wait, the less chance we have to use it."

The staff was spot-on about one thing: Franklin gained seven yards before being swarmed by a trio of disciplined Jayhawks. And although Pinkel admittedly let his emotions get the best of him, he was at the same time making a statement to his players. The Tigers weren't going to sit back and figure out a way to win this game at the end. They would stay aggressive and keep pedaling downhill. Fast.

Daniel loved the call. "So what we didn't make it," he says. "We'll go score the next time."

They did, methodically driving 78 yards in 11 plays for the first strike of the night. Temple rushed for 12 yards, Daniel got out of a second-and-15 hole when he found Alexander for 20 yards and Temple ripped off a 23-yard run with a slick pirouette. Two plays later, Alexander turned a potential loss on a double reverse into a first down, breaking three tackles on a four-yard run. The biggest play of the first quarter came four snaps later. It occurred on third-and-goal from the KU seven, and it didn't even result in a first down. Daniel looked into the end zone, then slid to his right before dumping the ball to Temple in the right flat. "He's not even in the route," says Yost.

Temple buckled Rivera with a sharp cut, got a nice block from Saunders on nickel back Sadiq Muhammed and plowed over Talib to get inside the one. It would be a recurring theme: Not only did the Tigers possess more speed and athleticism, they were also the more physical team. If there was any question whether the players had read the memo from the night before, this play answered it.

"Our kids showed up and played extremely physical that night," says Christensen, sounding one part proud and one part appreciative.

The game was only 14 minutes old, yet Pinkel had another significant call to make. Thanks to Temple, the decision to go on fourth-and-goal was a no-brainer. "Fortunately I've been right a lot more than I've been wrong," Pinkel says, rapping his knuckles on his desk. "Again, that's an attitude call that we're going to try and win this game."

The play call was Christensen's, and from the coaches' booth, he opted for *Fast Ball, Quads Left, Sparks Left*. He made the call without hesitation and was confident it was the perfect play for the situation. He also remembers the reaction he got from his boss, who surely was still second-guessing his decision to follow through with the fake field goal.

"Coach Pinkel said, 'Is that our best play?' " Christensen says, his recollection interrupted by a prolonged laugh. "In my mind, I'm thinking, 'No, Coach, I'm saving it [for later].' "

The Tigers went empty. Empty! Coffman was split wide right, opposite Talib. Four receivers lined up to the left, the inside three in a bunch set.

"Great call," Daniel says. "Just a little bubble screen. Go block."

The formation, however, also screamed quarterback draw, so KU countered the quads left with only three defenders. After a quick shoulder fake to Coffman, Daniel spun back to his left and released the pass. Alexander and Maclin walled off their defenders, backup left guard Monte Wyrick pulled and sealed the edge on Mortensen, and Rucker, the outside receiver in the three-man bunch, made a bobbling catch while tumbling into the end zone.

"The first thing was, 'Catch the ball,' " says Rucker, harkening back to the TD he scored on the first reception of his college career. "I knew the end zone wasn't too far away. After I caught it, I said, 'They trusted you to get it into the end zone. That's what you have to do.' "

Many would roll their eyes at the notion of throwing the ball—out of an empty set, no less—on fourth-and-goal from inside the one. Yost doesn't blink. He points to the script and to the down-and-distance situations from the phonebook-thick game packet. "There it is. Right there," he says, pointing to the script. "I get, 'You're on the half-yard line and you line up 6½ yards deep in the gun with quads, and empty?' Yeah. Did we score?"

According to Christensen, the empty look was a formation the Tigers had never run a screen out of. "We go into a game with six to 10 alignment plays or formation adjustments that [the defense] hasn't seen," he says. "At that point, we'd played 11 games, and they'd seen 60 or 70 plays one time."

"The story of the game [is] the Missouri defense," Musburger said. "They've given up no points and 42 yards to this high-flying Kansas offense."

It took all but 29 seconds of the first quarter, but Mizzou had broken the ice. Christensen tips his hat to the guys on the other side of the ball. "Our defense played so well," he says. "It gave us a chance to get going."

Herbstrcit was duly impressed. He sounded almost surprised. "What I'm seeing in these first few series is something that Kansas has not seen for a long time," he said. "Missouri has decided to be the aggressor. Instead of sitting back and waiting for Todd Reesing to establish himself and dictate the tempo, they're attacking downhill."

With but a single first down in the first 15 minutes, KU couldn't get anything going. That was especially true for Reesing, who curiously decided to combat the cold by wearing a pair of synthetic gloves. "It didn't seem like him," says Keegan. "He's such a tough guy."

In the first quarter, Reesing was four of seven for 25 yards. Incompletions were low or fell short of their intended targets. A couple of the completions didn't seem to have the customary zip on them. Yet he dismisses any suggestion the gloves were a mistake.

"It was a decision made early in the week," says Reesing, who at some point scrapped the glove on his left hand. "With the really cold weather and my really small hands, getting a good grip is tough when there's no moisture on the ball. That's why you see guys licking their hands when it's cold. In practice, there were similar temperatures all week. I tested it out just in case I thought [the cold] would be a problem, and I liked how much grip I had on the ball. The risk I'd run not wearing gloves is that you don't get a good grip and you throw a really bad pass. Or you fumble a snap.

"For me, it was just the confidence of knowing that wasn't going to happen. In terms of throwing the ball, I didn't think there was any difference."

Perhaps it was simply time to credit Missouri's defense. The thought wasn't lost on Herbstreit. "One of the first times all year I've seen some frustration out of Todd Reesing," he said. "He looks downfield, he thinks he has an open man, but again, very good coverage. There is something we have not seen from No. 5 very much at all this year."

As the first-quarter clock wound down, Musburger noted, "So far the story of the game [is] the Missouri defense. They've given up no points and 42 yards to this high-flying Kansas offense."

Added Herbstreit, "They are not intimidated by Todd Reesing."

The Jayhawks trailed for only the seventh time all season, and on all but one of the previous six occasions, they immediately answered with a tying or a go-ahead touchdown. Reesing, for one, wasn't overly concerned.

"We were never a great first-quarter team," he says. "We usually started pretty slowly. We were a great second-quarter team."

Reesing was right. The 98 points the Jayhawks scored in the first quarter of their first 11 games were their fewest for any period, and the Mizzou game marked the fourth time in their eight Big 12 games they had failed to register a point in the initial 15 minutes. On the other hand, they had been their most productive in the second quarter, with 154 points, and in the seven conference games, they averaged 33.6 points in the last three quarters alone.

Everybody on both sidelines and in the standing-room-only crowd knew that one touchdown wasn't going to win this thing. The offenses were simply too good, too efficient, too explosive.

It was time to settle in for a long night of football. Fans at Arrowhead and those watching on ABC were in for a treat. These were two of the top six scoring offenses in the country, so the points were coming. Everyone was just going to have to be patient.

Chapter 16

Second Quarter
"I baited him so good"

The teams moved to the other end of Arrowhead, and Reesing wasted absolutely no time getting the KU offense on track. On the first play of the second quarter, on a second-and-nine from the KU 35, he beat the blitz with a bullet to Meier, who was streaking down a seam along the left hash. The play went for 39 yards, four shy of the total the Jayhawks had struggled to gain on 13 first-quarter snaps. The KU faithful rose as one and unleashed an ear-splitting roar. *This* was the offense they had come to know and love. Game on.

It was only one snap in a game that featured 164 plays from scrimmage, but you could immediately sense a seismic shift. Football can be a funny game that way. Momentum turns on a dime. The Jayhawks suddenly had it. They rushed to the line. They were about to take their first snap in Missouri territory, from the 26-yard line. It was time to get the equalizer.

KU went three wide, and Missouri was in man coverage. Moore was the nickel back—opposite wideout Dexton Fields, who was in the right slot.

"I'll never forget it," Moore says. "I'll *never* forget it. I've played it back in my mind so many times."

At the snap, Fields headed on a straight line upfield. Through film study, Moore knew exactly where he was going, and the natural thing would have been to follow in close pursuit. His mind told him to do otherwise. "Once he crossed 10 yards, I knew he was going vertical," Moore says. "Then he started speeding up, so I came off like he was open. I had the right to turn around and run with him. I did, but I kind of sloughed off on him."

Reesing saw two things: Fields running free down the middle of the field and a pocket that was collapsing. Quickly. Linebacker Brock Christopher was coming on a blitz from Reesing's right, and he had a free run at the quarterback.

"Because of pressure, I had to throw it a little off my back foot," Reesing says. "I didn't get to step into the throw as much as I needed to. When you can't step into your throw, you get a little less oomph on it. That, combined with the fact that William Moore is a hell of a player and had enough speed to make up the ground he had lost on Dexton, is why it happened."

"That was probably the biggest play of the first half," Reesing says. No, it was the biggest play of the *game*.

It was a goal-line interception. As Fields cupped his hands to make the catch, Moore cut in front and reached high over his head to pull the ball in. It was his seventh interception of the season, tying the school record held by Pro Football Hall of Famer Roger Werhli, and his fourth consecutive game with a pick. It was also Reesing's first interception in 213 attempts. Since throwing three picks in the Big 12 opener against Kansas State, he had gone six games without one.

"The All-American safety does what he's been doing all year, since the injury sustained by Pig Brown," said Musburger. "He snuffs out the Kansas scoring drive."

As he walked the TV audience through the replay, Herbstreit added: "Brent, William Moore proving week after week that he's a ball hawk. Missouri not slowing down. They're still coming after Todd Reesing, despite the big play by Meier. And for good reason."

When he let the ball go, Reesing was confident he had thrown a game-tying touchdown. He was sure of it. Worst-case scenario, he thought the pass would fall incomplete. "If I get to step into my throw, it's a touchdown, no problem," he says.

That comes as news to Moore. Told that Reesing was preparing to celebrate with one of his signature upper-cut fist pumps, he laughs. "As soon as I saw the quarterback release the ball, I broke in front of [Fields]," Moore says. "I didn't overrun the pass. I undercut it.

"I baited him so good. I made it look like my man was wide open. He was jogging his route, he was running a go route, and I read it the whole way."

At halftime of his games at Hayti High, Moore would exchange his helmet for a tuba. "I don't think Coach [Jerry Bethune] was too fond of it," he says, "but he knew how much I liked the band." Moore is humble and respectful, but over the course of a two-minute dissection of the play, he proudly uses a form of the verb *bait* a half-dozen times.

"I'm not tooting my own horn," Moore says, "but I remember baiting him."

The significance of the play wasn't lost on Reesing. Everyone knew how important turnovers would be in a game of this magnitude. The Jayhawks had made the first big mistake. They had grabbed the momentum on the Meier reception. Missouri needed only 18 seconds to seize it back.

"That was probably the biggest play of the first half," Reesing says.

No, it was the biggest play of the *game*. Although there would be 128 more plays from scrimmage, none was more pivotal than the Moore interception. And on their next snap, the Tigers rode their newfound momentum to produce the second biggest play of the night. Officials originally ruled the interception a touchback, but the replay judge determined that Moore had established possession before crossing the goal line. The ball was placed at the Missouri two-yard line. "I still think it was a bad spot," Daniel says. "I would have liked to have started at the 20."

From the shadow of his own end zone, he went under center. This was no time to be daring. Missouri had dodged a missile and was just glad to have regained possession with the lead. Had the ball been spotted at the one, Christensen would have called *Whale*—a quarterback sneak. But because the Tigers had those extra three feet of real estate with which to operate, he went with *Under Doubles Right Cut Check*. It was a two-tight-end set. The line splits were squeezed foot to foot, and Temple was standing four yards deep in the end zone.

"We ran it in practice," says Christensen, "but we never got in a situation where we used it that much."

Adds Daniel: "We had one back-up [situation] play. Give it to Tony and let him run."

Temple didn't exactly have fond memories of *Under Doubles Right Cut Check*. He remembers getting dumped for a game-changing safety in the fourth quarter of a 2005 loss at Kansas State. "It is not a play to bounce to the outside," he says.

The play was designed to go behind Spieker, but after taking the handoff near the goal line, Temple *did* bounce it to the outside, and to his left. Considering he was so perilously close to the goal line, it was a risky move. It was also the right one.

"That's part of the read," Yost says. "He's got to read the A-gap, but he's got to see the end."

That was John Larson, who crashed inside. Though he was effectively taken out of the play, he tied up two blockers: Rucker and Luellen. Plus, Larson had help behind him. Or so he thought. The problem for the Jayhawks arose when free safety Darrell Stuckey took a horrible angle—a straight line from the nine-yard line to the line of scrimmage. He got pinched inside, and Temple had the corner.

"The safety gets himself out of position," says Yost. "He screws himself."

Temple saw the play unfolding in front of him. There was no back-side pursuit—Gregory and Brown saw to that—and then Temple's instincts took over. "I remember that end coming down and bouncing it to the outside," he says.

As he continues to rewind the play more than three years later, Temple is sitting in a coffee house on State Line Road in Prairie Village, Kan., directly on the Missouri-Kansas border. He estimates that he ran for about 40 yards. Pinkel has about the same recollection.

"He had a feel for it," Pinkel says. "They closed it off inside and it bounces. How huge was that play? All of a sudden, the ball is at the 35-yard line, and you're rolling. You've got the field position back.

"It was huge. *Huge*—bigger than the average fan would think. That was a field-position game, and that was also a hit-you-in-the-mouth momentum play."

The run down the left sideline that knocked out a few front teeth covered all of 17 yards. But considering the situation, it was much bigger than that. Temple may as well have run for 98 yards.

Pinkel, it turns out, was simply a play ahead of himself, because on the next snap, Jackson ran off right tackle for 18 yards. In less than a minute, Missouri went from potentially having to give the ball back to KU with great field position to flipping the field to shifting into scoring mode. Old Mo was back with the black and gold, and it wouldn't be leaving for some time. A long time.

Still, seven plays later, the Jayhawks were in position to force a punt. Missouri was facing a third-and-12 at the KU 40 when Daniel threw deep down the middle into two-safety coverage. Stuckey arrived a split second after the ball and de-cleated Franklin with a bone-rattling shot. "He's got to get the ball there sooner," Yost says of Daniel. "He gets Franklin killed. The safety's right on top."

The ball and the receiver hit the ground, but Franklin bounced right up.

"That was part of that team's mentality," says Yost. "They were never going to let anybody think they got the best of them. That's part of Coach Pinkel's philosophy. You can be dying inside. Just don't give them any credit."

The Jayhawks celebrated the big hit and the third-down stop, unaware that a yellow flag lay limp on the field back near the line of scrimmage. Officials stepped off a 10-yard penalty against Holt, who had bear-hugged Derrick Washington coming out of the backfield. It would be one of only two penalties called against KU, but it would prove huge. After four unsuccessful attempts, Mizzou had its first third-down conversion of the night.

Five plays later, the Tigers were facing another third down, and Yost admits there weren't a lot of passes in the playbook for the predicament. "We called this with the expectation we would get four guys in the end zone, and we might make a play," he says. "We don't have a great play for third-and-11 from the 11-yard line."

What Daniel and his receivers did have was time, because for one of the few instances all night, the Jayhawks obliged by rushing only three. Opponents trying to defend Daniel faced a double-edged sword. Come with the blitz, and he would get the ball out quickly, almost always to the open man. But giving Daniel any amount of time was also asking for trouble, and on this play he had an eternity. He started left, then circled back to his right, his eyes trained downfield. At one point, he retreated to the 32-yard line. "If he had taken that sack," says Yost, not needing to finish his sentence.

"I don't remember seeing anything," Daniel says. "It was five verticals, trying to get somebody open in the end zone. It didn't work out. It was just instinct. I had to go make something happen with my feet."

As Daniel circled back toward the line of scrimmage, Larson was drawing a bead on him, but Brown peeled back and delivered a crushing block. Then, finally, Daniel saw something.

"I was running, running, looking," he says, "and all of a sudden I see Danario waving his hands."

Alexander, the middle receiver in a three-wide package to the right, had looped down the right sideline, then floated to middle. Now, he was working his way back from left to right. He caught Daniel's pass in stride at the two and hopped into the front-right corner of the end zone.

Much had been made of Reesing's ability to keep a play alive. Daniel one-upped him.

"A play that took a half dozen seconds to unfold, it seemed," said Musburger. "And Chase Daniel strikes again."

Check that. The time from snap to release of the football was 10 seconds (10:53 to be precise, according to Yost). From snap to touchdown signal, the 11-yard pass play took 14 seconds.

It was Daniel's Heisman moment. "I watched that play unfold," Moller says, "and I remember thinking, 'We're going to New York.' "

"One of the reasons we were so solid that year was that we had a good running game," Reesing says. "But against Missouri, our running game was not there."

The 13-play, 98-yard drive burned 5:04 off the clock—slow by Missouri standards but equally deflating to most every opponent. Not the Jayhawks, who in their first 11 games never trailed by more than seven points. Fearful of Marcus Hereford, the nation's leading kickoff-return man, the Tigers repeatedly opted for pooch or squib kicks. After another short kickoff, Reesing went to work from his 37-yard line, moving KU 33 yards in four plays. A third-down holding penalty against cornerback Carl Gettis kept the drive alive, but three plays later Dezmon Briscoe dropped a pass that would have given the Jayhawks a first down inside the 10. Looking to get on the scoreboard, Mangino summoned Webb, but his 33-yard field-goal attempt bounced off the right upright.

The Jayhawks were making all of the mistakes—the biggest ones, anyway—and the Tigers weren't interested in waiting for their rivals to find their rhythm. Daniel rescued Mizzou from a first-and-20 hole with a 16-yard, blitz-beating completion to Rucker on third-and-11. Saunders caught a pass for 20 yards, and Temple turned a potential loss into a five-yard gain. The KU defense was on its heels. In its first 11 contests, the Jayhawks allowed an average of 88 rushing yards a game. This game was barely 25 minutes old, and Missouri had already matched that total. Temple alone had 68 yards—on just nine carries.

"They're seventh in the nation coming into this game stopping the run," said Herbstreit. "But they've never seen an offense like this. They're getting exposed. They've never seen this kind of talent."

The Jayhawks dug in, however, and on fourth-and-one at the KU 36, Pinkel rolled the dice again. Christensen called another bubble screen to Rucker, this one to the right. Temple was supposed to go in front of Daniel, but instead he went to the right flat. Most of the Jayhawks followed, and Mortensen led a swarm of tacklers to Rucker, who was dropped for a two-yard loss.

"We got yelled at," says Yost as an ABC camera caught Pinkel talking into his headset. His message: You can't go with a bubble screen every time.

With 2:52 left in the half, Kansas had life—and pretty good field position. Reesing connected with Fields for 31 yards, and when referee Jon Bible tacked on a 15-yard penalty against Stryker Sulak for roughing the passer, the Jayhawks were suddenly at the Mizzou 16. Sulak quickly made amends. On first down, he deflected a pass at the line. Two plays later, he chased down Reesing from the blind side and chopped the ball out of his right hand. KU recovered, but as a result of the 11-yard loss, a manageable field-goal attempt turned into a 45-yarder. Mangino seemed to hesitate before sending out Webb, and this time he sailed the kick wide left.

"You're trying to get some traction, and you can't do it," Mangino says. "We were backed up a bunch in the first half. When we did get it across the 50, we missed two field goals and threw an interception. You can't do that against a team like Missouri."

What happened next spoke volumes about the respect Mangino and his staff had for the Missouri offense. The Tigers got the ball back with 1:29 left, yet when Daniel was sacked for an eight-yard loss on second-and-10, the Jayhawks didn't call timeout, even though they had their full allotment.

"They didn't take a timeout here, because they're worried we're still going to get a first down," Yost says. "We do it all the time."

Missouri punted, Kansas took a knee and the teams headed to their respective locker rooms. The Tigers had won the first half convincingly, on the stats sheet (272 yards to 139) and most important, the scoreboard: 14–0. Not surprisingly, the mood in the two locker rooms was markedly different.

"The feeling was that we played shitty the whole half, we didn't make plays, we missed field goals, we had a turnover, but we're still in the game," recalls Reesing. "This thing is not out of reach. Because of that, everybody had to refocus."

And adjust. The Missouri defense was the star of the first half. Eberflus' aggressive plan to make KU one-dimensional was working. McAnderson carried seven times for 24 yards—and a dozen of those yards came on one first-quarter jaunt. Sharp ran once for no gain. Reesing? He didn't even think about tucking it and taking off.

"One of the reasons we were so solid that year was that we had a good running game," Reesing says. "But against Missouri, our running game was not there. We couldn't get any rhythm going because we couldn't get our running game started. They had a good game plan. We knew they wanted to stop the run."

On the Missouri side, it was business as usual.

"The energy in the locker room was really, really high," says Pinkel. "Our leaders were doing their thing too."

Everyone was throwing around a six-letter verb: *Finish!*

Chapter 17

"He reminds me a little
of a Peyton Manning"

Eberflus knew his defense was playing ridiculously well, but he also knew the Jayhawks would come out of the locker room firing. KU's offense had shown signs of life in the second quarter, and it was too explosive to bottle up for 60 minutes. Plus, this was more than just another football game. The No. 1 ranking was on the line. There was also the whole rivalry issue. No one wanted to be remembered for being on the losing side in the biggest sporting event the two schools had ever played.

"With that school and that head coach, it's always the same," Eberflus says. "It doesn't matter."

So his message was quite simple: Prepare for each play as if the score was 0–0. And take the last 30 minutes one snap at a time. "Play for six seconds," Eberflus recalls telling his troops. "Play with intensity. Play together. Turn the page and do it for the next play."

The Mizzou defense was tested immediately. KU got the ball to start the second half, and again the Tigers insisted on kicking it short. This time, tight end Derek Fine scooped up Wolfert's indifferent squib kick at the KU 37 and returned the ball 11 yards. The second half was only seven seconds old, and already the Jayhawks were setting up shop two yards short of the 50. It would be their best starting field position of the night.

On third-and-third, Reesing found Fine along the right sideline for 13 yards. When cornerback Castine Bridges was called for a facemask penalty away from the play, Kansas was knocking on the door again, 17 yards from the end zone.

Again, the Kansas crowd made itself heard. Another momentum swing was looming. You could feel it. But no one could have envisioned the haymaker that came next. The Tigers immediately put the six inauspicious seconds that resulted in a 28-yard KU gain behind them; they turned the page.

Under heavy pressure on first down, Reesing unloaded a pass out of the back of the end zone. On second down, McAnderson was fortunate to gain one yard before being stoned by Weatherspoon. On third down, Reesing threw across the middle from off his back foot. The pass was high and a little behind Henry, who could only tip the ball with his left hand as he reached back for it. Bridges was in close pursuit and he too reached back for a football that was floating in the air. He snatched the ball with his right hand as if it were a flyswatter. Almost in the same motion, he did a 360 spin and set sail down the right sideline with a convoy of blockers. He was finally knocked out of bounds at the Kansas 40, after a 49-yard return.

Talk about your unlucky 13. After going 212 passes without an interception, Reesing had been picked off for the second time in 13 attempts. "They definitely made some adjustments for us," he says. "They played some coverages in the secondary that they hadn't used all year. They gave us some different looks."

Flashing back to those pre-season battles against Daniel and Co., Eberflus doesn't sound overly surprised that his unit was having so much success. "It wasn't real hard to get that defense excited to play hard from the first snap to the last," he says. "Those guys were geared up for that game."

After going 212 passes without an interception, Reesing had been picked off for the second time in 13 attempts. "They definitely made some adjustments for us," he says. "They played some coverages that they hadn't used all year."

Given some of their best field position of the night, the Tigers wasted no time punching it in. The seven-play drive featured five runs, a couple of Daniel completions and more sloppy KU tackling. Washington broke four tackles on a four-yard run, and Franklin turned a potential third-and-four into first-and-goal at the one when he shook free from Talib on a 10-yard catch-and-run. Missouri was simply the more physical team.

"Again, the Tigers showing a tenacious attitude, fighting for that second and third effort," Herbstreit said. "That time, Franklin almost takes it into the end zone."

On the next play, Missouri did. Unveiling the Pistol formation for the first time all night—Daniel was four yards behind the center and the running back three yards behind him—Jackson walked in on a run up the gut. He was a yard into the end zone before a Jayhawk laid a hand on him.

KU, which in its first 11 games had trailed for a total of 28:01, was staring at a 21–0 deficit. The good (or bad) news was that the third quarter was only 4:24 old.

"You get the feeling that Kansas is shell-shocked," Herbstreit said. "It's almost like they don't know what has hit them."

The Jayhawks' problems were two-fold. First, the three linebackers were the strength of the defense, and Young made the decision early in the week to put his 11 best defenders on the field. He didn't think twice about it. Why sit Holt or Mortensen or Rivera for the biggest game of the season? Why insert a nickel back for the sake of having another defensive back on the field?

"If we took a James Holt out, we would have just been playing a defensive back with a number on his jersey," Young says. "The coverages we wanted to run worked better for us with those guys on the field."

And why change now? The Jayhawks had played with their base defense for 11 weeks, and played spectacularly. What coordinator in his right mind would revamp a unit that was ranked seventh in the country against the run, eighth against the pass and eighth in total defense? It made perfect sense to Christensen.

"First of all, they were good, and they were confident in what they were doing," he says. "I think it was probably their best 11 to put out there. In a week, you can't put in a whole new scheme. You're better off using what you have in."

Still, Missouri featured five-receiver sets with burners on the outside in Maclin, Alexander and Franklin. Saunders was an excellent possession receiver who was adept at finding soft spots in the zone. And the biggest nightmare of all might have been the two-headed monster of Rucker and Coffman. They both stood 6-foot-6, and they were as athletic as they were physical.

"Those two big old guys," says Mangino. "They're trying to get matchups on your corners. They're trying to get matchups on your safeties. They do a good job of finding holes in the zone, catching the ball and getting yards after the catch."

That only made the decision to maintain the status quo all the more perplexing. *Nobody* played its base defense against the Tigers. At least nobody played it and got away with it.

"It was surprising," Daniel says of the three-linebacker look. "You might have a plan going into a game, but who can react best to the other team's plan and fix it on game days and at halftime? That's something that Coach Pinkel, Coach C and Coach Yost did a hell of a job with that year."

The Jayhawks were big on the zone blitz. They also played a lot of cover-four, dropping their safeties deep and leaving cushions on the outside. Taking the opposite tact of Eberflus, KU seemed to be saying it would do everything it could not to get beat deep. Bend but don't break.

"That was kind of our philosophy," Young says. "We didn't have the big-time pass rusher up front. We didn't have that guy to come off the edge."

In fact, for all of their gaudy defensive statistics, the Jayhawks ranked only 80th in the country in sacks. Daniel was more than happy to take advantage. He points out that the goal going into most games was to average about 10 yards per pass attempt. Against KU, the number was a shade over seven—even on a night when he completed 81.6% of his attempts. "We didn't throw a lot of balls down the field," he says. "There were a lot of quick slants, a lot of bubble screens, a lot of stuff like that. Get players in space, and go make some plays."

Adds Pinkel, "They played a cover-four. That opens up a lot on the outside if your quarterback's patient enough to take it. And he was."

KU's other issue involved its inability to adjust to the Swan, the formation in which Missouri slid one of its tackles to the other end of the line. The unbalanced front featured three linemen on one side of Spieker, only a guard on the center's other. Unlike Texas Tech, which refused to shift its front, KU simply was slow to recognize it. The Jayhawks knew the Swan was coming, and they practiced for it (and practiced well). Yet when the Tigers went unbalanced, the front seven was slow to react.

"The linebackers were running into the backs of the defensive linemen," says Young. "You've got to kick your front over to compensate. It sounds so simple."

All told, Missouri called 18 plays out of the Swan (including three passes), gaining 111 yards and scoring a pair of TDs. Daniel laughs when he thinks back on it. "If it was Swan right, teams had to make the right guard the center," he says. "They weren't doing that. They were still making the center the center. We'd run to the right, and it was just numbers. We had more blockers than they had defenders."

A few weeks after the game, Christensen and Young crossed paths on the recruiting trail. "I asked him, 'Why is this formation so difficult for people?' " Christensen recalls. "He said, 'I can't answer that because we lined up perfectly in practice all week, but we couldn't do it once in the game.' "

Asked about the Swan almost five years later, Young still sounds baffled. "I've been coaching 40-something years," he says, "and I've never seen that done anywhere but at Missouri."

Nor had anyone staggered the KU defense like this. In their first 11 games, the Jayhawks surrendered 21 points or more only three times.

Missouri needed only 34:24 to get to 21 and had already racked up 312 yards of offense, a dozen yards more than KU had been allowing. Young's defenders needed a blow. A little help from their friends on offense would have been nice as well. Something. Anything.

The transformation started with a couple of Mangino adjustments.

"With them showing pressure, we tried to get the ball off quicker with shorter routes," he says. "When they dropped to a two-shell, we tried to drop the ball in front of the safeties. We got the safeties to tighten up a bit, and then we got a vertical down the one side."

Williams sensed a momentum shift. "You could feel it coming," he says. "Those dudes started lighting us up."

The fireworks commenced on the Jayhawks' second possession of the third quarter. The biggest play came on a spectacular 39-yard catch by Briscoe, whose diving reception put the ball at the Mizzou five. Just as significant was the eight-yard pass to Fine on the previous play, because for the first time all night, KU moved the pocket at the snap, with Reesing sliding to his right before making the throw.

Asked about the Swan almost five years later, Young still sounds baffled. "I've been coaching 40-something years," he says, "and I've never seen that done anywhere but at Missouri."

"Give credit to Mangino," says DeArmond. "He moved Reesing. He got him to roll out. Missouri didn't adjust to that. Reesing was a lot better when he did that."

Adds Pinkel, "That quarterback was just a great player. [In 2009] I went up to him after the game and said, 'I'm so glad you're leaving.' He just gave me a smile."

McAnderson scored the touchdown on a one-yard run, dragging Moore into the end zone. But even that didn't come easily. The Jayhawks needed three plays to cover the five yards, the clock running all the while. Still, they were on the board, they were back within 14 and the third quarter was barely half over.

"This stadium's starting to come alive," Herbstreit said as the teams lined up for the ensuing kickoff. "You really felt that Kansas needed to get that score and have a reason to believe. They've got their crowd back in the game, and their defense is jumping up and down on the sideline."

Alas, the excitement was short-lived, because the Jayhawks had no answer for Daniel. "All I remember is that neither defense was stopping anybody," says Mangino. "It was like a track meet."

While the Jayhawks assumed the sprinter's role, the Tigers settled in as the patient, calculating distance runner. Missouri drove methodically down the field, running for five yards here and throwing for seven yards there. Taking a handoff out of the backfield, Maclin scored on a 35-yard touchdown run around left end, beating a couple of Jayhawks to the edge before zigging and zagging and diving into the end zone. However, the highlight-reel dash was wiped out by a holding penalty, announced against Franklin. The replay showed he was nowhere near the play and *looking* for somebody to block. It also caught Alexander locked up against Rivera in what appeared to be a perfectly legal seal of the edge. It was one in a series of eyebrow-raising infractions against a team that entered the game second in the nation in penalty yards, with 32.8 a game.

No worries. Daniel was in a rhythm. You might even say he was bobbing and weaving. On the next play, KU sent six, and he threw across the middle to Alexander for 17 yards. After Temple was dropped for a three-yard loss, Daniel found Saunders for 10 yards, again beating the blitz. On third-and-three from the Kansas 16, Missouri lined up in the Swan, but Daniel didn't like the look the defense was giving him, so he called time. He shook his head as he walked to the sideline.

Out of the timeout, going empty against a three-man rush, he looked right, then across the middle before throwing to Saunders on the left side for five yards. Mr. Reliable, a one-time walk-on from Kearney, Mo., who would catch 41 passes in 2007 and 72 as a senior, was at least Daniel's third read. The QB gave a quick fist pump, recognizing the significance of another third-down conversion.

"He reminds me a little of a Peyton Manning of the college game— the way he's in total charge out there," Musburger said. "He looks over to the sideline, he moves his players around, he's very confident in how he does things."

Added Herbstreit, "Don't get caught up in the height. He makes every throw you want to see made on a college football field."

On cue, Daniel delivered a 14-yard strike across the middle to Alexander, putting the ball at the two. Two plays later, again out of the Pistol and again out of the Swan, Daniel dumped a swing pass to Washington, who caught the ball at the 10 and skipped virtually untouched into the end zone.

"You're between a rock and a hard place," Mangino says of trying to defend Daniel. "You want to put some pressure on him and disrupt him, but he'll find the open guy. He was real good at finding the hots and finding the check-down. Damned if you do, damned if you don't."

If what Pinkel witnessed from Daniel in Boulder was "not normal," how would one characterize his quarterback's play against the Jayhawks? In the third quarter alone, he was 10 of 10 for 85 yards. He spread those 10 completions around to seven receivers. He was three for three on third-down conversions.

"He was lights out," says Christensen. "It was a phenomenal performance considering the stage it was on and the magnitude of the game. His whole career was like that. He showed up for every game the same and competed his ass off. That just happened to be No. 2 and No. 4 playing."

Considering the Tigers bled an additional 3:23 off the clock after Maclin's touchdown was taken off the board, the Jayhawks would have been better served if the flag for holding had never been tossed. Only 79 seconds remained in the third quarter. Mizzou had stretched its lead again. It would win this quarter just as it had the first two—by a touchdown. It was 28–7. Almost everything was going the Tigers' way.

And with 45 minutes complete, this much was apparent: Missouri was the better team. The Tigers were faster and more physical. They had the better quarterback. They had more playmakers. They ran when they wanted and passed when they wanted, and they continued to make KU one-dimensional.

Then there was the whole experience factor. Sure, the Jayhawks had won at Kyle Field, but the arena they walked into at Arrowhead was unlike anything they had encountered. The Tigers had been there, done that. The tests against Illinois in St. Louis and Oklahoma in Norman and even Ole Miss in Oxford were serving them well.

"They had proven it so much more," says Matter. "It wasn't Kansas' fault. They had played the perfect schedule. You don't get punished for playing the perfect schedule as long as you don't lose."

The Tigers were close. But they had been close in El Paso in '06 and close again in Norman just six week earlier.

There was but one lingering question to be answered: Could they finish?

Chapter 18

Fourth Quarter
"The border belongs
to the Tigers"

Fifteen minutes. Fifteen minutes stood between Mizzou and its first No. 1 ranking in 47 years. But Kansas was on the move and facing a fourth-and-three at the Tigers' 35. Had it been a seven- or even a 10-point game, Mangino most likely would have punted. But he was down 21, and his defense had shown nothing over the previous 2½ quarters to suggest it could so much as slow Daniel.

On the last play of the third quarter, Reesing had scrambled for the first time, running for seven yards. And on the first snap of the fourth period, he kept another play—and the drive—alive with his feet before throwing to Henry for 12 yards. That the reception was the first of the night for KU's leading receiver spoke to the job the Tigers were doing defensively. Still, the Jayhawks had life, even a little momentum. Daniel knew it.

"They were a good team," he says. "They were No. 2 in the nation for a reason. We knew they were going to test us."

Adds Keegan, "You'd seen Reesing pull off amazing things. You knew he had more bullets in his gun."

On the next play, Moore was flagged for pass interference, moving the ball to the Mizzou 13. But with the clock stopped, KU had to burn a timeout it wished it would have had in its pocket later, and on the next snap, left tackle Anthony Collins drew a personal-foul penalty for separating Hood's helmet from his head. The Jayhawks were in a hole, and when Reesing's first-down pass fluttered to the ground after he was hit on the release by Sulak, the Tigers seemed on the verge of slamming the door.

Thinking the pass might be ruled a fumble, Moore sauntered over to pick the ball up, but as he reached down, he was jostled by Kansas right guard Chet Hartley. Whistles were now blowing, and Moore flipped the ball at Hartley. It grazed off his left shoulder. At least two officials witnessed the incident, but only umpire Wiley Willingham saw fit to reach for his flag. Granted, Moore had violated the letter of the law, but the ball had barely tickled the 315-pound Hartley. Plus, like Franklin's first-quarter penalty, it was a case of the retaliator getting caught. Things were starting to get chippy, but would anybody have expected anything less in a rivalry game with so much on the line?

Given new life, the Jayhawks took advantage. On fourth-and-two from the five-yard line, Reesing deftly faked to McAnderson, sucking linebacker Steve Redmond inside. He then dashed around right end on a bootleg, beating Weatherspoon to the pylon. KU was back within 14, and there was still 13:02 left.

The problem was that the Jayhawks still faced the issue of finding a way to slow the Missouri offense. Even after officials missed a blatant pass interference call on a deep ball to Maclin, even after Temple's 19-yard dash was wiped out by a substitution infraction and even after the Tigers were put in a first-and-20 predicament due to a holding penalty, Kansas couldn't force a punt.

The Jayhawks took just 1:23 off the clock, and they were suddenly only 10 points down. Musburger posed a question that was on everybody's mind: "But now, can they stop Missouri?"

Daniel completed passes of 18 and 10 yards to Maclin, and on consecutive plays he hooked up with Saunders and Rucker for 10 and 16 yards, respectively. When the drive stalled at the KU 25, Pinkel didn't hesitate to send out the field-goal unit.

"I was really confident for that game," Wolfert says. "I had good warm-ups and good mental preparation, and when that comes together, I'm able to make a lot of kicks. I wanted [Pinkel] to be able to rely on me. I said, 'Give me a range and I'll make it.' "

Wolfert converted the 43-yard attempt. The Tigers were up three scores again and, most important, they had taken another 3:44 off the clock.

Again, Kansas, playing faster than it had all night and wisely working the sideline to conserve time, came storming back. More specifically, Reesing was heating up. He completed six of seven passes in a 57-yard drive, the touchdown coming on a 10-yard pass to Fields. For the first time all night, the Missouri defense was on its heels. After being the aggressor for three-plus quarters, Eberflus admits he may have gone too soft while playing with a big lead.

"Looking back on it, I think I did," he says. "You're playing the clock a little bit. You want to make sure you keep everything in front of you. Part of that is the function of the quarterback being able to extend plays and the coverage breaking down."

After getting off 46 snaps in the first three quarters, KU had 25 in the fourth. "I think our rushers got a little tired, because it was a volume of two-minute offense," Eberflus says. "We could have done a better job of rotating our d-linemen and putting fresh bodies in there to get after the passer."

The Jayhawks took just 1:23 off the clock, and they were suddenly only 10 points down—as close as they had been since early in the second quarter. Then Musburger posed a question that was on everybody's mind: "But now, can they stop Missouri?"

The answer was simply no. On a night when he threw for 361 yards and three touchdowns and saw the ball hit the ground just nine times in 49 attempts, Daniel was at his best on the ensuing drive. Considering the situation, it couldn't have come at a better time for the Tigers. The momentum was most definitely back with the blue and red, and who knows how the last 8:23 would have played out had the Jayhawks gotten a quick stop. But Daniel threw for 18 yards to Maclin, and three plays later, on third-and-14, he subtly eluded the rush with a slide step to his left before threading a throw between a linebacker and a defensive back to Alexander. It was the sophomore's eighth catch, and his 117 receiving yards were a career high.

"Where's Marlin?" said Musburger, a man who always does his homework but apparently had been blindsided by Alexander's sudden emergence.

"You know, I'm not sure," Herbstreit replied. (It's south of Waco, guys.)

The better question: How does a player with 44 career receptions have a breakout performance in Missouri's biggest game?

"I throw to the open guy," says Daniel. "I don't care what the read is. If a guy is open and I see something in the defense, he's getting the ball. That's something the receivers told me they liked. They said, 'Hey, I can be open on every play, and even if I'm the fifth read, Chase can get me the ball.' They had confidence in me."

On second-and-12 from the KU 44, Maclin happened to be the open guy. Daniel rolled right and delivered another dart, this one for 14 yards. Talib's ankle tackle prevented a bigger gain, if not a touchdown.

"All this hype, all this talk about the winning team was going to move to No. 1," Herbstreit said. "I wondered which of these quarterbacks and which of these teams would handle it and play with poise. And Chase Daniel almost looks like he's out on the practice field."

The next three plays netted only five yards—KU burned its second timeout after second down—and Wolfert was called on to attempt another 43-yarder.

"He came over when I was talking to Chase during the timeout and said, 'Coach, I guarantee I will kick that thing through there,' " Pinkel recalls.

Wolfert drilled it. The Tigers led 34–21, and this time they had burned 4:52 off the clock. They were only 3:31 from the rematch with Oklahoma.

Depending on which sideline you stood, the fourth quarter was either interminably slow or blindingly fast.

"I kept looking at the clock and thinking, 'Geez, is this thing ever going to get over?' " says Rucker.

Says Reesing, "It seemed like the minutes were flying by. I was looking at the clock like every 30 seconds, especially when I was on the sideline."

Though he got away with a couple of ill-advised throws, Reesing wasted no time marching the Jayhawks back down the field. Twice over a three-play stretch, strong safety Justin Garrett got both hands on a potential interception, and on fourth-and-three, Reesing scrambled for seven yards. Five plays later, he threw a five-yard touchdown pass to Henry. It was a second straight 83-second drive.

Only 2:03 remained, but at least KU was back within a touchdown, at 34–28. Down to their last timeout, the Jayhawks had no option but to attempt an onside kick. Webb produced his best boot of the night, a skidding kick that took a couple of crazy bounces along the frozen turf. Unfortunately for the Kansas faithful, the ball was headed directly at Saunders. Without so much as a bobble, he smothered the kick at the Kansas 40.

Still, simple math said the Jayhawks were going to get the ball back if the Tigers didn't pick up the first down. Three conservative running plays into the middle of the line generated only five yards—KU stopped the clock after second down—so after taking a delay-of-game penalty that moved the ball back to the Kansas 40, Pinkel sent out the punt team with 28 seconds left. Crossett, the kid unceremoniously benched in favor of Wolfert in 2006, made his brother-in-law proud with arguably the best punt of his career.

It covered all of 33 yards. In any other situation, Talib undoubtedly would have let the ball bounce, hoping it would tumble into the end zone. But the one thing the Jayhawks didn't have was time, so Talib caught the ball at the seven. He got only four yards upfield before meeting Van Alexander. The clock read 0:17, enough time for Kansas to get off two plays, maybe three.

Eberflus called *Straight*. The scheme is as simple as it sounds.

"Straight cover-two with two high safeties," he says. "We didn't want to give up big-chunk plays."

More precisely, it was a cover-two with a twist. "I was really deep," Moore says. So deep he wasn't even in the TV picture when the ball was snapped.

The Tigers' goal, of course, was to keep everything in front of them—regardless of how much time Reesing had to throw. And then wrap up. Otherwise, a slant pass to Henry or Briscoe coupled with a missed tackle

"I wondered which of these quarterbacks and which of these teams would handle it and play with poise," Herbstreit said. "And Chase Daniel almost looks like he's out on the practice field."

or two could produce an 89-yard catch-and-run, a 35-34 Kansas victory, another Missouri did-that-really-happen? defeat that would rival—no, exceed—the Fifth Down Game and the Flea-Kicker. The thought crossed Rucker's mind. "I've seen crazier things happen," he says. "Especially at Mizzou. Do. Not. Let. Them. Score!"

Nevertheless, the Jayhawks were in dire straits—89 yards from the end zone, 17 seconds left, no timeouts. "In the back of your mind, you're holding out hope, even if you have 90 yards to go," Reesing says. "It's something you practice at the walkthrough every week during the season, just in case you get in that situation. The idea is that I'm taking a three-step drop out of the shotgun, then rolling out. You're trying to buy some time for your receivers to get down the field. You have a designed pass 25 or 30 yards downfield, to get in range for a Hail Mary."

If only it were that easy. "Keep pedaling downhill," Patton remembers thinking of the catchphrase the players had adopted in their stated quest to finish games. And after riding the brake for much of the fourth quarter, the Tigers let loose.

Sulak, one of those Texas-two-star, Garmin-aided recruiting finds, had spent much of the night beating Collins around the edge. At the snap, he blew by the consensus All-American one last time, coming off the corner from Reesing's blind side. It was as if Sulak knew the snap count. "That was a great move," says Williams. "We went back and looked at it a hundred times."

Williams was lined up next to Sulak, across from left guard Adrian Mayes. "He tried to soft-set me," Williams says, explaining that Mayes attempted to make it appear as if he was dropping into pass protection, only to surge forward with an aggressive block.

"I was pretty good at reading feet," Williams says. "He tripped over one of his feet, because I could see him trying to stop and come back. As soon as he threw his hand out there, I decided to run around him."

The first part of his assignment complete, Williams glimpsed another guy in a white jersey barreling in from his right. It was Sulak. Reesing saw him coming, too.

"I didn't have a chance to digest what was happening," he says. "Before I knew it, they were in the backfield. I was just trying to dodge getting sacked."

Now three yards deep in the end zone, Reesing spun back to his right. There was Williams, eyes wide. It was hard to tell which player was more surprised.

"My first thought was, *I need to get my left hand up, because he's going to throw this ball*," Williams says. "He's not going to take the sack. I wanted to tip it. I got my hand up, but it was the wrong one."

The misstep threw Williams a bit off balance, but then he didn't commit the sin made by so many defenders who have a sack within their grasp.

"Every quarterback has a way he wants to get away from you," he says. "They try to make you jump, and when you do, they pick a side and get away. The hand in the air was a fake-out move I had developed. Coach Kul [Craig Kuligowski] is a great D-line coach. He was big on me learning all these moves. You've got to have a move and a counter to everything."

Reesing may have been trapped, but Williams knew his work wasn't finished. The most emphasized aspect of the defensive game plan was not only to pressure and contain Reesing, but also to get him on the ground when presented the opportunity.

However, not even Reesing could Houdini his way out of this box. Just as Sulak was about to pounce, Williams wrapped up Reesing and drove him face-first into the turf, planting the quarterback in the gold-painted end zone bearing the Missouri name. Sulak arrived a split-second later. Then came Hood.

"Ballgame! Kelly screamed to his listening audience. "Bingo!"

In a game that featured 64 points, 51 first downs and 910 yards of offense, the signature play came courtesy of Williams, Sulak and the Missouri defense. It was as if they were saying it was time to go home. Six seconds? From snap to tackle, five ticks elapsed. On their final play of the night, the Tigers' defenders pedaled downhill. Fast. They *finished*.

"Everything kind of stopped for a second," says Williams.

Then he heard a roar. "It was nuts."

Not for the quarterback at the bottom of the pile.

"You've got these big guys excited and pushing off of you, your face is in the dirt and the reality sets in," says Reesing. "After fighting so hard in the second half, getting back to the point that it was a one-possession game and then to come up short after having to fight so hard to get back in it ..."

He slowly rose to his feet, a divot of gold-painted turf wedged in the upper reaches of his facemask. He had never experienced defeat as a starter at Kansas. Now he was trudging off the field, a memento embedded in his helmet for a national TV audience to see. The swagger was gone. He was out of bullets.

"The lasting memory I have of that game is Reesing trying to dig the sod out of his helmet, and he can't get it all," DeArmond says. "It's packed in there. Hence, Sod Reesing. That poor boy, in Missouri lore, is forever going to be known as Sod Reesing."

"I still see pictures of that all over the place," Reesing says, sounding somewhat resigned.

As is his custom, Alden had made his way to the field to take in the end of the game. Win or lose, he is always there to shake Pinkel's hand. Watching nervously with his wife, Rockie, and Alnutt, Alden had a perfect view of the clinching play. He was standing under the goal post in the east end zone, so close to the action he could have assisted Williams on the tackle. Reesing went down in a heap, and like that, Alden was the athletic director of the No. 1 college football team in the country.

Amid the bedlam, he was inexplicably drawn to a black-and-gold attired Mizzou fan celebrating in the first row of the end zone seats. Alden's voice quivers and his eyes well up as he relives the moment. He is sitting in his office at Mizzou Arena, almost five years later. He has to stop several times to collect himself.

"Rockie and I are standing there with Alnutt," he says. "I turn around and there's a guy, he's 70-plus years old, probably 80-plus. He's a Mizzou guy. He's crying like a baby. And he's yelling at me, saying, 'I never thought I'd see this before I died.'

"I'm looking at this guy, and Rockie is hanging on me crying and Mark is crying and this old man—I have no idea who he is—he's crying and yelling, 'Mike! Mike! Thank you! Thank you! Thank you!' Not just to me, but to all of us."

> **"I turn around and there's a guy, he's 70-plus years old, probably 80-plus," Alden says. "He's a Mizzou guy. He's crying like a baby. And he's yelling at me, saying, 'I never thought I'd see this before I died.'"**

A dozen seconds remained, and KU needed to recover the ball farther downfield to have any chance for a miracle score. Mangino called for a squib kick, but Webb booted the ball far too hard. Marcus Woods recovered and fell to the ground 45 yards downfield, at the Missouri 35. Daniel took a knee.

Just this once, Brian Brooks was O.K. with that.

"The border belongs to the Tigers!" Musburger proclaimed.

It was over: Missouri 36, Kansas 28.

Pandemonium reigned. Matter wasn't surprised as much by the players' euphoria as he was by what he saw in the coaches' eyes. "A few of them were sobbing," he says. "Others seemed blown away by the moment, didn't know how to react. It was like they had won more than a national title."

After the early recruiting rejections, the first-game loss to Bowling Green, the debacle at Troy, the 50-point beat-downs, the death of Aaron O'Neal and hearing loud whispers that they weren't capable of—or shouldn't even dare consider—ascending to such heights, maybe Pinkel and his staff had.

"It was seven years of wondering whether this was the right group to take the program where it's never been," says Matter. "That night, at least, they were. It was more than winning the division, more than beating Kansas, more than a national championship. It was everything. It was seven years of skepticism. *What's good enough for Missouri football? Is eight wins good enough? Is there a higher ceiling?* That night affirmed everything they were doing."

Gregorian says the celebration was unlike any other he had witnessed.

"Andy Hill was going out of his mind," he says of the Tigers' receivers coach. "He was hugging and kissing everyone he saw. It speaks to the Missouri athletic experience. That whole thing came from a bigger place, a place that had never had anything to celebrate like that in generations. Here they were against the Evil Empire and having this incredible breakthrough. My Missouri tenure has involved covering some bad football, and you know the usual catalog of Missouri disappointments— all that stuff that is emblazoned on the minds of Missouri fans. It's part of the DNA. To have this grandest of moments was unbelievable."

At a brief midfield ceremony, Pinkel accepted the Lamar Hunt Trophy from Peterson and Clark Hunt. Daniel did a quick interview with ABC's Lisa Salters, then was hustled to the ESPN set. Rucker headed straight for the War Drum, the traveling trophy that went to the winner of the oldest college football rivalry west of the Mississippi. ("I scouted where it was before the game," he says.) Some Tigers climbed the Arrowhead walls and exchanged hugs and high-fives with delirious fans.

Zo Williams went to the 25-yard line.

Chapter 19

Orange Crush

The ride back to Lawrence was quick. It only seemed to take as long as the Jayhawks' odyssey to Arrowhead. "The bus was quiet going home," Mangino says. "It always is when you lose. It's a time for reflection."

As he sat in his customary seat at the front of the bus, Mangino thumbed through the game book—the thick packet of statistics that Strauss and his crew had compiled for the media. One number jumped off the page: 37:25.

It was the amount of time, in minutes and seconds, the Missouri offense had been on the field. The Tigers got off a staggering 93 snaps, six more than they had in any of their first 11 games and almost 14 above their season average. As for the time of possession, seven times Mizzou had controlled the ball for 30 minutes or less, often because touchdowns came quickly in the hurry-up attack. At Arrowhead, the Tigers scored touchdowns *and* bled the clock. KU was in uncharted waters as well. In its first 11 games, the Jayhawks' defense was on the field an average of 69 snaps and for never more than 78 plays (versus Colorado) or 32:41 (Southeastern Louisiana). The other telling stat: For the first time all season, Kansas, which led the country in turnover margin, didn't produce a takeaway. There were also those two costly interceptions.

"I knew we would throw the ball decently because we had all year," Mangino says. "I felt like we needed to establish a run game so we could control the clock. On defense, we knew if we let Chase sit back there, find a receiver and throw it, he would be really dangerous. We had to get some pressure on him, and we had to do a good job of disguising some looks.

"I know this: We left our defense out on the field all night, and you can't do that. We didn't have enough sustained drives, we didn't control the ball, we had too many three-and-outs."

And despite being the beneficiaries of an uncharacteristically high 14 Mizzou penalties (while being flagged only twice themselves), the Jayhawks couldn't capitalize.

Herbstreit was right. No offense was more dynamic than Missouri's, and no quarterback was hotter than Daniel. For the 12th time in 12 games, the Tigers surpassed the 30-point mark; they were the only team in the country to accomplish that. As they had done to so many opponents before, they gashed KU with their underrated and often overlooked ground attack (151 yards on 43 attempts), and Daniel spread his career-high 40 completions to nine receivers.

"The linebackers didn't do a good job of rerouting middle routes and seams," Mangino says. "They ran some seams that should have at least been rerouted or disrupted. The bottom line is that if we hadn't left those kids out on the field all night, they would've done a better job."

Some of the Jayhawks insisted they simply ran out of time, that the outcome would have been reversed if the game had been just a few minutes longer. Yet while there is no debate that Reesing and the offense got in a rhythm in the fourth quarter, the fact remains that KU's eighth-ranked defense couldn't stop Daniel and the Mizzou offense. Consider that over the final 55:37, the Tigers punted twice—once when they went hurry-up at the end of the first half and not again until they ran three plays into the middle of the line while bleeding the clock in the final minute. Plus, the play-calling was especially conservative when Mizzou got into range for Wolfert's two fourth-quarter field goals.

"We left our defense out on the field all night," Mangino says, "and you can't do that."

Christensen admits as much. "I had a tendency to do that because we had so much confidence in our defense," he says.

Another hot topic was whether the result would have been different had the game been played in Lawrence. Mangino would have none of it. "That's not an excuse," he says. "I got upset with people trying to say we got cheated. Baloney. They outplayed us in the crucial areas of the game, and that was it."

Young was never crazy about the notion of moving the game to Arrowhead. "I thought it was a huge mistake, because Kansas City is in Missouri," he says. "But I'm just a peon. I'm not the one who makes the decision to move those games." At the same time, he's not sure a change of venue would have mattered. "They probably would have whipped our butts in Lawrence, too," he says.

In the end, Daniel was the difference. "Reesing was good," says Kelly. "Daniel was terrific."

That would be an understatement. The video-game statistics—40 of 49 for 361 yards and three TDs—only begin to tell the story. Many cynics may have rolled their eyes, but this was the kind of performance Daniel had come to expect from his team. Flash back to Rucker's recollection of how Daniel talked about winning championships as a freshman and the impromptu conversation with Kelly in the El Paso airport 11 months earlier. Why couldn't the Tigers aspire to be like Oklahoma and Ohio State and LSU and the other household names in college football? They just needed someone to show them the way.

"Chase cemented himself in Missouri's psyche," says DeArmond, speaking not only of Daniel's teammates but also of a fan base that had been programmed to think that when things could go wrong, they usually did. *"I won't let you lose. I won't."*

As the Tigers boarded their buses for a raucous ride back to Columbia, they did so confident they would be sitting at the top of the college football world when the polls were released on Sunday. So what if West Virginia had hammered Connecticut, 66–21. The Mountaineers were playing in Morgantown, while Mizzou had impressively dispatched No. 2 on a neutral field.

Christensen made the two-hour ride home with his wife and three children. The kids were old enough to attend the game and understand the summit their father had climbed. Buffalo Wild Wings? "I'm sure we had the conversation on where we were after that first game at Missouri and where we were now," he says. And what was Susie Christensen's state of mind?

"She was pretty fired up," says Dave.

Rucker thought about his older brother, Mike. "He had experienced it all throughout college, and that's what I was used to," T says. "He won three national championships. I was finally on the team that had No. 1 next to its name. He and I had something else in common."

Sure enough, when the AP poll was released on Sunday, Mizzou was a comfortable No. 1. The Tigers received 45 of 65 first-place votes and were 30 points clear of the Mountaineers. Most important, Missouri was No. 1 in the BCS standings. Unranked at the start of the season and even after wins over Illinois and Ole Miss, the Tigers were a victory over Oklahoma in the Big 12 championship game from playing for a national title. Or as Pat Forde, j-school Class of 1987 and then of ESPN.com, put it: "four quarters from the French Quarter."

Business took Alden back to Kansas City on Monday, and he opened the door to his hotel room at the downtown Marriott early that morning to find a copy of *USA Today* sitting at his feet. He was rushing to the gym for a workout, but the headline on the front page of the newspaper stopped him cold. Then he looked up and down the hall.

"They were lined up in front of every room, and every one of them had Mizzou on the front page," he says. "Not the front of the sports page. The front page! I went down to work out and I'm thinking, 'Every place in America that has one of these promotions, some person is waking up, getting that *USA Today* and Mizzou, No. 1 in the country, is on the front page.'"

The headline was significantly smaller than the task Pinkel and his staff had on their hands. Just a week earlier, the message to the players was that they were about to participate in the biggest game of their careers. What would the coaches say now?

"That Kansas win was like a national championship game," says Pinkel. "We're No. 1 in the nation. You talk about the week before being a big game. This was bizarre."

It was also markedly different.

"It seemed like we were on an island that week [against KU]," Ivey says. "Everyone else was away. We were able to focus really well. You talk about the perfect environment to prepare for that game, that was it. Now the students are back, and everybody wants to tell you how great you are. It didn't seem real. It was an awesome feeling, but I think it lasted too long. We didn't know how to refocus for the next one."

It was slow in coming, but the Tigers had finally unseated the Jayhawks as the surprise of college football. The media wanted to know about Mizzou's chances against Oklahoma; the players pointed out that Temple was healthy and would be ready for the rematch, that they'd most certainly play better than they had in Norman. Daniel appeared on the cover of *Sports Illustrated*, fist pumped, with the headline: "Mizzou, That's Who." He was billed as a Heisman contender. Turn in another performance like the one he had against KU and he just might overtake Tim Tebow.

(Though they didn't know it at the time, the Tigers even had the full attention of a former Commander in Chief. Stumping on the campaign trail in the spring of 2008, Bill and Hillary Clinton visited Columbia. Dave and Susie Christensen were invited to the on-campus reception and, figuring they might never get another opportunity to rub elbows with a U.S. President, they decided to attend. In the receiving line, Christensen told Clinton what he did for a living, and the ever-personable 42nd President became especially engaged. Clinton mentioned the showdown at Arrowhead.

"He said, 'I watched every minute of that game,' " Christensen recalls. "He said it was the best football game he had ever seen." Then, without missing a beat, Clinton asked: "Coach, is Chase Daniel as good a person as he appears to be?")

Lost in the excitement was concern over the health of Chase and Chase. So efficient was the offense at Arrowhead that nobody much noticed Coffman was on the field for only a handful of snaps in the second half. He limped around the practice field all week, the result of a right ankle he sprained in the second quarter. It wasn't just that Coffman turned his ankle; it was the way it happened.

"I twisted my ankle during the Oklahoma game [on Oct. 13]," he says. "It was getting better and better. Then I stepped on somebody's foot during an extra-point attempt [against Kansas], and I retwisted it."

Daniel wasn't feeling much better. The flu had knocked him off of his feet.

"I was absolutely as sick as a dog," he says. "Oh, my gosh. I barely got to practice that week. It was bad—the worst timing. You're one game away from playing for the national championship."

Just Missouri's luck. In the first meeting against Oklahoma, Daniel wore out the middle of the field with the two-headed monster at tight end. Coffman caught a team-high 10 passes for 102 yards, and Rucker chipped in six catches, including a last-second touchdown reception. Now as the Tigers boarded the charter for San Antonio, Coffman was in a walking boot, questionable for the biggest game in program history. Oklahoma was installed as a three-point favorite, and on the GameDay set, with the Alamo serving as a backdrop, Herbstreit said the keys to victory would be turnovers and red-zone offense. Corso slipped on a Tigers' head for the second consecutive week. "I *love* Missouri," he said. "I think they're going to New Orleans."

Coffman tested the tender ankle during pre-game drills, but he knew almost immediately he couldn't go. "I couldn't push off," he says. More than five years after the fact, he adds, "It's hard to talk about because it was such a big game, and it's hard not to be able to participate in something like that."

It was especially painful having to stand helplessly on the sideline and watch the game play out. Missouri scored first, on a 28-yard Wolfert field goal, and after the Sooners answered with a touchdown, the Tigers marched 75 yards. Again, the drive stalled, this time at the one-yard line, and Wolfert was summoned for another chip shot. "I don't like kicking 18-yard field goals," he says. "I knew that against Oklahoma we needed more than three points. An 18-yard field goal—that's as short as it gets."

Lamenting the absence of Coffman, Daniel says, "He was a great red-zone receiver. Tall dude. Great target."

Even after another Oklahoma touchdown, Mizzou was hanging around, and 14 seconds before halftime, Daniel capped an 84-yard drive with a four-yard touchdown run. Conventional wisdom said it was too early to be chasing points. But Christensen had a trick up his sleeve, and he used it on the two-point attempt. Maclin rocketed right on a double reverse—it was the same play on which he had scored twice in the first meeting, only to the other side of the field—but this time he pulled up at the five-yard line. Before being swallowed up by three Sooners, Maclin flipped a pass to Rucker, who was standing alone in the end zone. T crossed his arms as if to say, "Punked!"

In a mere 1:28 and over a combined 11 plays from scrimmage, 14–14 became 28–14. "When the momentum turned, it was like, 'Wow!'" Kelly says.

Mizzou gained 192 yards on 44 snaps in the first half, but the rushing total (95 yards on 20 attempts) was deceiving—Daniel ran for 20 on a scramble and another 19 came on an Alexander reverse. The Tigers had played their worst first half of the season on offense, yet as they headed to the locker room, the score was knotted at 14. They had weathered the early storm. They were 30 minutes from playing for the national championship.

"Here we go," says Rucker.

Missouri got a stop to start the second half, and taking over at its own seven-yard line, needed only seven plays to move across midfield. The offense was in a rhythm, and when Maclin ripped off a 22-yard run on a sweep left, the Tigers had a first down at the OU 25. As the third-quarter clock wound under eight minutes, the momentum was all on the side of the guys in black. The next score would be huge.

"You settle into the game," says Rucker. "You get comfortable and you play football."

Next, however, came the play that swung the momentum to the other sideline and started the spiral to a defeat that was as deflating as the previous week's victory was exhilarating. Out of the Swan formation,

Daniel rolled right. He was a step from getting outside when he was tripped up for a 10-yard loss on a shoestring tackle by defensive end Jeremy Beal, who had beaten the block of Gregory, the only lineman to Spieker's right. "We ran naked, just like we did against KU," says Yost. "The over route had a chance."

In other words, Mizzou may have been a shaken shoestring tackle from a 21–14 lead. In fact, Beal's tackle may have resulted in a 14-point swing. That's because the Tigers punted three plays later, and the Sooners responded with a seven-play, 80-yard touchdown drive.

The deficit was only seven points, but two snaps later, on second-and-one, came the play that broke Mizzou's back. It was eerily similar to the miscommunication that did in the Tigers in Norman. Daniel threw short over the middle to Rucker, but he was late to look back. "I turned real quick, and all I could do was get my hands on it," he says. "Mr. Johnny on the Spot was there again, and it fell right into his hands."

That would be Curtis Lofton, the Big 12 defensive player of the year, he of the fourth-quarter fumble return for a TD in Norman. This time Lofton returned the interception 26 yards, to the seven.

Rucker might have been late to turn around, but Daniel also took responsibility. "It was a high throw, too," he says. "An offense's worst nightmare is a tipped ball. It can go anywhere."

This time, Oklahoma scored in two plays. In a mere 1:28 and over a combined 11 plays from scrimmage, 14–14 became 28–14. "When the momentum turned, it was like, 'Wow!' " Kelly says.

Again, the Tigers had a quick answer, but for the third time a drive stalled inside the 20. Coffman was sorely missed, and now Missouri was playing without Alexander, who injured his left knee after coming down awkwardly at the end of his second-quarter run. Wolfert kicked a 32-yard field goal, but OU answered with 10 fourth-quarter points for a 38–17 victory.

Herbstreit had been on the money again. Missouri made four trips inside the 20 and kicked three field goals. Oklahoma produced five such drives and scored four touchdowns, while converting the game's only turnover into another TD.

In the end, OU was simply a bad matchup for the Tigers, or most any other team. Stoops' program was loaded with talent—17 Sooners who played in San Antonio would be selected in future NFL drafts, including four first-round picks, three second-rounders and three third-rounders.

"They had a fast-paced offense, they could run the ball, they got big on you, they'd change personnel groups," says Eberflus. "Certainly we should have played better than we did."

Oklahoma, says Yost, was the one defense that could account for the run *and* pressure Daniel with its front four, leaving the back seven to flood zones and disguise looks against Missouri's four- and five-receiver sets. "We lost our running game early," Yost says. "We couldn't beat them up front. They could run the ball when they wanted to, and we couldn't. You watch them against everybody else and then watch them against us. They're different. They have an [understanding] of what we do."

The fourth quarter was ugly. OU controlled the clock for 12:23. Mizzou ran six plays—a pair of three-and-outs—for a total of eight yards. "OU is OU," says Williams. "Stuff just didn't go our way."

As was the case with KU at Arrowhead, the moment may have been just too big for the Tigers. Seven days earlier, they had played an epic game against a bitter rival. Now they were facing a seasoned Oklahoma team with a coaching staff that had made a habit of appearing in the Big 12 title game—five of the previous six, to be exact.

"Not to take anything away from Oklahoma," says Kelly, "but I've always wondered if so much went into preparation for KU that Missouri didn't have a lot left in the tank."

Like Devine after the 1960 loss to the Jayhawks, which cost the Tigers a national championship, Pinkel is quick to take responsibility. "To get your guys ready to come back and play, to get rest and have that edge, play like we did the first time [against Oklahoma], I just didn't do a very good job," he says.

If there was any consolation, it was that the Tigers were headed to their biggest bowl game since the 1970 Orange Bowl. Most everyone penciled Mizzou in for a return trip to the Sunshine State. In the national championship game, Ohio State would face LSU, which backed in after West Virginia, a 29-point favorite, lost at home to Pitt. The Sugar Bowl took undefeated Hawaii to meet Georgia. The Rose Bowl stuck with tradition, using an at-large berth on three-loss, Big Ten runner-up Illinois to play USC. The Fiesta paired Oklahoma and West Virginia, the Big East champ. That left the Orange Bowl, which was looking for a team to match against Virginia Tech, the ACC champion. At No. 7 in the BCS and still a spot ahead of Kansas, Missouri seemed like a slam dunk.

In the week leading up to the Big 12 championship game, Alden talked by phone with Eric Poms, the Orange Bowl's executive director.

Alden says Poms wished him good luck and told him the folks in Miami were pulling for the Tigers to get to the BCS title game. "There was never any, 'If you win the game, you're playing for the national championship. If you lose it, we're taking you,' " says Alden. "There was never any of that. Nor did I ask them."

Big 12 rules require schools to channel any communication with the bowls through the commissioner's office. So if Alden wanted to talk to Poms, he was obligated to call the league, which would contact the Orange Bowl on his behalf. Likewise, the school is required to notify the league if a bowl reaches out. Both before and after the Oklahoma game, Alden says he followed protocol.

"Commissioner [Dan] Beebe reminded us that he and his staff would coordinate any communication with the bowls, because what they wanted to make sure was that people weren't lobbying," says Alden. "That's what our understanding was."

Big 12 bylaws don't allow for lobbying—specifically a school guaranteeing ticket sales, thereby making it more attractive to a bowl. Alden continued to follow protocol, but that didn't mean he wasn't feverishly burning up the phone lines. He stayed in constant contact with the Big 12 office, but around noon on Sunday, he began to hear rumblings that he shouldn't be booking any dinner reservations on South Beach. He remembers asking Beebe where his school stood with the Orange Bowl.

"'The way I took it was, 'Don't assume you're a lock for the Orange Bowl,' " Alden recalls. "'They can pick whoever they want.' I said, 'Commissioner, I understand that. But we want to make sure [Orange Bowl officials] know that we're 11–2 and we were the No. 1 team in the country not more than six hours ago. I'm hoping that's going to be an opportunity for us.' "

Perkins saw an opportunity for the Jayhawks as well. Could you blame him? Even if its 11 victories had come against teams that received exactly zero votes in the final regular-season AP poll, and even if it had been throttled for 36 points, 29 first downs and 539 yards in its most recent game by a team it was fighting for a lucrative bowl bid, KU was nevertheless the only one-loss, BCS-conference team in the country. This would be one of Perkins' easier sells.

"Lew Perkins, pulling whatever strings he did to get Kansas to the Orange Bowl," says Keegan, "even though it's not technically legal to pull any strings …"

Asked point-blank if he believes the school across the border failed to follow Big 12 protocol, Alden replies without hesitation: "I'm not saying that. I'm just saying that we were consistent in everything we were doing, and we were really disappointed when we found out the Orange Bowl had not selected us."

Beebe phoned to break the news. The next call came from Poms, and shortly thereafter, Cotton Bowl executive director Rick Baker happily extended the Tigers an invitation to Dallas. "There was a process, a system in place," Alden says. "I'd been communicating with Coach all morning. I think our kids, rightly so, assumed that they'd be going to the Orange Bowl, because we earned that."

It was as if Orange Bowl officials had witnessed only the fourth quarter of the game at the Alamodome ... and the last two minutes at Arrowhead.

KU's invitation was met with skepticism by most everybody outside of Lawrence—and even some inside the city limits. It would have been one thing if the Tigers had beaten the Jayhawks in, say, the middle of October, and Kansas had responded by reeling off a half-dozen victories. But Mizzou had beaten KU just a week earlier. Poms indicated that the Big 12 championship game had gotten away from the Tigers. Fair enough. At the same time, it was as if Orange Bowl officials had witnessed only the fourth quarter of the game at the Alamodome ... and the last two minutes at Arrowhead.

"That was Missouri's game," says DeArmond. "They should have been in the Orange Bowl. [Alden] played by the rules. And he shouldn't have. You want to know why Missouri left the Big 12? That's part of the reason."

Keegan agrees. "In a fair world, Missouri should have gone to the Orange Bowl," he says. "The fact that they didn't made their anger against the Big 12 so intense that they made an emotional decision and went to the SEC [in 2012]."

Poms was grilled on Kansas City radio, and even back in South Florida, the media questioned the selection. In a *Palm Beach Post* column headlined "Orange Bowl picked the wrong Big 12 team," Greg Stoda wrote, "The Tigers have a Heisman Trophy finalist in quarterback Chase Daniel, beat Kansas straight up and, despite the second loss to Oklahoma, remain ranked ahead of the Jayhawks in The Associated Press poll, the coaches' poll, the Harris Interactive poll and—here's the juicy Orange part—even the BCS rankings!"

"Missouri was where we were headed," Poms told Stoda, "but then that game [against Oklahoma] got away from them in the second half."

Actually, there were signs in the third quarter of a 14–14 game that the Tigers were going to be in trouble if they didn't beat the Sooners. KU and Oklahoma hadn't played during the regular season, of course, so in a live interview with Beebe during the telecast from San Antonio, Musburger threw out the possibility of a Sooners-Jayhawks meeting in the Fiesta Bowl. Musburger was prodding, but that didn't stop Beebe from saying that such a matchup could be "spectacular."

Asked by Herbstreit what he would say to the Missouri fans if the Tigers lost to Oklahoma and were "somehow" left out of a BCS bowl, Beebe replied, "That's a tough issue. … And with Kansas, the team they just beat going in [to a BCS game] perhaps, I'm sure that's hard. But this is what it's all about. It's about competition. I got the sense these guys wanted to play this game no matter what, no matter what's at risk."

You think? And if the selection process truly was all about competition, how were the Jayhawks even an option for a BCS bowl—at least when weighed against the Tigers?

Common sense said KU would have been best served by a Missouri victory in San Antonio. Each conference is allowed only two BCS selections, and three-loss OU would have effectively been eliminated from consideration. Now it sounded as if the Jayhawks couldn't lose. And they didn't, though the potential Big 12 showcase went kaput when West Virginia went down. Picking ahead of the Fiesta, the Orange Bowl snatched up Kansas.

The selection made no sense, but it was pretty simple, Kelly says. The moral of the story: Don't get beat on the night before BCS Selection Sunday, and most certainly don't get beat by 21 points on national television. "It brings the human element into the process," he says. "I think they thought that would have an impact on Missouri's ability to sell tickets for the Orange Bowl."

At least Daniel was headed to New York City for the Heisman ceremony. He may have lost the opportunity to win the most prestigious award in college football, but he was still invited to the party. Two days after the loss to Oklahoma, Daniel was notified he was one of four Heisman finalists, joining Tebow, McFadden and Hawaii quarterback Colt Brennan. Tebow became the first sophomore winner in the 74-year history of the award, while Daniel was a distant fourth. It was the highest finish by a Missouri player since Pitchin' Paul Christman was third in 1939.

"I've been around a lot of great quarterbacks," says Pinkel. "Not only that game [against KU], that was a signature for his season. He had a tremendous year. He was a finalist for the Heisman Trophy. I'm sitting there in New York City for the ceremony. How many coaches get a chance to do *that*?"

Still, the Orange Bowl snub left a bad taste in the mouth of every Missouri player, coach and fan. It was one thing to be passed over, but it was another to be shunned in favor of a team you had just soundly whipped. That the team was Kansas made the situation especially difficult.

"To this day I don't know how that happened," says Rucker. "I don't know how college football allows stuff like that to happen. Why would you send Kansas over us? We're ranked higher, we beat them and we ended their season."

The Tigers found a sympathetic voice in Strauss, of all people.

"They were *really* good," he says. "Kansas not only got the conference spotlight but also the national spotlight because they came out of nowhere. Everyone was overlooking Missouri, but they were *really* good. I remember that whole year feeling bad for Missouri. I was probably the only Kansas person who felt that way."

Later in December, Strauss flew to South Florida for an event to promote the Jayhawks' matchup with Virginia Tech. In the middle of the festivities, he recalls being pulled aside by an Orange Bowl official, and asked a curious question.

"Do you think we made the right choice?"

Chapter 20

Homecoming

The Cotton Bowl wasn't a bad consolation prize. Leigh and I may have left for the Northeast in late 1989, but we still called Dallas home. We had met in Big D, married there and still had family in the area. Mom couldn't travel, having suffered a debilitating stroke in the fall of 2004, so for the fourth consecutive year, we made the trek south to celebrate Christmas.

Dad would have undoubtedly demanded a ticket to the game, but he had left us—far too early, in 1993. His health had been in decline for a couple of years. It was tough to watch a man so full of life slip away. Best I can remember, the last football game he and I attended was the 1990 matchup between Princeton and Brown. He and Mom had come for a visit, and the two of us snuck off to historic Palmer Stadium on a splendid fall Saturday afternoon to watch the Ivy League programs square off. The game was uneventful; I had to resort to Google to find out who won (Princeton, 27-23). But it was football, and most important, I was taking it all in with Dad.

One thing I do remember from that afternoon was returning home and turning on the TV just in time to hear ABC's Keith Jackson say something like, "They'll be talking about that one in Columbia, Mo., for a long time." Other than the fact the Tigers had lost another football game, this time to Colorado, Dad and I had no idea what Jackson was talking about. Only later that day would we learn about the Fifth Down Game.

The year after Dad's death had been difficult for the family, but we were heartened when Leigh and I learned we were going to be parents. Steven Luke Godich was born in October 1994, one year and one day after Dad died. I'd say the timing was coincidental, except that Steven arrived two weeks early. Leigh went into labor at three o'clock on a stormy Friday morning in Norwalk, Conn., and Steven entered the world at 1:04 that afternoon, sun shining brightly. It's like Dad was saying, "I'm O.K. Get on with your lives already!" Leigh and I named our only child after his Grandpa Steve. The following day, my sister, Deborah, made a surprise visit from Dallas to meet her new nephew, walking into Leigh's hospital room on a Saturday afternoon to find the TV tuned to a college football game. Hey, the sound was muted.

Steven would develop a passion for sports that rivaled mine as a youngster. And, naturally, there was the small but significant generational connection. Just as I had quizzed Dad about the 1967 Richardson Eagles, Steven would interrogate me at every opportunity about the prospects for the 2007 Missouri Tigers.

We scrambled to find tickets for the Cotton Bowl, as the school's 17,000-seat allotment for the game against Arkansas sold out in 20 minutes.

Just as I had quizzed Dad about the 1967 Richardson Eagles, Steven would interrogate me at every opportunity about the prospects for the 2007 Missouri Tigers.

Not that it should have come as a surprise. The Tigers were playing in their first New Year's Day Bowl since 1969 (when Bob Dudney got his Orange Bowl watch). Dallas was also home to one of the school's largest alumni bases. No wonder 5,000 fans attended a pep rally at the Hilton Anatole, the team hotel, several days before kickoff.

Everything was falling into place. Sure, it stung to lose a BCS bid to Illinois (Rose) and especially Kansas, but in the grand scheme of things, the Tigers couldn't have picked a better bowl destination. The Lone Star State had become the recruiting gold mine Pinkel envisioned when he took the job. Seventeen Texans were on the 2007 roster, including starters Daniel, Weatherspoon, Alexander, Sulak, Hood and Tommy Chavis. Pinkel invited three dozen high school coaches to a pre-bowl practice at Texas Stadium, and every one of them attended.

"If you had to fall somewhere, that was a really, really good place to fall, because of the tradition and because of the masterful job the folks at the Cotton Bowl do with the teams," Kelly says.

That was all well and good, but Pinkel understandably feared a letdown. The Tigers had been 22 minutes from playing for the national championship. They had been passed over for a more prestigious BCS bowl in favor of two teams they had beaten. So Pinkel the psychologist went to work. At one of the first meetings after the players learned they were destined for Dallas, the coach mentioned three other national-title contenders that had been snubbed by the BCS over the years. Each of them laid an egg in its bowl game, including Kansas State, which fell to Purdue as a double-digit favorite in the 1996 Alamo Bowl.

"I'm going to tell you a story," Pinkel recalls saying to his players. "This is what happened because guys were moaning and crying and complaining about getting screwed over."

Not that they needed to be reminded, but the players got the message. "It was our chance to show why we should have been in the Orange Bowl," Rucker says. "If we had tanked that game, everybody would have said, 'Same ol' Mizzou. Why would we want them? They couldn't even beat Arkansas in the Cotton Bowl.' "

If the Tigers needed any extra motivation, they got it from a program that was in disarray, to say the least. The Razorbacks may have been coming off the upset of then-No. 1 LSU, but in the days after the game, embattled coach Houston Nutt took the Ole Miss job. The Hogs got an upgrade in Bobby Petrino, but the hire raised eyebrows most everywhere outside the state. Petrino, who has never seen a job interview he didn't like, had abruptly bolted after 13 games with the Atlanta Falcons, informing players of his departure by leaving a note in their lockers. (Petrino would watch the Cotton Bowl from the press box, with linebackers coach Reggie Herring calling the shots on the sideline.) Yet even amid the chaos, Arkansas fans were beating their SEC chests and making themselves heard around town.

"It was clear the Arkansas fans thought it wasn't going to be a game," Kelly says. "Even in the press conferences and the events [the Cotton Bowl] had for the two teams, it was pretty clear the Arkansas players didn't think it was going to be much of a game either."

If only they had taken a minute to consider what the Tigers were playing for. The highest end-of-season ranking in program history was within reach. There was the bitter taste left from the Big 12 title game, a taste that had been lingering for almost a month. And were Williams and Rucker really going to stand for ending their college careers on a two-game skid?

For a segment that aired during the pre-game show, Kelly invited Zo and T to sit down for one last interview. It was taped a couple of days before the game, in the cavernous atrium of the Anatole. There were some laughs —there always were when those two got together—but it was mostly a time for reflection. Among other things, the two cornerstones talked about what the college experience meant to them, the state of the program when they arrived in Columbia and the indelible mark they were leaving.

"It was striking to listen to those guys talk about the things they had dreamed of," says Kelly, "because they came to Missouri on a dream."

On the day before the game, the Cotton Bowl hosts a luncheon. Every bowl has one. The coaches shake hands, speak glowingly of each other's program, pose for pictures. Captains are introduced. Slick highlight videos are shown. The cheerleaders might cheer; a band might fire up the fight song for each school. Williams says he was standing next to Pinkel when a Cotton Bowl official approached the coach and said he would be asked to make a few general comments.

"So [Pinkel] says, 'Here are my coaches, here are my captains, here are my seniors, happy to be here, great opponent, back on the bus,'" recalls Williams.

As these things go, the affair was uneventful. At least it was until Herring stepped in front of the mike. First, he butchered Pinkel's name, calling him *Pinkney*. Then Herring sang the praises of his two star running backs: McFadden and Felix Jones. Herring said he felt sorry for anybody who had to defend the dynamic duo. Herring wasn't being arrogant. Maybe he was just trying to be funny. Whatever his intention, the comments could not have come across any worse. The Razorbacks most certainly had the Tigers' full attention.

"It was no big deal to me," Pinkel says. "But I had players come up to me and say, 'That pisses me off. He doesn't even know your name?' I'm thinking, 'Guys, lighten up. Are you kidding me?'"

As the Tigers boarded the buses for the trip back to their hotel, Pinkel sensed they were ready to play. By the time they convened for meetings two hours later, there was no doubt. "Our guys were ready to play that minute," he says. "It was pretty cool."

The Tigers arose early on the first morning of 2008 to bitter cold temperatures. It's for that reason the Cotton Bowl, one of the original four New Year's Day bowls, was left out of the national-championship rotation. January weather in Big D is too unpredictable. There have been years when players have sweltered in 90-degree heat. Then there have been times like 1979, when an ice storm crippled the city and flu-ridden Joe Montana famously led Notre Dame to a comeback victory over Houston.

I had been to too many Cotton Bowls to count. I was there on New Year's Day 1970, when James Street rallied Texas to the national championship with a 21-17 victory over Notre Dame, the Irish's first bowl game in 45 years, and for the rematch the following year. I also remember the 1974 matchup between Nebraska and Texas. As luck would have it, my family had gone to a dinner theater with out-of-town guests, and the Cornhuskers football team happened to be there. During intermission, Dad struck up a conversation with a Nebraska offensive lineman, and the next thing I knew he was digging in his pocket to buy four tickets to the game. Then there was the 1978 meeting between Texas and Notre Dame. I was a junior at Mizzou, and Neys got his first taste of Texas.

For this game, our seats were on the Missouri side, 15 rows up on the 20-yard line. They came from Brooks, who was sitting somewhere near the 50. Neys and Karen were tucked in an end-zone corner. Leigh, Steven and I were joined by Steve Rocca, a 1987 graduate of the School of Journalism who had flown in from Virginia. Through mutual friends, Rocca-mon and I became friends in the late 1990s. He was equally invested in the '07 Tigers, and every Saturday included a phone call to discuss that week's opponent. Dudney was watching from his home in McLean, Va. Steven didn't know it, but his GrandPa Steve was sitting right alongside us.

As we settled into our seats, I wasn't surprised to see the sea of red on the other side of the field. Arkansas fans travel well, and they already were in full throat, warming up by calling the Hogs again and again. But I was stunned—stunned!—by what I saw on the north side of the stadium. It was packed in black and gold, 35,000 strong. I wondered if the Orange Bowl officials were watching.

With its strong Dallas-area alumni base, Missouri had long been on the radar of Cotton Bowl officials, but as he stood on the field with Alden during pre-game festivities, Baker had to do a double-take.

"It was crazy," Alden says. "You go in the Cotton Bowl, that venerable stadium. And you knew that Razorback fans were going to show up. You *think* your fans are going to show up really well. And then you turn around … Rick Baker's standing next to me saying, 'Son of a gun. You guys really showed.'

"We're playing in the Cotton Bowl, Pat Summerall is calling the game, and we've got 35,000 fans in black and gold having the best time in Dallas, Texas."

Again, Alden gets emotional, having to stop a couple of times to collect his thoughts. "You brought me back to a place I haven't been for a while," he tells me. "In this business we get so caught up in, O.K., what do we do next? All of a sudden you look back and think, 'Son of a buck. Five years ago, that was something.' "

One of the features of the Cotton Bowl is the ramp at the east end of the stadium that leads from the locker rooms to the field. It is not an especially wide piece of real estate, maybe a dozen yards wide. Fans squeeze against the wall to glimpse the players, so close they can almost touch them. When the two teams left their respective locker rooms at the same time, Ivey found himself in the middle of an unplanned pre-game festivity.

"That was intense because we had to go through the same tunnel," he says. "They had a coaching staff that was gone, an interim coach. If there was ever a chance for there to be an altercation … Their players were yelling over our coaches as we tried to keep everybody separated. It was the closest I have been to physical chaos."

It was also about as close as Arkansas came to putting up a fight. T called tails, because, as we all know, "tails never fails." The Razorbacks won the toss and took the ball, and though they moved 48 yards, the drive stalled and Alex Tejada missed a 35-yard field goal. For much of the rest of the day, Arkansas' performance was a comedy of errors, made only worse by the all-red uniforms the players wore to honor retiring athletic director Frank Broyles. Consider:

• Trailing 7–0 late in the first quarter and facing a fourth-and-four at the Missouri 35, the Hogs called a fake punt. It appeared the play was going to work, but a split-second after the snap, whistles blew. Somebody on the Arkansas sideline had called timeout. So the Razorbacks lined up in punt formation and … Ran. The. Same. Fake. Again! This time the Tigers stuffed the play for a one-yard loss.

• Kicking off to start the second half, Arkansas attempted an onside kick. The Tigers recovered and needed only six plays to cover 48 yards and take a 21–0 lead.

• Four plays after thwarting a third-quarter Missouri threat with a fumble recovery, the Hogs returned the favor. Weatherspoon blitzed off the edge and tipped a pass to the right flat to Moore, who returned his school-record eighth interception of the season 26 yards for a touchdown.

• And in the fourth quarter, linebacker Adrian Davis intercepted a Daniel screen pass, only to fumble the ball back after a hard hit by Daniel, of all people.

Pinkel knew the Tigers were walking a fine line against the Razorbacks, who were playing for an interim coach who had already made it known he wouldn't be returning to Fayetteville in 2008. "If they got going, I thought they'd build on the momentum," Pinkel says. "But if you hit them in the mouth a few times, it could also go the other way."

Did the Tigers ever hit the Razorbacks in the mouth. Arkansas was intent on shutting down Daniel and the Tigers' passing game. That meant playing man to man all over the field, employing press coverage, bumping receivers off their routes before they could get off the line of scrimmage. The problem was that Daniel was perfectly content taking whatever the defense gave him. Exhibit A: Mizzou's Oct. 20 game against Texas Tech, when Daniel threw it 20 times and the Tigers ran it 50. Certainly the Razorbacks had studied the video from that game.

The Missouri coaches, on the other hand, didn't have a lot of video on how Arkansas defended empty- and one-back sets, but they knew this much: The Razorbacks played what's called a man-free press, so when Tigers receivers were jostled at the line, they were instructed, Yost says, to "just run off"—or down the field.

The next concern was the defensive end, who, Yost adds, "was really, really good about watching the quarterback, because it's man coverage and there's nobody else there." At that point, it became a case of simple arithmetic.

"Now you're blocking five on five," Yost says. "If we get five on five with our splits and our size and let our back have space, we knew we're going to be in good shape. They were so committed to stopping the pass. They lined up one time with three linemen and a 'backer. We thought, 'We can run on that.' "

And run it the Tigers did. More specifically, the Cotton Bowl turned into the Tony Temple Show. In the days leading up to the game, Temple, perhaps more than anybody, had grown tired of the hoopla over McFadden and Jones. Nary an interview passed without Temple's having to answer a question about the pair. The first of his career-high four rushing touchdowns came on a 22-yard dash that he took off tackle and then down the left sideline. In the first three quarters, Temple also broke off runs of 22, 22, 38, 19, 14 and 14 yards. So dominant was the Tigers' offensive line (and so stubborn if not clueless were the Razorbacks) that at one point Daniel got on the phone and told Christensen and Yost, "Run it on every snap. They've got no answer for that."

Though he was excited about the opportunity to showcase his arm in the shadow of his hometown, Daniel was perfectly happy to cede the stage.

"I was off, and they weren't allowing us to throw," he says. "Two-man coverage is one of the hardest things to throw against. But with two-man coverage, there's no one responsible for me or the running back. You have to go with your hot hand. Sometime it was going to be me. Most of the time it was going to be us and our receivers and Tony and all of us working together. But that game it was unbelievable."

In the days leading up to the Cotton Bowl, one of the objectives the Tigers talked about was sending Temple out with a 1,000-yard rushing season. He held out faint hope of a medical redshirt after the ankle sprain limited his freshman campaign to those six carries in Lincoln, but Temple says, "I had to go into the Cotton Bowl thinking it would be my last game."

Considering he needed 242 yards to hit the magic number, the ambition seemed far-fetched. Yet Temple excelled in big games, and as the fourth quarter started, Missouri was leading 28–7, and he was sitting on 232 yards. Yes, sitting. His left hamstring had tightened up; in fact, after ripping off a nine-yard run on the second play of the fourth quarter, Temple pretty much figured his day—and his career—was over. He had given way to Jackson.

It was some way to go out: On the final carry of his college career, Temple got his 1,000 yards, broke one of the game's most storied records in style and scored a touchdown.

On the Missouri sideline, however, Saunders was lobbying to get Temple back on the field. Not only was he a yard shy of 1,000, but Temple also was closing in on one of the most storied records in Cotton Bowl history: the 265 rushing yards produced by Rice's Dicky Maegle in a 1954 New Year's Day victory over Alabama. (Maegle was famously credited with a 95-yard touchdown after helmetless fullback Tommy Lewis sprang off the Bama bench and tackled Maegle as he streaked down the sideline.) It was no secret where Temple stood. His rushing total was flashed repeatedly on the giant video board above the east end zone.

"I remember Tommy saying, 'Just four first downs to the record,'" Temple says. Actually, 2½ first downs would have sufficed, but Temple didn't even know if he could run two yards on his tender hammy. So he told his teammate, "Tommy, I have one play left."

From the Arkansas 40 with 8:43 left, Temple limped onto the field. Christensen called *Rhino Left*. Three receivers were flanked to the left; one to the right. The play was designed for Temple to run left, behind Madison and Luellen. Temple, however, didn't know if he could cut off the left leg, and at the snap his instincts took over. It was not unlike the momentum-changing run from the goal line against Kansas. This time he ran directly behind Spieker. Just as he was coached, the defensive end darted straight upfield toward Daniel. The middle of the field was wide open; Temple ran a good 10 yards before he even saw a red jersey. At the 27, bad leg and all, he eluded a tackler with a pirouette. He was still running free, but when he got inside the 10, he began dragging his leg as if he were a contestant in a three-legged race. At the five, an Arkansas defender jumped on his back, but Temple dragged him across the goal line and collapsed in the end zone. Exhausted and his leg basically numb, he had to be carried off the field, by Daniel and Luellen. It was some way to go out: On the final carry of his college career, Temple got his 1,000 yards, broke one of the game's most storied records in style and scored a touchdown.

"I thank God for giving me peace," Temple says. "He gave me peace with that last game—that last carry, that last touchdown, the record."

It was a run and a rushing performance that symbolized what these Tigers were all about. Playing a half-hour from his hometown, Daniel, who in terms of completion percentage would have his worst game as a collegian (12 of 29 for a season-low 136 yards with completions to only four receivers), could easily have demanded center stage and insisted that Christensen and Yost open up the offense. Yet Daniel saw what was working and urged the coaches to stick with the run. In the final game of his college career, Rucker caught three passes for 19 yards, yet the co-captain wasn't about to question the play-calling. "We were there to win the football game," Rucker says. "I caught 84 balls that year. What was I going to complain about?"

During the fourth quarter, a party broke out on the sunny side of the Cotton Bowl. The Missouri faithful alternated between chants of "Toe-NEE! Toe-NEE!" and "M-I-Z" "Z-O-U." One bearded gentleman strutted up and down our aisle flashing a sign that read, "Razorback tastes a lot like Jayhawk!" The Tigers and their fans were in the sun, a glittering sea of black and gold (and a stark contrast to the cold, shady, ghost-town-of-a-scene across the field). Daniel gave way to Patton, and after the clock hit zero in a 38–7 victory, the Tigers accepted the Cotton Bowl trophy in the northeast corner of the stadium, a stone's throw from where we were sitting. Nobody wanted to leave. Rucker hoisted the hardware over his head. So did Williams. LaRhonda Alexander was there to see it, thankful she kept trucking up I-44 on that December day in 2002.

Almost five years later, Pinkel points to the events of the previous afternoon in a ballroom of a downtown Dallas hotel. "It was a get-your-mind-right luncheon," he says. "It shows the power of the mental side of competition. Ultimately when you get to our level, that generally is the difference in the outcome—where you are focus-wise and the ability to handle that and play at a high level."

At the post-game press conference, Temple, who ran for 281 yards on only 24 carries, said all the right things, thanking his coaches and his offensive linemen. He reflected on his four years at Mizzou, content that if this was where his college career had to end, he couldn't think of a better way to go out. Asked about breaking a storied record, Temple innocently replied: "Who's Dicky Maegle?" (Contacted at his home in Houston, the 73-year-old Maegle said he thought if anybody was going to break his record, it would have been one of the two Arkansas backs. He added that the Razorbacks could've done a better job of tackling.)

Ford and Kelly embraced in a long hug, and then Ford said, "You know what's special about this? Every single person in our program is on the same page.'"

Not a word was mentioned about how fortunate Temple was to be on the field from the first snap, that he had been late to a team meeting after falling asleep in his hotel room on the eve of the game, that Christensen told Pinkel he believed a suspension was in order. "I was madder than a hatter at Tony Temple," Christensen says, adding with a laugh, "Coach Pinkel was calmer than I was, which is unusual."

The Gary Pinkel of 2004 very well may have benched his running back, maybe for the first quarter (when Temple ran five times for 52 yards). But this was a different Gary Pinkel. He says the situation would have been handled the same way had it occurred before a non-conference game in Columbia. He is quick to add that he has never suspended a player for being late to a meeting. But Pinkel had to know the Cotton Bowl would be Temple's last game. And maybe, just maybe, Pinkel had a flashback to that 2004 game in Lincoln, where a redshirt was burned and a heralded recruit finished with a freshman stat line that read: one game, six carries, 13 yards.

As Pinkel, Temple and the Missouri traveling party boarded the buses for the trip to the airport, Kelly bumped into Ford, the cornerbacks coach and lead recruiter in St. Louis. He was one of the assistants Pinkel had brought with him from Toledo. Toledo! So long ago, it now seemed. Ford and Kelly embraced in a long hug, and then Ford said, "You know what's special about this? Every single person in our program is on the same page."

Christensen, who in late 2008 was named the head coach at Wyoming, reflects fondly on the special season. "The part that people don't realize is they were great kids," he says. "My wife brings this up all the time. I would come home with this big smile on my face, and I would tell her how much fun it was going to work and to practice. We had no prima donnas. At all.

They were great kids to work with. They practiced their asses off. Every day. They never complained.

"That year was the most fun I've had coaching."

Six days after the Cotton Bowl, LSU, which backed into the national championship game only after Mizzou and West Virginia lost on the first Saturday in December, defeated Ohio State, 38–24, in New Orleans. As I watched those Tigers stroll to victory, I grew convinced that the Missouri Spread would have run circles around the Buckeyes, that the Tigers' defense would've swarmed the lead-footed Big Ten champs.

Mizzou would have to be satisfied with a school-record 12 victories and a No. 4 ranking in the AP poll, the best finish in program history. Along the way, the Tigers ascended to No. 1 in the poll and the BCS standings. Fans for seventh-ranked Kansas still like to gloat about getting the BCS invitation at Missouri's expense (KU validated its season with a 24–21 victory over Virginia Tech), but any Jayhawks follower in his right mind will tell you he would gladly trade that trip to Miami for a 2007 victory at Arrowhead. Instead, the folks in Lawrence will have to forever live with the fact that Missouri prevailed in the biggest athletic event the two bitter rivals have ever played against one another.

"People still talk about that game," Mangino told me five years later. "Even down here in Florida, people stop me on the street and say, 'I remember that game.' "

On the day Pinkel was hired in November 2000, not long after the jarring introductory press conference, alumni and fans made sure he understood the intensity of the rivalry, of the importance of beating KU. Every game against the Jayhawks was significant, but in 2007? The stakes could not have been higher.

"I'm glad I was a part of it," Pinkel says. "That will go down as the greatest game between those two schools ever."

He pauses, then cracks the slightest of grins.

"I'm glad we won it."

Acknowledgements

This project began in July 2010, on a steamy Thursday in Columbia, Mo. In the morning I laid out my vision for the book with Gary Pinkel and Chad Moller. After lunch at Booches and a visit to the state historical wing of Ellis Library, I stopped at a Starbucks across the street from the School of Journalism. The heat was unbearable—even for this native Texan. The respite also gave me a chance to ponder whether I really had it in me to write a book. Where would I even start?

As I sipped on an iced tea lemonade, a gentlemen took a seat in the cushy leather chair next to me. He mentioned he had seen me in Ellis and was curious to know what I was up to. I told him about my idea and that I was doing some very preliminary research on the Border War. He introduced himself as Mike Snodgrass and mentioned he taught history at the university. He said he couldn't be of any help on the early feud between Missourians and Kansans, but he was quick to add, "I know somebody who can. He's doing his doctorate on guerilla warfare during the Civil War. Would you like his name?"

That was the moment I knew I had to write this book. Mike passed along Joe Beilein's phone number, and I was on my way. I didn't cross the goal line without a lot of help.

I wrote this book without taking any time off from my job at *Sports Illustrated*. I will forever be indebted to Terry McDonell, Jim Herre, Paul Fichtenbaum, Chris Stone and David Clarke for their patience and understanding. Thanks also to Jim Gorant, Richard Demak, Mark Beech, Hank Hersch, Gabe Miller, Dick Friedman and Steve Fine. Jack McCallum, Tim Layden, Michael Bamberger, Bill Nack, Peter King, Austin Murphy and Stewart Mandel coached this neophyte through the book-writing process. Without hesitation, former SI colleague Joe Posnanski graciously agreed to write the foreword. Miriam Marseu, Nate Gordon and Don Delliquanti searched frame after frame from the game at Arrowhead to find the perfect images. Karen Carpenter tutored me on photo rights, while Bill Frakes and David Klutho generously donated images. Chris Hercik drew up a game plan for the photo act, and Liana Zamora executed it.

Not many publishers would take a flier on a rookie author, but Bob Snodgrass (no relation to Mike) of Ascend Books did. Jeffrey Flanagan treated my copy with kid gloves and patiently heard me out on all of my manuscript revisions, Beth Brown pulled me through the production process and Cheryl Johnson designed the eye-popping cover and made my words easy on the eyes.

This project would not have been possible without the cooperation of Gary Pinkel. Quite simply, Gary adopted me into the Missouri football family. Likewise, Chad Moller was always introducing me to people and digging up phone numbers, statistics and photographs, among other things. I would have been lost without Chad's guidance. Dave Christensen, Dave Yost, Matt Eberflus, Pat Ivey and John Kadlec shared insight and anecdotes. And even as he was overseeing the athletic department's move to the SEC, Mike Alden, with an assist from Sandy Matthew, made time for an extended sit-down interview. Later, Mike dug through his notes and supplied meticulous details about his coaching search.

The impact of Lorenzo Williams and Martin Rucker in the turnaround of Missouri football can't be overstated. Zo and T were cornerstones of the program. I saw it firsthand in the summer of 2010, at Zo's benefit golf tournament in Springfield. I was invited by Brian Cheever, the event chairman, and more than a dozen Tigers were in town to help Zo raise money for local charities. When I mentioned to a player how impressive it was to see such a strong turnout for a former teammate, he replied, "We'll follow Zo anywhere."

I talked to many Tigers for this book: Zo, T, Chase Daniel, Chase Patton, Jason Ray, William Moore, Tony Temple, Chase Coffman, Jeff Wolfert, Sean Weatherspoon, Jeremy Maclin and Danario Alexander. They are more than great football talents; they are also outstanding representatives of the University of Missouri.

I never had the opportunity to meet Aaron O'Neal, but I felt as if I knew him after visiting with Bob Bunton. I was lucky to meet Lamar Hunt. I was still finding my way on the NFL beat at SI when Leigh and I attended the league meetings in the spring of 2000 in Palm Beach, Fla. We were sitting alone at a dinner function one night when Lamar and his wife, Norma, asked if they could join us. The Hunts and the Godiches—shooting the breeze. Picture that. Carl Peterson saw Lamar's vision through. Then he outlined for me how he brought the historic game to Arrowhead.

The folks across the border were equally gracious with their time and insight. I made a new friend in Mark Mangino, who enlightened me on the finer points of football. Todd Reesing was as fiery on the phone as he was on the football field. It was a treat to talk to Bill Young, a straight shooter with an encyclopedic knowledge of the game. Tom Keegan, a former colleague at *The National*, and Mike Strauss were invaluable sources on all things KU. Finally, what can you say about Don Fambrough? He invited me into his house in November 2010, and before I could finish briefing him on my background, he groused, "I know. You're one of them." Then he spent the next 90 minutes regaling me with stories. Sure, Don despised all things Missouri, but he also had a passion for his alma mater that was unrivaled. What's so wrong with that?

I thought I knew everything there was to know about Missouri football, but I got schooled by a quartet of long-time followers of the program. Dave Matter is only the best college football beat writer around. The *Columbia Daily Tribune* was lucky to have him, and the *St. Louis Post-Dispatch* was smart to hire him away. Vahe Gregorian painted a vivid picture of the recruiting struggles in St. Louis. Nobody holds court like Mike DeArmond. Fittingly, we met at Willie's in Kansas City. He talked. I listened. And Mike Kelly's storytelling is as entertaining as his call of a Missouri football game.

I also leaned on media relations directors around the country. Thanks to Tim Harkins (Wyoming) and Gavin Lang (Oklahoma State), as well as Rich Dalrymple (Dallas Cowboys), Reggie Roberts (Atlanta Falcons), Greg Bensel and Doug Miller (New Orleans Saints) and Harvey Greene (Miami Dolphins).

Vince Doria and Ken Boudreau opened the ESPN vault to find game film dating back 35 years.

Joe Beilein's perspective on the Border War was fascinating, and he was among my biggest fans when my reporting was in its infancy. Paul Stuewe passionately gave his take from the Kansas side, and Richard Sunderwirth took me back to Osceola. Amy Brachmann did the heavy lifting with her reporting on the Civil War and the early years of the rivalry. And Bob Dudney helped get me started in journalism and shared memories from his days at Richardson High and Mizzou.

Last fall, I recruited Steve Rocca as my editor and therapist. When I was kicking around the idea to write a book, Steve was the one person who suggested I think really hard before diving in. When I made the leap and I asked him to be the caretaker of my copy, he kept me on track, subtly asking where the hell I was going with a thought and always available for those midnight phone calls when I was stuck, frustrated or just plain pissed off at a player or an agent who wouldn't respond to my queries. Katherine, you can have your husband back.

Karen and Pat Neylon run the best bed and breakfast in mid-Missouri. Their door is always open, and the beer is always cold. Neys and Karen are like family. Leigh, Steven and I are grateful to have such special friends.

Mike Bevans has been a colleague and a mentor dating to 1984, but more than that he is a special friend who has always been there for my family. Brian Brooks, an invaluable source for this book, took me under his wing in 1975, lined me up with two interviews when there were no jobs to be had and has always had the answers to my tough questions. I've worked with many great people over the years, none better than good friends Greg Stoda and Tim Murphy.

Just as it has become a signature of the Missouri football program, family is foremost in my life. I was blessed to have two parents who dared me to dream. They were always there to help me up when I fell, and they were then quick to remind me I could do anything I set my mind to. I felt Mom and Dad's presence with my every keystroke.

Deborah is the best sister a brother could ever ask for. She is a friend and a mentor, and she has always been spot-on with a timely piece of advice or practical thinking. Deb is always assessing where she is in life, always challenging herself. Occasionally she'll mention that she feels the need to reinvent herself. The opportunity to challenge myself was the genesis for this endeavor. I'd also like to think I've reinvented myself.

Steven is my pride and joy. I wrote this book with him in mind, because I wanted to show him that his grandparents were right: You can do anything you set your mind to. I can see him writing his own book or doing play-by-play for the Cowboys or the Red Sox, if not calling the Super Bowl or the World Series.

Finally, there is Leigh. I have had a lot of cheerleaders on this project, but none has been bigger than my wife of 27 years. My intent was to roll out this book on the fifth anniversary of the game, but our world was rocked on Aug. 1, 2011, when we learned that Leigh had a grade-three brain tumor, an anaplastic astrocytoma. The diagnosis came out of nowhere. Leigh underwent surgery and bravely faced 33 radiation treatments. There were setbacks along the way, but Leigh soldiered on. Now she is back to her active lifestyle—smiling, laughing, enjoying life again.

Not once have I heard Leigh complain. Nor have I heard her ask, "Why me?" After almost a year of idling, it was Leigh who encouraged me to get back on the horse. In fact, she demanded I finish the book. This is the selfless woman I married.

Hero gets thrown around too casually in sports. Quarterbacks and defensive linemen who play with bum knees or sprained shoulders may be tough, but they are far from heroes. The military and their families, police officers and firefighters—those are heroes. In my book, in their own way, brain-tumor victims fit the profile as well. Leigh inspired me to finish this project, and she continues to inspire me. She is my hero.

M.G.
July 2013
Plainsboro, N.J.

Biography

Mark Godich has been a senior editor at *Sports Illustrated* since 1995. In 2007, he was the magazine's college football editor. A 1979 graduate of the University of Missouri's highly acclaimed School of Journalism and a former instructor there, he started a career in sportswriting and editing at the *Abilene* (Texas) *Reporter-News*. Before landing at SI, he also made stops at the *Dallas Times Herald*, The Associated Press, *The National Sports Daily* and *Golf Shop Operations*. He lives in Plainsboro, N.J., with his wife, Leigh, and son, Steven.

Visit www.ascendbooks.com for more great titles
on your favorite teams and athletes.

www.ascendbooks.com